ELBERT W. STEWART
Chairman, Department of Sociology and Anthropology
Bakersfield College

JAMES A. GLYNN
Assistant Professor of Sociology
Bakersfield College

INTRODUCTION TO SOCIOLOGY

McGRAW-HILL BOOK COMPANY
New York   San Francisco   St. Louis   Düsseldorf
Johannesburg   Kuala Lumpur   London   Mexico   Montreal
New Delhi   Panama   Rio de Janeiro
Singapore   Sydney   Toronto

This book was set in Linofilm Helvetica
by Applied Typographic Systems, and
printed on permanent paper and bound
by Peninsula Lithograph Company. The
designer was Janet Bollow; the drawings
were done by Richard Leech. The editors
were Ronald D. Kissack, Eva Marie
Strock, and Ronald Q. Lewton. Charles A.
Goehring supervised production.

INTRODUCTION TO SOCIOLOGY

Printed in the United States of America.

Library of Congress catalog card number: 76-139564

234567890 PEPE 7987654321

07-061327-5

There is no single way to capture the totality of the
madness and mirth of human society, of its heroism and
its foibles, of the daily rhythm of its routine activities,
and the shocks of its recurrent tragedies. Folk tale,
proverb, and prophecy have made shrewd comments on
the human scene; philosophy has searched it for meaning,
and poetry and drama have heightened its emotional
impact and sensitized it with an empathic touch.

Sociology examines the same human scene in
another manner—the systematic, objective manner of
modern science. The drama of human life is in no way
deadened by the sociological approach; in fact, it is
often enlivened by new discovery, but there is always an
insistence on regularity and order in method and
explanation. Although all sociologists search for an
understanding of the development and cohesion of
human societies, their detailed studies are wide-ranging,
and their total field of interest is enormous. How, then,
can the sociological view of the vast social milieu be
brought within manageable proportions for a brief,
introductory book?

To a great extent our introduction to sociology will
center on three facets of human society, or, possibly,
three faces of reality. In the mythological genius of
Hinduism, three great principles are presented as a triad
of gods: Brahma the Creator, Vishnu the Preserver, and
Siva the Destroyer. Sociology must also look into these
three faces, for they are as real to the modern world of
science as to the world of Hindu religion. The forces
that mold human groups into societies and cause them

to develop their distinctive cultures represent the creative force, the Brahma, of sociological science. The socialization processes and the institutions that tend to become rigid and encrusted with age represent the sociological Vishnu, the Preserver. Perhaps the most important god of modern society is Siva, the force of change and the subverter of old orders, who constantly seeks to redesign the societies' fabric, a fabric that the other gods have woven and sought to preserve. Although only our final chapter speaks of social change in its title, "Siva" will be found constantly at work in this analysis of society, changing socialization patterns, altering religions, undermining economic systems, broadening and changing political orders, ripping up the old and time-honored, and lending voice to a hundred movements of protest.

Social institutions also are discussed at length in this text, although they are presented always in a framework of change. They are given considerable space because they are the culmination of the creative processes of society and the servants of its values. Institutions, in an age of challenge, can also be the vortices around which swirl the forces of social change. In an age of polarization and economic conflict, it seems highly appropriate to give ample space to the institutions of government and economics. When society fears a decline of its religious values, such values cannot be ignored as irrelevant. Religion changes as it struggles with the secular, scientifically oriented society, but the personal and societal needs that gave rise to religion remain. The prevailing belief in and concern over generation gap and family instability must be examined and explained, and so must the charge of irrelevance in the educational institution. All institutions must be examined in terms of their contribution to the social order, and their required changes must be seen in the same terms.

To be faithful to sociological perspectives, social systems must be shown as on-going concerns, with self-preservation mechanisms that operate even in times of disturbance. This view is necessary also to prevent making sociology nothing more than a dreary recitation of societal failure. Nevertheless, we who inhabit today's world see it as a planet of strife, uncertain of its future, convulsed by war and internal conflict. We are antagonized by any evasion of problems and challenges. For this reason the present text invades the field of social problems to a limited degree, for it has seemed the logical and natural way to illustrate sociological concepts and endow them with life and meaning.

We have spoken of the gods of creation, preservation, and change, but perhaps have said too little of the god of science—a hard master to serve. Sociology prides itself on scientific method and theory and strives for objectivity. Attention has been given to several great theorists of sociology: Durkheim, Weber, Simmel, Merton, and Parsons. Many have been omitted, of course, partly because this book is too brief to include them all, and partly because writers, try as they will to be objective, are more engrossed in one man's ideas than another's. This book does not attempt to be a compendium of sociological knowledge but only a brief introduction, and, hopefully, a goad to further study. Where opinions have inevitably crept in — those of the authors or of the authorities cited — they should add heat to the discussion, and the discussion itself can generate the light.

A major purpose in keeping an introductory book concise is to give it flexibility. The basic concepts introduced here can be supplemented by studies of the surrounding community or by revealing and relevant articles in journals or books of readings. There are many specialty books available — books about the black rage, deviants and contracultures, student movements, conservative suburbia, the urban crisis, and the hundreds of issues that are the reason for a constantly growing interest in sociology. Hopefully, this introduction will add to that interest and help to bring the patterns and details of the social order Into sharper focus.

ELBERT W. STEWART
JAMES A. GLYNN

contents

INTRODUCTION TO SOCIOLOGY

*Know that the problems of social science . . .
must include both troubles and issues, both
biography and history, and the range of their
intricate relations. Within that range the life
of the individual and the making of societies
occurs; and within that range the sociological
imagination has its chance to make a
difference in the quality of human life in
our time.*[1]

C. WRIGHT MILLS
The Sociological Imagination

DEVELOPING A SCIENCE OF SOCIETY

In many ways the twentieth century seems to be the
ultimate age of enlightenment. New knowledge Is
produced in hundreds of laboratories and research
centers throughout the world, with all the brightest
scientific minds drawn Into the investigative effort.
Science is undaunted by the vastness of the heavens,
the depths of the oceans, or the invisibility of atomic
structure. Everything is researched, from the amino
acids that build the proteins of life to the processes
of decomposition of life and of matter itself; from the
communications systems of dolphins to the visual acuity
of the lowly slug; from the pecking order of chickens to
the memorles of flatworms. The mind of man is similarly
researched: emotions, senses, neurons, origins,
capacities, and genetic structure. Everywhere the thirst
for knowledge grows faster as the amount of knowledge
expands. As the old French proverb says, "The appetite
comes with the eating."

Yet the feeding of the appetite for knowledge never
results in satisfaction. Much of the knowledge of the past
seems unimportant to a world that moves so fast, and the
new knowledge gained can hardly be digested and
assimilated before it becomes obsolete. Furthermore,
the new knowledge seems to have less effect on many
areas of life than might have been expected.

[1] C. Wright Mills, *The Sociological Imagination*, Oxford University Press, Fair Lawn, N.J.

Though the knowledge of the outer universe expands, in the inner world of his emotions man can still remain a creature of suspicion and fear, answering his own misunderstandings by building bigger guns, bigger prisons, and bigger asylums. The genius of man seems to be increasingly dangerous in an age of unlimited possibilities, and science, whatever its intentions, adds to the dangers. The tools of science can be used by fools and oppressors as well as by the friends of mankind. This lesson has been driven home so forcefully in recent history that some people grow suspicious of science itself. Science, however, is but a means to knowledge; the decision of how to use knowledge is a societal decision. Perhaps the most fruitful field for scientific research is therefore in the field of human societies.

WHAT IS SOCIOLOGY   What is clearly needed is an approach to knowledge that attempts an understanding of society, that seeks the constant and relevant in social systems, and that tries to increase man's understanding of his fellow man. From its very beginning, sociology has aspired to accomplish this task. Sociology has also been interested in the dilemma of rapid material progress that seems to outrun society's capacity to adjust, as well as the search for basic principles of social organization. Sociology is a systematic and scientific discipline seeking knowledge of man as a social animal: his societies and subsocieties and his adjustment to them, his customs and institutions and the patterns of stability and change that they develop.

Characteristics of sociology   As Peter Berger[2] noted, not all that sociology says will be startlingly new, but it will cast a new light on things barely noticed before. The student of geology or physical geography suddenly discovers new interest in a landscape that he has often passed without notice because now he is trained to see the features of erosion, uplift, and volcanic activity. The student of paleontology finds that the old sediments he has observed before are full of treasures revealed to him only after he had been trained to see them. Similarly, the student of sociology will discover a new world around him, a world that was always there, but previously was little observed: the ethnic groups of his city, the social-class divisions, the blighted areas, the varied religious denominations, sects, and cults, the distinctive and little-observed worlds of poverty. He will find the world of deviant behavior closer to his own world than he cares to know. He will see many variations in life-chances for the young. He will discover that education—the open sesame for the majority of people—is a closed door for some, regarded either as unimportant or

[2]Peter L. Berger, *Invitation to Sociology*, Doubleday & Company, Garden City, N.Y., 1963, pp. 20–24.

as impossible. He will find that a nation pledged to equality has a type of stratification that many informed observers have called "racial caste." He will find that the emotions roused in mobs and riots are not as foreign to his nature as he would like to believe. He will, perhaps, agree with Emerson that there is no type of behavior too low for him to have followed had the circumstances been different.

Relation of sociology to the other social sciences   The social sciences all seek greater understanding of man and society, although their approaches are somewhat different. Sociology and anthropology are both extremely broad in their perspectives; they try to study societies in their entirety, not just as political systems, economic systems, or systems of belief and value. Anthropology has focused a majority of its studies on preliterate societies, and sociology has focused on contemporary societies, but both look for universal patterns of human relations behind the varying details. The other social sciences are somewhat more specialized, but their areas of investigation are also important to the total understanding of human societies. Psychology studies the mental and emotional side of man; economics studies the systems of production and distribution of goods; and political science studies the systems by which social power and authority are institutionalized, exercised, and regulated. History, in its careful recording of the past, gives all the social sciences a body of evidence from which to draw. The social-science disciplines are interrelated, of course, and profit from each other's studies; sociology cannot ignore any of them.

The distinctive field of sociology   Although sociology can profit from the findings of all the social sciences, it has a distinctive field, a field that was clearly defined by one of its founders, Emile Durkheim, long ago. Sociology's distinctive field is the study of group life: how the individual is influenced by others and how he influences them; how human societies develop and change, and how they are swept by such social contagions as fads, panics, hysterias, and ideologies; to what degree society is a tyrant and to what extent it is a friend of the individual. Unlike anthropology, sociology does its studies mainly in modern industrial societies rather than in preliterate societies. Unlike history, sociology looks mainly for explanations and developmental trends when it studies the past rather than searching carefully for the details of the story. Sociology differs from psychology in its greater emphasis on the group rather than the individual. All the social sciences are of value. We believe that for the college student sociology offers particularly useful insights for the understanding of self and society. As we turn to an analysis of the types of questions pursued by sociologists, this point will become increasingly clear.

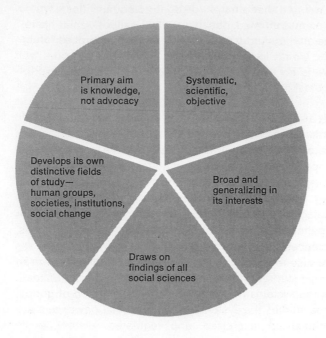

WHAT QUESTIONS DO SOCIOLOGISTS ASK   Sociology encompasses so many areas of research that in some respects it seems impossible for a brief text to introduce the entire discipline. In a more important respect, however, a concise introduction to the field remains possible, because all phases of society and its problems are interrelated. A study of any major part of society sheds light on the whole; a study of the problems of any ethnic group reveals much about the entire human race. The problems of the family and of the education and socialization of the young are the problems of the total society. The ghetto casts its shadow over the affluent world beyond its borders; poverty and malnutrition are the problems of all people, contributing to crime rates, welfare costs, and hostility and despair. Intergroup conflict, whether it grows out of hatred of class for class, race for race, or nation for nation, sends its shock waves throughout the world and threatens all humanity. Industrialization, an almost imperceptible force in the eighteenth century, now sweeps the entire world, crushing older production systems under its weight of goods and uniting much of the world in the common paradox of miraculous productivity and rapid despoliation of the natural environment. The questions sociologists ask, then, range all the way from the nature of man himself in all his social-class and ethnic variability, to his major institutions and the forces of change that disrupt old meanings, relationships, and values.

The roots and growth of society   The first questions must be asked about man as a social being. What are the consequences of his social nature and the formation of social life? What is necessary for loyalty and cohesion and a sense of meaning and purpose? How do groups develop self-centered (ethnocentric) attitudes? Is there something basic about social systems that will cause man always to divide the world into those who are to be loved and those who are to be hated?

Another cluster of sociological questions centers around customs, values, and the other phenomena of what we call *culture.* Is man endangered by his tendency to follow traditions of the past? Why are human societies so different in their traditions, manners, dress, values, religions, and ideas of right and wrong?

How do societies perpetuate themselves, teaching their children to believe most of what they are taught until they think of the attitudes as their own? How does the attempt at internalizing the rights and wrongs of society sometimes produce unintended results? What are the functions of nonconformity?

Societies become differentiated in various ways, and differences and inequalities raise many more sociological questions. Why is social class almost always present? Is it a matter of human nature or of social organization and need? How prevalent is caste? What are the similarities between racial discrimination and caste? What is the meaning of race? Does race make any difference except in the prejudiced minds of men? How do social-class and racial problems help to generate riots and disorders in American cities? What are the possible solutions to the problems of riots and disorders?

Population and urbanization   There are a number of disturbing questions about the consequences of population increase and the manner in which populations are distributed. Are all societies, classes, and races threatened by a rising tide of people—a population explosion? Will the problem take care of itself, or is the world destined for starvation or war? Why do the ever-growing masses of people crowd together into giant cities? What is to be done about the problems of city congestion, blight, and contamination?

Social institutions   Institutions, those standardized and generally accepted patterns for achieving the essential needs of society, make up another area of intense questioning by sociologists. Family, religion, and

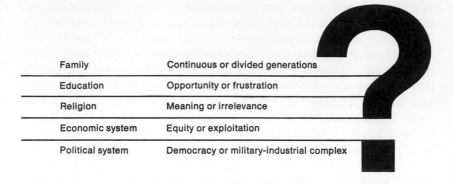

Family	Continuous or divided generations
Education	Opportunity or frustration
Religion	Meaning or irrelevance
Economic system	Equity or exploitation
Political system	Democracy or military-industrial complex

education function to give continuity, meaning, and opportunity to the people of this crowded, urban world. Why is there uncertainty even about these institutions? Why do many families give so little sense of continuity and security? Why are there such high rates of divorce and separation?

With the increasing secularization of society, what is the place of religion? Why is religion an inspiration to some and irrelevant to others? Why do different churches appeal differently to upper and lower classes?

Why are educational systems under increasing strain, and why is college youth so critical of society? Can education offer opportunity to all, or will some continue to know only frustration? Will the educational system provide all the manpower and specialties needed for a growing economy?

There are also questions about economic and political institutions to consider. Will the economy continue to grow and provide the funds for better education, more equality of opportunities, and city improvement, or will there be an "under class," feeling exploited, alienated, and rebellious? What will be the impact of automation and computerization on the future of employment? Is economic change leading us into an all-powerful government, or will a free economy prevail? Will our political system continue to mediate between interest groups and be responsive to the will of the people, or is some kind of military-industrial complex taking decisions out of the hands of the people?

Social change   All these questions are asked about a society in which the pace of social change increases, as does man's awareness of its consequences. What are the pressures of change that make modern society seem so disturbing and chaotic? Is the social system capable of keeping pace with scientific and technical change, or are dangerous disparities developing?

These questions will be explored in later pages. Few can be answered definitively at this stage of sociological knowledge, but an examination of findings and informed opinions of sociologists will greatly widen the student's perspectives on modern society, its organization, its trends, and its problems.

HOW SOCIOLOGISTS SEEK ANSWERS As the level of complexity of society increases, the wisdom of the past becomes less adequate and less relevant to sociological understanding. The common-sense answers which man once regarded as infallible are increasingly becoming open to doubt. Much of the common sense of the past turns out to have been common ignorance. Modern man recoils at the thought of burning "witches," trials by ordeal, torturing the insane, or bleeding the sick, but all these practices have at one time or another seemed like good common sense. More recently, such policies as denying voting rights to women, denying equal educational rights to black Americans, forcing Indians onto reservations and later off of the same reservations, and flogging mariners, criminals, and children have all been defended as common-sense policies.

Not all commonly held views of the past are as offensive as the ones just cited, and not all are to be repudiated; but all ideas and policies must be open to the light of scientific examination. Are present policies based on false premises? Were they ever useful and functional to the society? If so, are they still functional to the societies of today?

Observational studies The most obvious route to knowledge is through direct observation, but this does not imply that all observations are careful and accurate. The conflicting accounts of witnesses at trials, different accounts of the same event in newspapers and magazines, and even arguments over entries in autobiographies are good indications of the difficulties encountered in casual observation. Individual biases enter the picture, helping the observer to see mainly what he wishes to see; selective memory later helps to weed out other unacceptable details of observation.

In spite of its problems, however, observation must be depended upon, and many highly creditable observational studies are done. Observational studies depend upon training and reflection, knowing what to look for, and careful recording of all observed behavior so as not to select in terms of preconceptions. Some of the classical cases of observational studies in sociology are the studies of W. I. Thomas and

Florian Znaniecki involving Polish peasants adjusting to life in the United States, and William Whyte's *Street Corner Society*. In both cases, the researchers spent long periods of time with their subjects and came to know them thoroughly. Lewis Yablonsky's *The Hippie Trip* and Leon Festinger's *When Prophecy Fails* (a study of a flying-saucer cult) are interesting examples of more recent observational studies. Anthropologists make wide use of observational studies and require long periods of training for such studies.

Theories and concepts   Observation of events naturally leads to interpretation and the search for explanation. Some sociologists are more preoccupied with analysis and interpretation than simply with the gathering of data, but, as in any science, both the collection and interpretation of facts are important. New explanations make sense of the knowledge gained and can become the basis for policy. The germ theory of disease, for example, made the old practice of bleeding the patient seem absurd, and also it swept away explanations of disease as the result of witchcraft or sin. Environmental theories of delinquency suggest possibilities for correction, whereas older explanations of "bad blood in the veins" did not.

Sociology, then, as any science, looks for theoretical explanations. A *theory* is a logical and scientifically acceptable principle to explain the relationships between known facts. The theory of evolution, for example, is a well-known principle explaining the relationships between all living species. Some attempts have been made at broad general principles in sociology, but many theories are more limited in scope, explaining types of delinquency, variations in divorce rates, the appeal of new religious sects, social movements, urban riots, and many other social phenomena.

Not all sociological tools of analysis can be called theories. Sociology also develops a number of *concepts*, which are abstract ideas generalized from particular cases and usually having wide applicability. Many sociological concepts will be introduced later in this text, but some are already familiar enough in common speech to make recognizable examples: *norms* (behavioral expectations), *folkways* and *mores, status* and *role, culture, social class, elites,* and *subcultures,* to name a few.

Functional analysis   Similar to concepts in analytical value are models for the viewing of society. Sometimes the models are of an analogy type, as when society is compared to a living organism. A model that will be referred to in several of the later chapters of this text is that of *functionalism*—a model that views society as a system of interrelated parts and stresses how each part contributes to the whole. It is easy to apply a functional analysis of education, seeing how it contributes to the maintenance of the entire social system by such functions as passing along tradition, promoting citizenship, and training personnel. Functional analysis also leads to the perception of more subtle functions. What, for example, is the function of student activism? (This question will be discussed in Chapter 12.) Some sociologists are more interested in functional analysis than others and prefer, at least for some purposes, different perspectives. Social phenomena can also be studied in the light of historical cause or sometimes as the result of conflicting forces within society.

Statistical validation   When observation and logical analysis suggest a relationship between phenomena, some attempt must be made to validate the conclusion by examining all available evidence. Occasionally the offhand evidence may seem to point in opposite directions. For example, a welfare worker observing families in the poorer sections of town will note very large numbers of families broken by divorce. Another person, reading the society page, will be impressed by the number of divorces that occur in the upper circles of society. Is there an actual relationship between social class and divorce? Do wealthy people get more divorces than the poor, or does it just seem that way because more attention is paid to their social lives? The answer to the question is readily at hand in national statistics and can be stated very briefly: The higher the income and educational level, the lower the divorce rate. William J. Goode has collected statistics from the United States and many other countries that generally validate this statement. He finds that in most cases, the poorest levels have the highest divorce rates and the wealthy the lowest. The only exceptions occur where divorces are very expensive or desertion without divorce is extremely easy.[3]

A short introductory text cannot go into detail on statistical method. It should be mentioned, however, that usually the matter is much more complex than in the example just given. If the information is not available in Census Bureau reports, the researcher may have to develop his own statistics through extensive questionnaires and interviews. If he is trying to find a relationship between two phenomena (social class and premarital sex relations, for example), he will have to know enough about statistics to know whether his results are statistically valid, based on enough examples and showing a strong enough correlation to eliminate the possibility that findings are mere coincidence.

Experimental method   Experimental studies, as well as statistical and questionnaire studies, are possible in sociology. They depend upon

[3]William J. Goode, "A Cross-Cultural Analysis of Class Differentials in Divorce Rates," *International Social Science Journal*, vol. 14, no. 3, 1962, pp. 507–526.

formulating hypotheses, isolating a variable, and employing experimental and control groups. A *hypothesis* is a supposition or conjecture of a tentative nature to try to explain known facts. A *variable* is one of many factors of a changeable nature that might account for a particular phenomenon. An *experimental group* is a group in which one variable is deliberately changed. A *control group* is a group in which all variable factors are left the same so that the comparison with the experimental group can be made. A simple illustration will make these concepts clear.

Let us pose a hypothesis to account, in part, for the failure of low-ability students to improve their work in school. Our hypothesis will state that unfavorable self-image is an important cause of failure to improve. This hypothesis can be tested by dividing the students seeming to show low ability into two groups: one experimental and the other control. The experimental group will be given much encouragement, and many statements will be made to lead them to think that they actually have good potential. The control group will be taught in the same manner, except that this type of encouragement will not be given. We must watch to be sure that other variables do not enter the picture. Both groups should be equal in all significant ways, especially in measured ability and attitudes, and both should be given equally good teachers and equally favorable classrooms and periods of the day for study. Otherwise there will be no certainty whether we are measuring the variable of favorable self-concept or simply the difference between two teachers or classroom situations. If the hypothesis is proved, as sociologists would expect, we should find a measurable and statistically significant difference between the two groups in the amount of progress made by the end of the semester.

Scientific attitudes   Whatever the method of research used, scientific method depends upon several basic attitudes and practices. The first of these is *objectivity*—the willingness to accept the facts as ascertained and to avoid biases. It is a disappointment to do extensive research work and then find that one's treasured hypothesis is not proved, but objectivity calls for admitting such failures. Even disproving a hypothesis can make a contribution to knowledge, but distorting the facts cannot.

Precision, reexamination, careful attention to critics, and an open-mindedness, even about favorite theories, are all attitudes necessary for good scientific research. The task in sociology is more difficult than in many areas of physical science, partly because emotional involvement and prejudices are harder to overcome. It seems also to a student of the social sciences that the complexity of the field and the number of variables involved are much greater than in the physical sciences. It might be some consolation to the social scientist to know that the physical scientist can

Methods
Observation
Theories
Concepts
Analytical models
Experiments

Attitudes
Objective
Systematic
Open-minded

feel just as enmeshed in complexities. Such fields as physics and as-
tronomy become infinitely more baffling as greater knowledge is gained.
Sociology is not alone in such problems; as do all sciences, sociology
must refine its techniques of study to cope with growing complexities.

HOW DID SOCIOLOGY DEVELOP   To understand some of the concepts, interests, and methods of sociology, it is necessary to scan briefly the
history of its development. Man has always been interested in his societies,
but usually from the point of view of tradition, moral philosophy, or
religion rather than that of science. Historical forces had to focus man's
interest on social problems, give him a glimmer of hope for a better
future, and suggest some kind of scientific approach to societal studies
before sociology could be born. Not only is knowledge cumulative, but
better methods of pursuing knowledge are also cumulative. As a result
of an accumulation of knowledge, a very great difference in outlook and
method separate modern sociology from the speculations of the ancient
and medieval worlds and the social philosophers of the eighteenth and
nineteenth centuries.

The period of tradition   Since the dawn of recorded history, mankind has
sought greater knowledge about his species. The ancient Hebrew writers
contemplated a moral order for man and man's place in the universe.
The Chinese concentrated on man's relationship to man in perpetuating
the social system. Confucius (551–479 B.C.) taught that the status quo
of a society must not be disturbed, for only through changelessness
could social relations be orderly and moral. This thought so dominated

13

the values of the people that two centuries later Hsun Tse wrote "The essence of good conduct . . . is the unfailing repetition of tradition."[4]

During this same period of time Greek thought had centered on the political and legalistic aspects of society. *The Republic* of Plato and Aristotle's *Politics*, although ideologically different from one another, both investigated the patterns of government that men create for themselves. In tracing the development of these patterns of leadership, each philosopher concluded that the course of human history tended to repeat itself through the ages.

From theology to social philosophy   Early Christian ideas about society are best reflected in the work of St. Augustine (354–430 A.D.). In the *City of God* he describes the institutions of society as being either good or bad according to whether they motivate man toward salvation. Obviously, attention was focused too exclusively on the next world for the development of a real social science of this world. The theories of Augustine, and later those of Thomas Aquinas, dominated European philosophy until the seventeenth and eighteenth centuries. John Locke (1623–1704) in England and Jean Jacques Rousseau (1712–1778) in France began to devise theories emphasizing social factors and practically eliminating theological factors as the basis of social organization. A trend toward modern social thought was developing, born in a spirit of revolt against the injustices of the old social order.

The social philosophers of the eighteenth and early nineteenth centuries differed from modern sociologists by concentrating on ideas of what *ought to be* rather than on that which exists. But contentious arguments among many conflicting philosophers led to the realization of the need for a more exact knowledge of society. Early in the nineteenth century, the idea of an actual science of society was taking form in the mind of Saint-Simon, a French nobleman who helped Washington's cause in America and participated in the much less successful French Revolution. When he was not devoting his time to the cause of revolution, Saint-Simon was lecturing at the École Polytechnique, where he exerted a powerful influence on his students. One of these students was Auguste Comte, who became Saint-Simon's friend and collaborator. Comte later became discontented with the ideas of his former teacher and the partnership dissolved.

From social philosophy to sociology: Comte   Auguste Comte (1798–1857) went on to form a new school of intellectual inquiry. For this new discipline he coined the term *sociology* and began to pursue a science of society. Rather than speculating on things as they ought to be, he ad-

[4]Howard Becker and Harry Elmer Barnes, *Social Thought from Lore to Science*, Dover Publications, Inc., New York, 1952, p. 69.

vocated the study of society solely on the basis of observation. Since each science needs a father in order to be considered legitimate, today we claim Comte as the Father of Sociology.

Comte did not exemplify the scientific method in his writings, and he has been criticized as an "armchair philosopher" because he dealt in deductive logic rather than research and did not practice what he preached. However, he gave sociology its name, suggested directions for sociologists to follow, and became an advocate of the new science, awakening the interest of many other scholars of his day. His enthusiasm was boundless (so, unfortunately, was his conceit), and he saw himself as the founder of a new science that would eventually help man create a better world than he had ever known before.

Herbert Spencer   As the nineteenth century proceeded, it produced many new leaders in the field of social thought. *Herbert Spencer* (1820–1903), for example, became greatly interested in social evolution, and despite his denials, he seems to have been strongly influenced by the work of Charles Darwin. This darwinian bent was so intense that Spencer can be called a *monocausist*—one who looks for the *one* underlying explanation of social change. Other monocausists appeared, looking to theories of social conflict, cyclical interpretation, and other keys to the mystery of social progress and decay. In some ways Karl Marx fits this description because he analyzed human history almost entirely in terms of economic struggle between social classes. Of course, such approaches were significant and made some contribution to sociology, but modern sociologists are very cautious about accepting any theories that seem to oversimplify social issues.

Émile Durkheim   Perhaps the greatest single contribution to the early development of sociology was made by *Émile Durkheim* (1858–1917), the first Frenchman to hold the title of Professor of Education and Sociology. In 1898 he founded and edited the first French journal of sociology and thereby helped to publicize this new area of scientific investigation. By way of actual contribution to the fund of sociological knowledge, Durkheim added the statistical method, the concept of *anomie* or normative conflict (which will be discussed later in this text), the social causes of suicide, the relation of values to sociology, a theory on the origin of religion, an examination of the dynamics of social control, and an explanation of collective behavior. His interests reached into law, politics, education, familial relationships, psychology, and anthropology; from each of these areas of interest he was able to develop ideas relevant to the subject area of sociology.[5]

[5] An excellent and concise treatment of Durkheim's life and writings is presented in *Émile Durkheim*, George Simpson (ed.), Thomas Y. Crowell Company, New York, 1963.

Max Weber Durkheim's contemporary and counterpart in Germany was *Max Weber* (1864–1920), who was probably better known as an economist in the nineteenth century but is now almost always classified as a sociologist. Like Durkheim, Weber did much to improve methods of studying society. He used a historical comparative method of finding causal relationships among the institutions and processes of society and also advocated the *Verstehen* method which has proved to be equally valuable. Verstehen implies both objectivity and subjectivity. It is not enough to observe some problem of society objectively; to fully grasp its significance one must develop *empathy*, a sympathetic understanding of the problem.

Weber's use of the comparative method is evident in his examination of religious ideologies, and his Verstehen method is a necessary ingredient in his famous formulation of the Protestant Ethic and the Spirit of Capitalism theory. He also wrote extensively on such topics as social class, bureaucracy, and political leadership. A rebel of his times, Weber once remarked, "I do not care about the form of the State, if only politicians and *not* dilettante fools like Wilhelm II rule the country."[6] Capable politicians could learn from economics and sociology; the Kaiser could not.

American sociologists In the United States, sociology was first introduced through the writings and teachings of *Lester Frank Ward* (1841–1913). In his early and middle years Ward had been a botanist and geologist. Later in life he turned his interests to sociology, helped found the American Sociological Society (now called the American Sociological Association), and served as its first president. Although he accepted some of Spencer's theories about automatic social evolution, Ward was convinced that man could help direct the course of social change. Unlike so many people who fail to practice what they preach, he devoted a great deal of energy to the cause of social reform. He worked diligently to institute a system of free public education and championed the movement to grant full equality to women in the social and political system.

Probably the best known American sociologist of the nineteenth century was *William Graham Sumner* (1840–1910). Although Ward is known as the Father of American Sociology, it was Sumner who taught the first course entitled sociology in this country. In his famous work *Folkways* he gives a detailed description and analysis of social control that is considered to be his most significant contribution to the field. Sumner strongly advocated Spencer's idea of evolution and vigorously opposed Ward's idea of social planning. Few students of society would agree with Sumner today, but his ideas certainly stimulated thought

[6] J. P. Mayer, "Max Weber and German Politics: A Study in Political Sociology," in *Max Weber,* S. M. Miller (ed.), Thomas Y. Crowell Company, New York, 1963, p. 86.

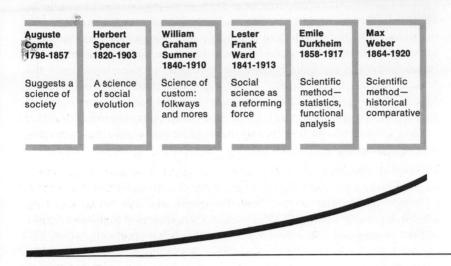

Auguste Comte 1798-1857	Herbert Spencer 1820-1903	William Graham Sumner 1840-1910	Lester Frank Ward 1841-1913	Emile Durkheim 1858-1917	Max Weber 1864-1920
Suggests a science of society	A science of social evolution	Science of custom: folkways and mores	Social science as a reforming force	Scientific method— statistics, functional analysis	Scientific method— historical comparative

among his students, some of whom are among America's most distinguished sociologists.

From its founding over 100 years ago, sociology has progressed as a discipline and has continued to refine its methods of inquiry. As do all social sciences, it has had its problems and its critics. As late as 1960 five of the nation's leading liberal-arts colleges did not offer any instruction in sociology. However, the great trend is toward sociology; the number of students enrolled in it increases yearly. There were fewer than 700 members of the American Sociological Association fifty years ago; today there are more than 12,000 members, and 200 doctor's degrees in sociology are added per year.[7]

WHAT OCCUPATIONS DO SOCIOLOGISTS PURSUE　In 1969 Raymond Mack reported that "seventy-nine percent of the sociologists whose primary employment is known are affiliated with colleges and universities."[8] (It is important to note that most of these people hold advanced degrees in sociology.) The beginning student who reads such statements might erroneously conclude that sociologists only teach others to teach sociology. This is far from true, because most teachers in the field also do research work, and large numbers of people who are not professional sociologists are engaged in sociological work.

[7] Alex Inkeles, *What is Sociology?*, Prentice-Hall, Inc., Englewood Cliffs, N.J., 1964, p. 107.
[8] Raymond Mack, "A Career in Sociology," *The American Sociological Association*, Washington, D.C., 1969, p. 7.

17

A student who graduates from college with a bachelor's degree in engineering is properly classified as an engineer, but the student who is granted a bachelor's degree in sociology is not usually classified as a sociologist. A master's degree in sociology is considered the minimum requirement for the employment classification of sociologist, and the Ph.D is usually the criterion for the more responsible positions in the field.[9] This helps to explain the apparent contradiction in the previous paragraph — that the majority of professional sociologists teach, but that college graduates with a sociology major enter many other fields of work involving sociological knowledge.

Sociology at the bachelor of arts level   Suppose a student in an introductory sociology class decides to set his sights upon the completion of a four-year course in this field. He might well ask "What can I do with my bachelor's degree?" The immediate response of many individuals is that he can become a *social worker*. This is a numerically minor occupational goal for the sociology major, although it is one possibility. Often social work is approached through psychology; as Peter Berger says, "American social work has been more influenced by psychology than by sociology in the development of its theory."[10] Also, many colleges and universities have established separate schools of social welfare, designed to produce graduates with specializations geared to meeting the needs of state and local welfare agencies. Such schools, of course, require considerable work in psychology and sociology.

A student with a bachelor's degree in sociology might also consider a career as a *probation or parole officer*. If he makes this decision, he should begin early in his junior year to enroll in course work relevant to this occupation. Many young graduates in sociology are particularly attracted to the field of youth probation because they feel that through their sociological understanding and personal guidance the young offender may be steered toward an adulthood of productivity.

Personnel work is an appropriate field of employment for a graduate in sociology. As a personnel assistant, one screens applicants for jobs in industry, helps in the preparation of job descriptions, and coordinates or mediates interdepartmental matters. Sociology students might qualify also for such related fields as public relations and advertising.

There are many other areas in which sociology will provide a valuable start. "An undergraduate major or minor in sociology will provide an especially valuable background for the student who plans eventually to become a *clergyman, attorney, economist, psychologist, political scientist,* or *historian*. . . ."[11] So, to answer the student's question as to what

[9] *Ibid.*, p. 8.
[10] Berger, *op cit.*, pp. 3–4.
[11] Department of Sociology, University of Kentucky, "Should You Be a Sociologist?," in Edgar A. Schuler et al. (eds.), *Readings in Sociology*, Thomas Y. Crowell Company, New York, 1967, pp. 839–844.

he can do with his bachelor's degree in sociology, we would respond, "You can do almost anything which, at a preprofessional level, is concerned with the direction, manipulation, or motivation of people."

The master's degree   Let us assume that the student decides to continue his study of sociology in graduate school. Should he be granted the master's degree, he may in some cases be qualified for the title of sociologist. At this level of competence he is acceptable for some of the more prestigious occupations. He may find an administrative or research position, or he may become an instructor at the junior college level. Some sociologists with the master's degree are employed in the state college or university systems, although most state colleges and universities require completion or near completion of a doctorate before hiring a sociologist. [12]

Often the master's degree is accepted in lieu of experience in many of the fields we have discussed. In this case the neophyte enters the occupation with an advanced status and pay commensurate with his position. For example, if an applicant with a bachelor's degree is employed as a probation officer, Class I, at a salary of $7,000/year, it may take him two or three years to increase his income to $8,000; but, if he holds the master's degree he may begin his career at Class III with a salary of $8,000 and also have greater possibilities for further advancement.

The doctor's degree   If the student is willing to invest another two or three years of his time in classes and seminars, he may earn the degree of Doctor of Philosophy. At this point he is a sociologist. Now he is qualified to direct research projects for private enterprise, educational institutions, or state and federal agencies, or he may be a specialist in urban problems, demographic trends, rural sociology, social gerontology, race relations, or any of a number of other categories of interest to sociology. As mentioned, most holders of Ph.Ds in sociology are affiliated with educational institutions, and of course the monetary rewards are greater. "Sociologists in teaching . . . averaged $11,000 annually in 1966. Sociologists working for non-profit organizations or industry averaged $14,000 and $15,000 respectively; in the federal government those with experience averaged $14,700." [13] Other fields are more lucrative economically, but few offer the intense challenges and potential growth evidenced in sociology.

Social service   The strongly idealistic student might be less concerned about the particular job he will hold, or even the pay scale, than he is

[12] Mack, *op. cit.*, pp. 8–9.
[13] *Ibid.*, p. 12.

Doctor's degree
Sociologist

Research for
  Government
  Industry
  Universities
  Foundations

Professor of Sociology in
  Urban problems
  Demography
  Race relations
  Criminology
  (And many more)

Master's degree
Research

Junior college
  instructor

State college
  instructor

Administrator in
  Social work
  Probation
  Juvenile work

Bachelor's degree
Personnel work
Probation, parole officer
Juvenile advisor
Social work

Higher degree increases pay and opportunity for promotion in all areas.

Sociological knowledge serves youth, minority groups, and the impoverished.

about what he can offer society and what he can do to improve the conditions around him. Although it should be made clear that sociology is not a synonym for social reform and that, as an academic discipline, it is concerned with investigation and understanding rather than advocacy, it nevertheless will have much to offer the young idealist. Sociologists often are called upon for help in the formulation of plans for reform in many institutions of society. Recently the specialist in urban sociology has been called upon to offer suggestions for relieving the pressures created by increasingly rapid urban growth; the criminologist is sought for advice on prison reforms; the individual with a background in medical sociology is called upon to help facilitate the rehabilitation of wounded veterans, mental patients, and people with physical handicaps caused by illness, injury, or congenital ailments.

The student with an undergraduate major in sociology is an excellent candidate for the Peace Corps or VISTA. Also, his understanding of human interaction is invaluable in working with Target Area programs in the nation's black communities. The specialist in race relations is asked for methods to alleviate the conditions that have given the black community the stigma of ghetto. The student with some understanding of sociology also is needed to work in programs directed toward the alleviation of poverty among migrant Mexican American farm workers, poor whites in Appalachia, and Puerto Ricans in New York. For some students of sociology such programs become short-term learning experiences, but for an increasing number of individuals these projects become lifelong occupations.

Therefore, to answer the question "What occupations do sociologists pursue?", we say "Use your imagination." By the time the student reading this book is ready to put his knowledge to use, new frontiers— frontiers unknown to us at the time of this writing—will be open to him.

SUMMARY All the social sciences become increasingly necessary in an age of rapid social change and expansion of knowledge. The special characteristics of sociology are its great breadth of interest in all aspects of the group life of mankind, in the trends and developments of social systems, and in the causes of social change and social problems. The questions asked by sociologists cover a wide range, including the reasons for the development of social cohesion and group-centered attitudes, the analysis of cultures, the socialization process, racial and ethnic groups, population and urbanization, and the major institutions of society.

The methods of sociology are similar to those of any other science or social science, stressing careful observation, the development of theories, concepts, other tools of analysis, and sometimes experimental designs. Whatever method is used, sociologists attempt to be systematic, objective, and open minded.

A brief glance at the history of sociology reveals much about its basic orientation and how it has changed emphasis to remain abreast of the times. Comte had several good suggestions for the development of a science of society, although he was not very scientific in his own methods. Sociology in his day, and to some extent for many years after his time, was seen as a key to controlling man's destiny for the purpose of societal improvement. Although the modern sociologist hopes his findings will help the human race, he sees his task as primarily the intellectual quest for knowledge and explanation. Several American sociologists of earlier times (especially Lester Frank Ward) were interested in sociology as a reforming field of knowledge. Sumner, on the other hand, contended that any attempt of man to improve social justice would end only in a decline of the human species. Later sociological thought has come somewhere between these two extreme views—the sociologist must study and learn; society, hopefully, can put his knowledge to use.

Sociology is a good background for a number of fields of employment, including some that are only indirectly sociological, such as welfare, probation, parole work, many kinds of juvenile work, and advisory positions in aid to the poor. For the person moving directly on to a higher degree, sociology offers opportunities for supervisory jobs in welfare, but more typically in college teaching, college research, and governmental and industrial research. Finally, it must be added that much of what sociology has to teach about society and social class will be helpful to any idealistic person going into community service, work with youth groups, or such organizations as the Peace Corps or VISTA.

The field of sociology has expanded rapidly in the last few decades, and until recently there has been a shortage of sociologists. Indications are that sociology will continue to be a growing field in the future in college, government, and industry. A complex, dynamic society requires study by experts, careful in their methods and objective in their conclusions.

Socially the hunting ape had to increase his
urge to communicate and to co-operate with
his fellows. . . . With the new weapons to
hand, he had to develop powerful signals
that would inhibit attacks within the social
group. On the other hand he had to develop
stronger aggressive responses to
members of rival groups.[1]

DESMOND MORRIS
The Naked Ape

two

THE HUMAN GROUP

Judging by all contemporary societies and by what little
is known of the remote past, man is and always has been
a social animal. Reasons for man's social traits are rooted
deeply in his biological nature, a nature in which sex
interest is a continuous rather than a seasonal
phenomenon; an extremely undeveloped and helpless
infancy calls for constant warmth and attention; and
a lack of instinctive ways of facing the problems of life
calls for a long process of learning from others. Although
nearly all primates, and a majority of other mammals as
well, are social In their habits, man has carried social
traits farther than any other species, subordinating and
controlling his biological urges for the good of the
group.[2] He creates his own rules regarding mating and
marriage and the duties and obligations of klth and kin, and
he defines his own groups, bands, tribes, and societies
in contrast to those of the outsider. In his evolutionary
past man had to learn cooperation in his constant search
for food, lest he be the hunted rather than the hunter.
One man alone was helpless. To be ostracized by the
group was to be virtually sentenced to death. Now, after
hundreds of thousands of years of human development,
the physical possibilities of surviving alone are greatly
increased, but it is a rare individual who chooses to live
alone. As John Donne wrote, "No man is an island, entire
of itself. . . ."

[1] Desmond Morris, *The Naked Ape*, Dell Publishing Co., Inc., New York, 1967, p. 23.
[2] Marshall D. Shalins, "The Origin of Society," *Scientific American*, vol. 203, no. 3, September, 1960, pp. 76–85.

THE IMPORTANCE OF GROUP IDENTITY In a society that has a tradition of individualism, it may seem strange to emphasize the study of groups of people rather than individuals. We like to see individuals with minds of their own, and we decry anything that looks like slavish conformity. Yet all of us are influenced in basic attitudes and values by our families, conform to some of the norms of our peer groups in childhood, and are sensitive to the judgments of our neighbors, associates, and fellow workers. We look to friends and kinsmen for moral support and for psychological security; the achievement goals that we seek are generally meaningful and worth our strife only if they are highly regarded by the groups to which we belong. Group pressures help us to obey the laws in most cases, but membership in deviant gangs can encourage disobedience. Group pressures can make cowardly conformists of us in some cases, and under other circumstances they can make us into self-sacrificing heroes. The group can impose its tyranny upon us, but it can also be our protector. It is not an exaggeration to say that the presence or absence of meaningful ties can be the determining factor as to whether we wish to live or die.

To live or die: Durkheim's study of group influence A major contribution of Durkheim was that of defining a distinctive field for sociology. Sociological facts, he believed, should be explainable in terms of sociological causes. One of his major works, *Suicide*, published in 1904, clearly demonstrates social causes for the desperate decision to take one's own life.[3]

First, Durkheim demonstrated with careful use of statistics that neither race nor climate had any bearing on suicide rates, although they were both rather popular explanations of suicide rates in those days. He also argued that to describe suicide as the result of a psychological malady, *suicidal mania*, simply was to supply a name for a puzzling phenomenon, but not an explanation. Durkheim reasoned that instead of examining the psyche of the person who killed himself (something nearly impossible to do), we should examine his group relations.

When a man commits suicide, he is not only destroying his own life, but he is severing his relationships with others. If these relationships mean enough to him, his emotional ties should surely act as a bulwark against suicide. Suicide, then, must be more characteristic of the isolated individual than of the man with a strong sense of belonging. In this negative sense suicide can be thought of as a social phenomenon.

Durkheim carefully checked all the available statistics relative to various indexes of social integration. What about married people as opposed to single? What about people with children as opposed to childless couples? In both cases, the importance of belonging was

[3] Émile Durkheim, *Suicide*, John A. Spaulding and George Simpson (translators), The Free Press, New York, 1966.

demonstrated. Married men and women are much less prone to suicide than single people, and married people with children are even less prone. Not only is family a protection against possible suicide, but Durkheim's statistics indicate that the same is true of belonging to closely knit communities, such as the old-fashioned European village. Even national group identity has a demonstrable effect. In war time the suicide rate consistently goes down; Durkheim explained that war, despite its ills, solidifies the nation, giving everyone a sense of belonging, identity, and purpose. Religious identification also has a measurable effect on suicide rates. The suicide rate in the France of Durkheim's time was highest for nonchurch members, second highest for Protestants, low for Catholics, and even lower for Jews, although all three religions teach that suicide is wrong. Durkheim reasoned that the differences between the three religious groups was a matter of the closeness of emotional union. The Jews are linked together by closer community feeling than either the Protestants or the Catholics. Catholicism, however, holds people into closer bonds than does Protestantism. Catholicism stresses organizational membership, spiritual leadership, and, in a philosophical sense, does not leave man alone before God as does Protestantism. Those not belonging to churches lack the group identity of the religious groups, and this, to Durkheim, was the major explanation of their higher rates of suicide.

Suicide rates also increase with age. Again Durkheim found the explanation in group solidarity, for old age tends to become a period of increasing isolation, as old friends die, and deafness and senility alienate the individual from others.

What about social expectations? Do feelings of right and wrong have their influence? After all, the family man is bound by duties as well as by love, and churchgoers would consider self-destruction a major sin. Durkheim's conclusion was that suicide rates are also higher among people who are not held in line by society's rules, either because they have never internalized the rules, or because they are plunged into a situation in which the rules they have learned no longer seem to apply. The problem of changing or inappropriate norms was part of the explanation Durkheim gave for the higher rate of suicide in the city than in the village. Suicide rates were highest among the recent immigrants to the city; it was they who were lost, rootless, and normless, not knowing the ways of urbanism. Other cases of suicide related to normative problems are those of people who were once well off and then lost status or sank into poverty (recently demonstrated in a New Orleans study).[4]

It was Durkheim's conclusion that suicide rates were increasing in

[4] Warren Breed, "Occupational Mobility and Suicide," *American Sociological Review*, vol. 22, no. 2, April, 1963, pp. 179–188.

Europe at the beginning of the twentieth century and that greater isolation of individuals from old home ties and greater detachment from the norms of an older society were part of the reason. Both types of detachment were typical of the growing industrial societies. The suicide resulting from isolation he called *egoistic*. *Ego* means self; the word "egoistic," as used by Durkheim, can best be thought of as referring to the isolated self. Durkheim applied the word "anomic" to the suicide resulting from detachment from the norms. *Anomic*, a word very much in the vocabulary of sociology ever since Durkheim's time, refers to normlessness or confusion over the norms. Durkheim also applied the word to the socially uprooted.

The concepts of egoistic and anomic suicide do not tell the whole story of self-destruction. Durkheim realized that there were societies in which people were closely bound by rules and regulations and by relationships to kinsmen, but suicide rates were, nevertheless, high. Japan was an important example. In Durkheim's days the practice of harakiri was more prominent, although it still exists. *Harakiri* is the practice of ceremonially taking one's own life by disemboweling himself with a knife. The reason for harakiri was not isolation or anomie but was essentially a matter of sacrificing for others. If the identification with the group is too strong, and, as Durkheim said, "the importance of life is beyond the individual life itself," then it is easy to die. This is the essence of sacrifice in war, but it is also the essence of harakiri. The Japanese died by his own hand if he had brought disgrace to his family, his community, or his nation. He could protect the honor of others only through the sacrifice of himself. Puccini expressed the idea correctly in *Madame Butterfly*, "If one can no longer live with honor, then one must die with honor." This form of suicide was termed *altruistic*.

Durkheim's three types of suicide are diagrammatically presented here. The "circle" indicates an optimum condition in which the individual is held closely in group bonds, but not so subordinated as to make life impossible without them. "Circle" indicates a nearly zero suicide rate (no country actually has this), and the arrows leading in three directions indicate an increasing suicide rate for each of the reasons given. Anomic and egoistic suicide are shown close together, because they are similar types. An individual might be both isolated and anomic, but the altruistic case is completely opposite.

In summary, group membership functions to give the individual a sense of identity and worth, obligation, and mutual benefit. So great are the psychological functions of the group for the individual that group membership can help usually to protect him against self-destructive urges, but under some circumstances it may even prompt him to lay down his life for the common good.

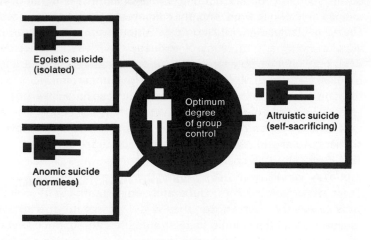

To fight or surrender   Durkheim's use of the term "altruistic suicide" comes very close to our term "heroic self-sacrifice" in some cases, especially when one willingly lays down his life for his country. Durkheim's study suggests that this type of heroism is most likely to occur when one's group is more important than his life. Research work from World War II bears out Durkheim's conclusions. In an investigation of why men were willing to face the enemy, several variables were tested.[5] Was indoctrination in love of country the primary source of bravery? Or was bravery most strongly developed as a result of hatred of the enemy? Neither explanation was primary. The strongest factor in this type of bravery was found to be group opinion. One cannot show cowardice in the eyes of his comrades-in-arms. Similarly, public opinion has pressured millions of men into joining the armed services in time of war; better to face the enemy than to face the contempt of one's peers. If the Vietnam War has been unsuccessful in attracting many volunteers, it may be because group pressure has been far from unanimous, with opponents of the war ready to give moral support to those who resist the draft.

A study of the German Wehrmacht shows how strong can be the influence of close group organization and sentiment.[6] The German army was organized with group integration in mind. Squads were trained together for long periods, went on furloughs together, and, if transferred, were reassigned together. Everything was done to maintain the

[5] Samuel A. Stouffer, "A Study of Attitudes," *Scientific American*, vol. 180, no. 5, May, 1949, pp. 11–15.
[6] Edward A. Schills and Morris Janowitz, "Cohesion and Disintegration in the Wehrmacht in World War II," *The Public Opinion Quarterly*, vol. 12, 1948, pp. 280–294.

social solidarity of the fighting team. Seldom has fighting morale remained so high for such long periods, even after ultimate defeat began to
seem inevitable. After Stalingrad fell there were no reassuring German
victories, only a long series of reverses. Yet desertions were rare, and
it took an unbelievably long time before demoralization set in. The surrenders were most likely to occur among units hastily formed toward
the end of the war and among those whose intensive primary-group
identity had not emerged. Others with a high surrender rate were those
men who had never fit in with the group or the unwillingly recruited
soldiers: Austrians, Moravians, Czechs, and other outsiders.

Soldiers were constantly reassured that all was well at home and
that they would be cruelly treated by the enemy if they surrendered.
There were even cases of deliberately cruel treatment of civilian populations to assure the men that they could expect no quarter. A common
rumor was that they would be castrated if captured, but eventually Allied
propaganda leaflets and counterrumors led the Germans to believe that
reasonably humane treatment would be given them. Even under these
circumstances surrenders were rare among well-integrated groups, except for occasional squad decisions to surrender. The study attributes
the high-morale factor to group solidarity more than to any other factor.

In the analysis of effects of the group on the individual, no distinction has been made yet among types of human groups. The importance
of our relationships with people has been emphasized, but some of these
relationships are much more important than others.

GROUP CLASSIFICATIONS   The term "group" has a special meaning in
sociology because it represents a concept which is central to any sociological analysis. A *group* is a collectivity of people sharing some common interest or having some basis for interaction. The possibility of
reciprocal communication is also an essential element. Therefore,
families, friendship circles, and close neighborhoods are usually classified as groups. Their interaction and communication extend over rather
long periods and are generally inclusive.

Associations are organizations of people bound together for
relatively limited and specified purposes. People enter associations to
promote or satisfy their individual interests. Clubs, protective and benevo-
lent organizations, and certain business organizations are associations.
The proliferation of associations in the United States accounts for the
fact that many foreigners view us as a "nation of joiners."

Chapters 10 to 14 will examine the five major institutions found in
every society. An *institution* is an established pattern of behavior which
is organized to perpetuate the welfare of society and to preserve its form.

The family, religion, education, economy, and government are the major social institutions, although many minor institutions develop in some societies.

A *society* is the largest meaningful group to which the individual belongs and is almost identical to nation or nation-state. There are some exceptions to the identity of nation and society, however, as when strong feelings of brotherhood cross national boundaries. Such feelings of societal identity bound Zionist Jews together long before they had succeeded in creating the present state of Israel. Some of their Arabic enemies are also bound together in the cause of Islam and Arabic unity more than by mere identity as citizens of Jordan, Saudi Arabia, or Kuwait.

There are also collectivities of people that do not constitute groups, such as a statistical category of "all people over sixty-five years of age" or "all middle-income families." There are also differences in degree of group identity. People generally feel more loyal to their family and close friends than to the companies for which they work. The small, intimate groups are so important in some respects that they are called *primary.*

Primary groups   Charles Horton Cooley In 1909 was the first to use the term "primary groups" to describe such groups as family, neighborhood, and children's play groups. Such groups were, in Cooley's phrase, "the nursery of human nature," where the essential sentiments of group loyalty and concern for others could be learned. Cooley was not creating an entirely new concept, but he contributed the word "primary," along with a sensitive description of the meaning of primary-group relationships.[7]

The characteristics of the primary groups Cooley described are those of face-to-face interaction, sentiments of loyalty, identification, emotional involvement, close cooperation, and concern for friendly relations as an end in themselves, not as a means to an end. The primary group is usually rather small, but size is much less important than sentiment. The primary group gives the individual his "first acquaintance with humanity." To Cooley (and the idea is typical of sociological perspectives), the group is of overwhelming importance. "Human nature is not something existing separately in the individual, but a group-nature or primary phase of society."[8] Human nature "comes into existence through fellowship and decays in isolation." Primary groups are, obviously, a great source of emotional psychological security. They are also, for a child, a school for learning the ways of human interaction and the give-and-take of working and playing together. Quarrels within primary groups can and do occur, and feelings can be hurt, for the

[7] Charles Horton Cooley, *Social Organization*, The Free Press of Glencoe, Inc., New York, 1958, pp. 23–31.
[8] *Ibid.*, p. 30.

members are emotionally close to one another, but indifference is impossible. How often have we, as children, said to a brother or sister,
"I'll never speak to you again!," only to have our resolution collapse
within an hour?

Cooley concluded that the positive and good characteristics of
the human being grow in families, neighborhoods, and children's play
groups in all societies, and that hatred, bigotry, and intolerance are, to
a great extent, a failure of these sentiments to spread beyond the small
group. In later pages of his book *Social Organization* he speculates about
the possible spread of primary-group sentiments to wider areas of mankind as improved communication makes man more aware of his fellow
man and as social organization grows and improves to prevent the
division of man into hostile groups. Although Cooley's hopes have not
been realized, few would deny the desirability of his suggestion for a
more thorough mutual understanding of the peoples of the world.

Cooley's analysis of primary groups and their functions may be
even more relevant to society today than it was in 1909. The analysis of
the spread of something resembling primary-group sentiments to wider
and wider areas of the world has not been continued in Cooley's terms,
but some of the implications of primary groups have been stressed even
more by modern writers. A dichotomy between primary and secondary
groups, perceived, but not elaborated on by Cooley, has become an
analytical tool for describing certain types of societal change.

Secondary groups   *Secondary groups* are the more formal and less intimate types of groups to which people belong. To start with clearly
definitive examples, the United States Army, General Motors, and a large
state university are secondary groups. As organizations, secondary
groups do not give people the feeling of close identity that primary
groups do. Considerable effort must be devoted to making people proud
of the corporation for which they work, and this type of pride, if it is
achieved at all, is not a primary-group sentiment. One can still be lost in
the great organization; there is not the same sense of psychological security. There is a greater possibility of one feeling uprooted and alienated.

If large secondary organizations are completely replacing primary
groups, then there is much to worry about in modern mass society. Loss
of identity and alienation in the mass society are common themes in
literature. There are arguments for feeling that the drift of modern society
is toward the secondary group. The military service can seize the individual
and take him from his family, friends, and neighbors. The demands of
education also can take him away from his primary groups and lodge

him in a giant university, and often the demands of business can cause him also to move far from home. Primary groups are either helpless to resist or do not wish to interfere with the modern demands of career opportunities.

There are two observations that must be made about primary groups that lessen the dreariness of the picture just presented. First, primary and secondary groups are *ideal types*, that is, types represented as opposite poles for the sake of analysis. In concrete life situations, most relations are not purely primary or secondary but have characteristics of each, and the two groups become intertwined. A man who has just moved from Arizona to Detroit to take a new job with a giant corporation will take his family with him. He might also transfer his membership in the Elks Club from the chapter in his home town in Arizona to a club in Detroit. In this case he will still belong to a family (Cooley's prototype of primary group) and to an association that has certain primary traits.

The second reservation about primary-secondary group classifications is that primary groups form within secondary groups. The man from Arizona might make a number of close friends on his new job, even though the corporation remains a distant and aloof entity. In as gigantic a secondary organization as the army, friendship ties are sometimes unusually close, especially in combat crews. Clubs and little friendship circles form in the great universities of today, even though such large institutions of learning seem cold and impersonal compared with the small-town schoolhouse. Unfortunately, though, there are sometimes "loners" within such large organizations.

A recent study by Litwak and Szelenyi[9] indicates that in the industrial society primary groups are broken up more easily than they were in agricultural societies, but they are also formed more easily by most people. The better-educated people required by industrial societies are more accustomed to making new friends and even to forming neighborhood associations when needed. In a small, agricultural community, newcomers might be regarded as strangers for years; in the modern community, where the turnover is rapid, the newcomers are "old residents" almost as soon as they have finished unpacking. Litwak's research indicates that neighbors are still the first people to be called upon in short-term emergencies (especially in a disaster such as flood or earthquake), relatives still help with long-term problems, and newly found friends fill the need for sociability and a sense of belonging in the new community. Litwak's study says more about well-educated people, however, than it does about the less educated. The latter are less likely to

[9] Eugene Litwak and Ivan Szelenyi, "Primary Group Structures and Their Functions: Kin, Neighbors, and Friends," *American Sociological Review*, vol. 34, no. 4, August 1969, pp. 465–481.

join associations and adjust quickly to new circumstances. Many people miss the ties of the small community, in spite of its having been a place of gossip and intrusiveness. Nostalgia for a simpler way of life is quite common.

Societal analyses Communities and societies have been analyzed in a manner paralleling the primary-secondary types of group relationships just discussed, and sometimes the analysts show a nostalgia for an older order. The German sociologist Ferdinand Tönnies used the word "gemeinschaft" to describe communities characterized by many primary-group relationships. Picture an old-fashioned European village with its homespun games and entertainments, its traditional festivals, communal baking ovens, a village common for sheep or cattle, and achievement in arts and crafts measured by village standards, not national standards. In such a place, families have known each other for generations; it would seem unlikely that one would worry about alienation. One might, however, be hounded by village gossip and ridicule. The opposite type of society in Tönnies' analysis is called *gesellschaft*—a businesslike, contractual society, emphasizing efficiency rather than primary personal ties. Durkheim and Weber were both cognizant of such contrasting types of societies. Weber spoke of the trend toward bureaucracy and rationalization of means of production, and Durkheim described a shift toward organic solidarity. By *organic solidarity* he meant the kind of solidarity that arises in a society whose members are as interdependent as cells in a living organism, each doing a different type of work. The idea of organic solidarity is not entirely pessimistic. In time, Durkheim said, the new interdependent society would be better than the old, but much chaos could be expected for the immediate future—a period of adjustment to a new style of life.

In the discussion of primary and secondary groups and societies, attention has been focused on groups to which we belong. Primary-group loyalties are strong and affectionate. Secondary-group belonging can be based on purely utilitarian values rather than affection; but in both cases the individual is a cooperating member of the group. What about the outside group—the people across the tracks, or across the ocean? What feelings develop relative to the outsider?

INTERGROUP ATTITUDES Conflicts have been so frequent and terrible in the human race that we sometimes wish all people could be blended into the same social system and all differences disappear. Yet a little more reflection makes us realize that such a world would be dull, un-

Cooley's primary group concept

Primary group	Secondary group
Examples	Examples
Family	Giant corporation
Children's play groups	State university
Close-knit neighborhood	United States Army
Traits	Traits
Emotional involvement	Unemotional
Close cooperation	Competitive
Face-to-face interaction	Less intimate
Identity	Identity less relevant
Psychological security	Economic efficiency
Belonging an end in itself	Belonging a means to an end

Additional comments
Not all groups are strictly primary or secondary but come somewhere between: school, church, lodge.

Primary groups exist within secondary groups.

Societal types similar to primary-secondary relationships

Tönnies	
Gemeinschaft (person-centered)	Gesellschaft (business-centered)

Durkheim	
Mechanical solidarity (members all alike, as though turned out of a machine)	Organic solidarity (members all different, held together by interdependence)

differentiated, and devoid of the constant and largely unconscious experimentation with social systems that has been the major preoccupation of the human species. Some of these social systems insist upon maintaining their own separate identities even within larger societies. Those societies holding pluralistic values would say they should have this right.

Conflict groups Georg Simmel, an early German sociologist, wrote that "the unity of groups frequently disappears if they have no enemies."[10] In this phrase he was describing what are often called *conflict groups*, groups living within a society but in a state of normative conflict with it. Throughout many centuries of Western history, religious dissenters have been good examples of conflict groups. Such groups, especially if they feel threatened, close ranks, displaying great unity and cohesion. Throughout most of their history the Jewish people have lived as a conflict group in one society or another. By surrendering their ideals, perhaps they could have lived unmolested, but at the price of surrender of their religion and their cultural identity. Simmel tells us that many Protestant nonconformist groups resisted attempts at compromise with the established churches because "otherwise the solidarity of their opposition would disappear, and without this they could not further struggle." The very fact of opposition to others preserves group solidarity.

In-groups and out-groups Sumner used the terminology of "in-group" and "out-group" to describe similar types of group feelings, but Sumner's terms have wider applicability. The groups to which we belong are *in-groups*, and groups to which we do not belong are *out-groups*, especially if we look upon them with a certain amount of antagonism. The in-group versus out-group concept is applicable to friendly rivalries between schools, clubs, and associations, but it is also applicable to much more hostile groups. On a small scale, it is descriptive of violent neighborhood gangs; on a larger scale it is descriptive of wars between nations.

The in-group versus out-group concept is intimately linked to *ethnocentrism*, which means, literally, centered in the culture and can be characterized as the idea that one's own group is best and others are to be judged on its terms. Ethnocentric attitudes are mentioned most frequently relative to national rivalries, but ethnocentrism has many applications. One can be ethnocentric about his community, state, social class, or even about his race. Strong and exaggerated ethnocentrism regarding nation and race is fraught with danger and possible conflict. Sumner was a pessimistic thinker on the subject of human hostilities, concluding that man would always be ethnocentric, and divided into antagonistic groups and would always have wars.

The essential reason for ethnocentrism is that a society must teach the "rightness" of its ways to its young to give them a sense of values; and if the society's ways are right, other ways must be wrong. Furthermore, group morale demands loyalty and pride. Even the individual ego is bolstered by the belief that his society is best. The stories of heroes

[10]Georg Simmel, "The Sociology of Conflict," *American Journal of Sociology*, vol. 9, 1904, pp. 517–518.

are told and retold to emphasize the societal virtues, and rising generations are not allowed to forget the evil ways of the enemy and all his past
transgressions.

Isolated in the hills of Western New Guinea live the Dugum Dani, a
stone-age people, not contacted by Western civilization until the 1960s.[11]
Each tribe of the Dugum Dani is indistinguishable from the others, but
they are mortal enemies, each tribe seeing its people as good and the
outsiders as bad. Year after year intermittent war goes on between pairs
of tribes. A member of one tribe is killed and is buried amid impressive
ceremonies and agonies of tears. After the burial, as soon as a good day
for fighting arrives, the war is resumed, until a Dugum Dani from the other
side is killed to avenge the act of "those evil people." No one knows
when the war started, for it is older than the memory of any living man,
and its origin was unknown to his father or even to his father's father's
father. Nor is there any expectation that the war will ever end, for all
wicked deeds must be avenged so that departed spirits can rest in peace,
and the righteousness of the tribe can be reaffirmed.

The recent history of Western civilization also contributes many
examples of ethnocentric behavior. During World War II, both Axis and
Allied troops prayed to the same God to make them victorious over the
enemy. Each combatant nation was sure that it had "God on its side."

In fact, ethnocentric attitudes have often served as justification for
violent acts. The Ku Klux Klan has used the pretext of "protecting white
womanhood" to rationalize its lynching of Negroes, and in any major
city in the United States Black Panthers seem to be convinced that their
attitude is right.

Reducing out-group hostility   Is this account of the Dugum Dani actually
a kind of parable about the human race? Sumner would have said "Yes";
Cooley would have said "No." Sumner saw a destructive degree of ethnocentrism as inevitable, growing out of our respect for our own customs
and values. Cooley saw the possibility of the spread of feelings of sym-
pathy for our fellow man during an age of worldwide communication, and
he saw also the possibility for larger organizations that would sweep
old enemies together into common societies, as happened long ago in
England and Scotland.

Another possible hope for the human race is in greater education
and awareness of others. The most narrowly and dangerously ethnocentric individual is apt to be poorly educated and to have little experience
with other types of people. Such a person is often referred to as an
authoritarian personality, a term developed in the 1940s by Adorno,

[11] Robert Gerdner and Karl Heider, *Gardens of War: Life and Death in the New Guinea Stone Age*, Random
House, Inc., New York, 1968, pp. 135–144.

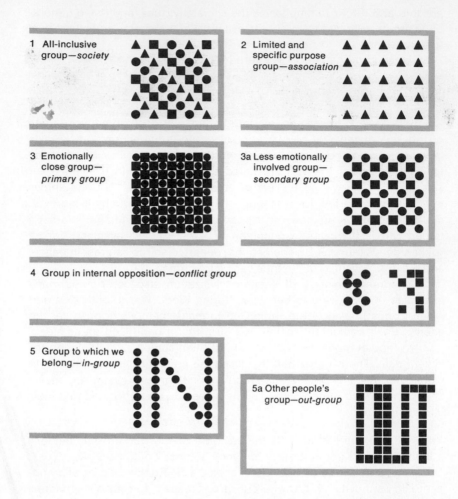

1 All-inclusive group—*society*

2 Limited and specific purpose group—*association*

3 Emotionally close group—*primary group*

3a Less emotionally involved group—*secondary group*

4 Group in internal opposition—*conflict group*

5 Group to which we belong—*in-group*

5a Other people's group—*out-group*

Flowerman, and others and widely used since. Authoritarian types tend to think that only one way is right, that there is not much room for argument, and that there should be strict obedience to leaders. Such people are usually highly intolerant of foreigners and draw complete and easy distinctions between "good guys" and "bad guys."

Education, especially education in the social and behavioral sciences, causes a decline in narrowly ethnocentric attitudes. Greater experience of the world and of various groups of people, not necessarily gained just in the classroom, is also helpful in broadening the mind. The type of perspective that social scientists would like to substitute for ethnocentrism is that of cultural relativism.

Cultural relativism *Cultural relativism* is the attitude that all people should be judged in terms of their own cultures and that various customs and practices that we would avoid might be appropriate in the context of the cultures that follow them. Nearly all present-day Americans are capable of seeing that such Indian leaders as Tecumseh, Joseph Brant, and Crazy Horse, although they fought against our ancestors, were great men as measured by their own standards. We are also broad minded enough to realize that in some cultures a man can have four or five wives because it is the custom.

Cultural relativism is a viewpoint that enables the student to step outside his own circle of values and see unfamiliar social customs as their practitioners see them. This does not mean, of course, that the cultural relativist is without values of his own, but he at least withholds judgment of other cultures as he studies them.

There are, however, some strains in the cultural-relativist concept. Most cultural relativists would find it difficult to remain purely objective about a society whose ideals call for conquering all of its neighbors or for practicing cannibalism, slavery, or head-shrinking; nor would they be objective about the atrocities of Nazism on the theory that they were part of a cultural system. Even the cultural-relativist view of human societies has its limitations, not in ethnocentric attitudes, but in terms of the common welfare and survival of mankind. The United Nations Declaration of Human Rights is a first faltering attempt to define rights and wrongs in terms of the welfare of mankind as a whole. The declaration avoids being a mere ethnocentric statement of the values of the Western world, and it also avoids the above-mentioned pitfalls of cultural relativism. Whether mankind can ever agree to certain human rights and make them more than an unenforceable statement remains to be seen. Many different cultural values would have to be considered, for cultures vary widely, as we will see in the next chapter.

SMALL-GROUP RESEARCH Considerable study has been done in the field of group research to test degrees of conformity and other patterns of group interaction. Are the judgments of people badly distorted by group pressures? Do patterns of leadership emerge naturally? Does interaction generally promote friendliness? Are there cases in which group and leadership pressures constitute dangers?

Conformity studies   One of the best-known studies in group conformity (conducted among college men) was undertaken by Solomon Asch.[12] The subject of the experiment compared the length of lines on white cards. He and several others sat in separate booths, and he was led to believe that the other people were also subjects of the experiment. The system was rigged in such a way that he could hear the judgments made by the other men being tested. What he did not know was that all the others had been instructed to give the same wrong answer. The question was whether the subject would have enough independence of mind to rely on his own judgment or whether he would go along with the opinions of the others. The answer was obvious enough so that errors could be expected in only about 1 percent of the cases. Yet under the influence of group pressure, 36.8 percent of the subjects gave the wrong answer.

Some variations on the experiment were also tried. If some of the people who were wise to the test were instructed to give a different wrong answer from that of the majority, then the subject's resistance to group pressure was increased. Standing alone against a unanimous group is more difficult than facing a disunited opposition.

A similar type of experiment was conducted by Muzafer Sherif, also with college men.[13] In Sherif's experiment, men were asked to watch a single pinpoint of light in a totally darkened room and to describe its movements. Sometimes four or five men watched it together, and sometimes individuals watched alone. The light actually did not move, but the circumstances made it very easy to imagine movement. The men got together to decide what the movements were. Those who had to watch alone readily agreed with the group about the direction of the light movement. It was as though under conditions of confusion and bewilderment there was a great reassurance in finding group norms. Sherif concludes that man may sometimes feel too constrained by group norms, but the absence of such norms is much more intolerable.

Building and resolving conflict   Sherif also did a lengthy study in group interaction among boys of junior high school age at a summer camp.[14] The boys chosen to attend camp were carefully selected so that such variables as bad reputation, ethnic-group antagonisms, and widely different abilities and backgrounds did not have to be considered. All the boys were intelligent, of good reputation, and from middle-class backgrounds. They were selected from different schools so that they did not know each other before summer camp began.

[12] Solomon Asch, "Opinions and Social Pressure," *Scientific American,* vol. 193, no. 5, 1955, pp. 31–35.
[13] Muzafer Sherif, "Group Influences upon the Formation of Norms and Attitudes," in Eleanor E. Maccoby, Theodore M. Newcome, and Eugene L. Hartley (eds.), *Readings in Social Psychology*, Henry Holt and Company, Inc., New York, 1958, pp. 219–232.
[14] Muzafer Sherif, "Experiments in Group Conflict," *Scientific American,* vol. 195, no. 5, 1956, pp. 54-58.

In the relatively unstructured first days of the experiment, friendships formed quickly, and leadership emerged. Leadership seemed to be natural and spontaneous. One experiment proved that the popular, leadership types were overrated in their performance in competitive games.

After friendship cliques were formed and leadership emerged, the boys were divided into two groups — the Eagles and the Rattlers — cutting across friendship lines. The Eagles and Rattlers were always made antagonists in sports and contests. Old friendships dissolved rapidly, with especially hard feelings toward former friends, who were now seen almost as traitors.

After antagonisms had grown strong, two attempts were made to resolve the conflict situation before it destroyed the summer camp. The boys were allowed to enjoy good times together: motion pictures and special treats at the cafeteria. This plan did not work. The two groups pushed and shoved in line and vented their hostility toward one another. The next part of the experiment was to see whether they could be brought back together by tasks in which they had to cooperate for their mutual good. It was arranged for the water supply to break down so that the boys had to work on the system. A truck was stuck in the mud, and everyone had to cooperate to get it out. Almost immediately, the antagonisms began to dissolve. The experiment had an acceptable outcome, and by the end of six weeks in summer camp old friendships were restored.

To what extent can the experiences of a group of boys in summer camp be generalized? Certainly there are many other situations in life where repeated contests rouse hostility. Sportsmanship is hard to maintain if tensions run too high between rival schools, for example. But what about the other side of the case? Can a need for cooperation unite people who have long been antagonistic? The experience of integration of the Armed Forces would indicate that the answer is generally "Yes."

Experiments in integration   Samuel Stouffer reports about the experiments in integrating the Armed Forces toward the end of World War II.[15] Previously, black and white troops had been assigned to separate units and separate tasks. It is appalling to think that we were fighting a war against the racism of the Nazis, but were fighting it with a racially segregated army.

Questionnaires were given to a control group and to an experimental group. The control group was a group of white soldiers who had had no experience with integration, and the experimental group was one in which integration had been tried.

[15] Samuel A. Stouffer, *The American Soldier: Adjustment During Army Life,* Princeton University Press, Princeton, N.J., 1949, p. 594.

The question posed to the control group was, "How would you like integration with Negro troops?" The replies were overwhelmingly negative, with approximately two-thirds saying they would dislike the idea very much, 11 percent saying it would be all right, and the remainder mildly opposed. In the experimental group, after integration had been tried for several months, similar questions were asked. The replies were almost the exact reverse of the control group. Sixty percent expressed approval; seven percent disliked it intensely, and the remainder expressed only mild disapproval.

Not all types of integration have worked out as well as that of the Armed Forces. It must be admitted that men in uniform are under orders that cannot be openly defied. There are, however, some of the same implications as those found in the study of boys in summer camp. The armed services bring men into a situation in which they have the same complaints, in which they are ordered around in the same manner, and in which they are deprived of the privileges of civilian life. They must cooperate for their mutual good in training and sometimes in a subtle defiance of the system through "gold-bricking" (looking busy without doing anything). Under combat conditions their lives depend upon each other, and color becomes completely irrelevant.

Neither the Korean nor Vietnam War has resulted in strong resistance to integration; attitudes change as customs change. It is not to be assumed that all is harmony at all times, but the quarrels between men are more personality clashes than racial clashes or the result of hard feelings over inequalities in assignments and promotions. Under combat conditions, color doesn't matter. Unfortunately, off the post, in Saigon bars and recreation halls, where the pressures of common interest disappear, a pattern of self-segregation is still noticeable.

Interaction and friendliness   George Homans has done an extensive study of continuous personal and group interaction and its influence on friendship.[16] In methodical, point-by-point analyses based on research studies by various writers, he shows the modification of opinions, the growth of sentiments of loyalty and friendliness, and the growth of leader-follower relationships through prolonged interaction. All of these sentiments decline if constant face-to-face interaction declines—probably one of the reasons why old-time reunions are enjoyable only for a relatively short time. Eventually the conversation begins to lag; there isn't enough in common to talk about because interaction has not gone on in recent years. Homans' work also helps to explain why people are seldom fired from jobs in which a personal relationship has developed. Even rather

[16]George Homans, *The Human Group*, Harcourt, Brace and Company, Inc., New York, 1950, and George Homans, *Social Behavior: Its Elementary Forms*, Harcourt, Brace and Company, Inc., New York, 1961.

difficult characters are hard to turn against completely. If they are fired at all it is likely to be before they have become part of the crowd.

The dangers of the group Durkheim's suicide study suggests that the control of the group can be too great. In other ways, the studies cited by Asch and Sherif are disturbing, for they make us wonder to what extent we surrender our minds to group opinion. The development of group conflicts and ethnocentric attitudes is also disturbing. Certainly the group can both mother us and smother us, and it can define our friends and enemies for us.

A disquieting thought about man's relationship to his fellow man was suggested by Raser in an article entitled "The Failure of Fail-Safe."[17] The term "fail-safe" refers to attempts to guarantee against human error in strategic situations fraught with extreme danger, especially in the handling of nuclear weapons. Many United States submarines are equipped with nuclear missiles which could be fired in retaliation against an enemy that resorted to nuclear warfare against us. To make sure, however, that no American commander fires a nuclear weapon on sudden impulse or in a state that the courts might call "momentary insanity," fail-safe systems are employed. A senior officer can fire a missile only with the consent of the other officers aboard and, ordinarily, only after receiving a set of radio signals. However, in case of an extreme emergency, it would be possible for the officers to make the fateful decision themselves. An important precaution in fail-safe is that a number of officers must decide jointly. The critical question the author raises is: knowing what we do of group cohesion, of group thinking, and of the close primary-group loyalty and "almost mystical sense of trust" that develops under combat conditions, can we really expect the junior officers to overrule their commander?

Raser further shows that human judgment grows more erratic and undependable under conditions of extreme emergency. Adrenaline enters the blood stream to prepare the warrior for fight or flight but not for meditation. It is also under emergency conditions that people look most strongly to leadership and seem least capable of rendering independent judgment. "Even if the subordinates have doubts, there is research showing that they will probably obey the captain's orders."[18] A combination of explosive ingredients develops: fear and hatred leading to restricted vision and imagination, and group training and loyalty leading to group thinking. Add to this combination greater power in a single Polaris submarine than has been exploded in all the wars of history, and we shudder in spite of all the reassurances of fail-safe.

[17]John R. Raser, "The Failure of Fail-Safe," *Transaction*, vol. 6, no. 3, January, 1969, pp. 11–19.
[18]*Ibid.*, p. 17.

SUMMARY   Man is a social animal who exists in groups, a collectivity of people sharing interests, interaction, and communication. He identifies with the group, influences it in some cases, and is influenced by it in others. The group itself exerts strong pressure to conform to the standards and behavioral patterns of the overall membership.

A study on suicide has shown that the individual's attachment or lack of attachment to a group may influence him to commit suicide. Anomic suicide occurs when there is loose attachment to the group or when there are simply no norms to follow. If one commits altruistic suicide, his motivation arises from the idea that in taking his own life he will serve the good of the group. If one is isolated from the group, he may commit egoistic suicide.

Groups, associations, and institutions make up the structural fabric of society, the largest meaningful group to which one belongs. However, the *most* meaningful relationship is that which exists between the individual and the primary group, a small, close, and emotional collection of people. Secondary groups are more formal, less emotional, and less intimate.

Conflicts between groups occur when members of a group think of themselves in ethnocentric terms. Ethnocentrism teaches the "rightness" of one's customs and patterns and may justify violent actions against anyone whose attitudes are too divergent from those of the group. However, the attitude of cultural relativism can help to reduce out-group hostilities by pointing out that other customs are the results of different value patterns.

Experiments in creating and reducing conflict between groups, as well as experiments in integration, have shown that it is possible to change hostile attitudes toward a group to friendly, or at least tolerant, attitudes. In each case, it is the nature of the group which is the decisive factor in influencing the attitude of the individual.

three

HUMAN SOCIETIES CREATE CULTURES AND SUBCULTURES

A *culture* is the total way of life of a people—their
customs, habits, beliefs, and values, the common
viewpoints that bind them together as a social entity.
It is what the old Indian in the above quotation meant by
the cup from which they drank their life. Cultures change
gradually, picking up new ideas and dropping old ones;
but many of the cultures of the past have been so
persistent and self-contained that the impact of sudden
change has torn them apart, uprooting their people
psychologically. When the old Indian said "Our cup is
broken now; it has passed away," he was not speaking
of physical death, "but of something that had equal value
to that of life itself, the whole fabric of the people's
standards and beliefs,"[2] the entire culture. Cultures of
the modern world sometimes change with such rapidity
that members of an older generation can easily feel that
"Our cup is broken now."

The concept of culture is one of the major interests
of sociology and anthropology. Much that was once
attributed to race and heredity is now clearly seen as
the result of cultural training. The Iroquois were not
savage fighters because it was in their blood but because
it was in their culture. The Hopi are not calm and
imperturbable people because it is in their blood (or more
correctly, chromosomes) but because it is in their culture.
Cultures train people along particular lines, tending to
place a personality stamp upon them, reading "Made in
the U.S.A.," or "Made in France," or "Made in Germany."

---

[1] Ruth Benedict, *Patterns of Culture*, Mentor Books, New American Library, Inc., New York, 1946, p. 19.
[2] *Ibid.*, pp. 19–20.

43

This is not to say that all people are alike in any particular culture, for each person has his own idiosyncrasies and is a blend of heredity, cultural experience, family experience, and unique, personal experience. Nevertheless, the total experience of growing up in one culture leaves its mark upon the individual, so that a Korean child reared in America can seem typically American, and an Anglo-American child reared in Korea can seem, in cultural respects, Korean. Men create cultures, but it is equally correct to say that cultures create men.

CULTURAL TRANSMISSION, ACCUMULATION, AND DIFFUSION   Culture is transmitted by language, one of man's most remarkable gifts. Man's ability at communication is so much greater than that of other animals as to be more a matter of difference in kind than simply of degree. A mother chimpanzee, for example, can warn her child of danger and can make a variety of sounds, but she cannot link present to past and future. She cannot say "There were lions there yesterday, so don't go near the place, and avoid it in the future." Man can say all of these things, linking past, present, and future through language, as well as describing the near and familiar and the strange and faraway. This makes the accumulation of knowledge from the past and from distant places possible. When language becomes written as well as spoken, great new possibilities for cultural accumulation are opened, and the process of cultural growth accelerates.

Cultures accumulate more techniques, ideas, products, and skills as time goes on, and the more traits a culture has, the more rapidly it grows. The pace of change in modern Western societies is often bewildering. At the same time that new cultural traits are added, certain old ones have to be dropped because they have outlived their usefulness. Buggies and most of the paraphernalia of the age of horses has dropped out of American culture. However, cultures sometimes accumulate customs that are outdated but very hard to drop, such as our cumbersome methods of spelling words, our dividing lengths into inches, rods, furlongs, and miles, and dividing weights into ounces, pounds, and tons. The adoption of a metric system would save hours of mathematical computation, and the adoption of an easier spelling system would make reading possible for many who have had reading problems all of their lives. Unfortunately, though, many of the traits accumulated by a culture become set and unchangeable.

Cultural ideas and inventions not only accumulate, they diffuse, that is, spread from one area to another. During the Middle and New Stone Ages, the knowledge of the bow and arrow spread to all parts of the world except Australia. An alphabet, developed by the Phoenicians, copied by the Greeks and Romans, and modified by them and various other peoples, has spread to encompass all Western civilization and much of the rest of the world. History books are full of illustrations of the spread of the use of gunpowder from the East to the West, and its devastating effects on medieval castles and feudalism. The diffusion of the automobile to all parts of the world in recent years is having a similarly drastic effect. Examples of cultural diffusion are so numerous that it is difficult to think of an important cultural trait that has not been involved in the cultural borrowing process.

Although distance is ordinarily a barrier to diffusion, sometimes elements can diffuse over tremendous distances and long periods of time. Versions of such Biblical stories as the Great Flood, the Tower of Babel, and the forbidden fruit of the Garden of Eden have traveled to various parts of Africa, with some changes in details, but with the plot recognizable. In an Ashanti version of the Garden of Eden story, for example, a pregnant woman is overcome with an irresistable urge for the fruit of the tahu tree, which the great god Onyonkopon has warned people not to eat. The moon sees her take the fruit, reports the incident to God, and death is sent down among men.[3] The Brothers Grimm found that many of the Germanic fairy tales they recorded were found in nearly all parts of the world.

A study of the gradual diffusion of Chinese ideas and products into the Western world reveals the ubiquitous nature of diffusion. Even back in ancient Roman times silk made its way from distant China to the courts of Rome where it was dyed purple and used for royal robes.[4] During that same period of history the peach and apricot trees spread to the West. In 751 the Moslems captured some Chinese paper makers, and the making of paper spread through the Arabic world and across North Africa, reaching Spain in 1150. The magnetic compass also spread to the West via the Arabs, as did porcelain and the orange and lemon trees. After the time of Marco Polo, the knowledge of gunpowder and coal spread to Europe, along with less portentous inventions such as dominoes, playing cards, chess (via Persia), and paper money. Later tea, wallpaper, the sedan chair, lacquer ware, kites, and folding umbrellas spread to Europe; and yet later, Chinese gardens, goldfish, azaleas, chrysanthemums, camellias, tree roses, papier mâché, soybeans, firecrackers, and a few of the thousand or more vegetables used by the Chinese were popular in Europe.

Interestingly though, it was only during the eighteenth century, when Europe was very critical of its own civilization, that the ideas and philosophy of China began to spread to the West. For a while Confucius

[3] Susan Feldman (ed.), *African Myths and Tales*, Dell Publishing Co., Inc., New York, 1963, pp. 118–119.
[4] Paul Frederick Cressey, "Chinese Traits in European Civilization: A Study in Diffusion," *American Sociological Review*, vol. 10, no. 5, 1945, pp. 595–604.

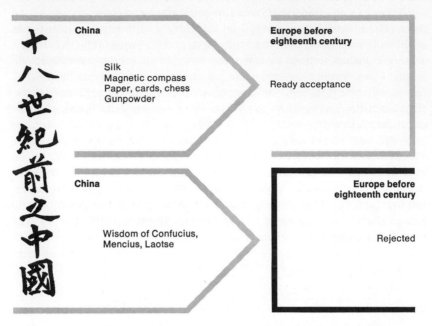

Foreign ideas are seen as more threatening than foreign products.

The wisdom of the East held no interest before the eighteenth century.

and Mencius were very much the vogue in France, hailed as the greatest sources of wisdom the human race had ever developed.

The fact that ideas spread only under the right circumstances is closely connected to the total understanding of culture. Some elements seem to fit a culture and others do not. Many people of Africa and Asia who have listened to the missionaries of the West have only halfway comprehended, for much of the message became confused with ideas of their own cultures. The leader of the Taiping Rebellion in China, for example, called himself the reincarnation of Christ, confusing Christian and Buddhist precepts and fighting with a savagery foreign to the thinking of both Buddha and Christ. Often old gods are retained and simply incorporated into the new religion brought to a people, whether that religion be Christianity, Islam, or Buddhism. Cultural diffusion of ideas tends to be limited, then, to ideas that can fit the borrowing culture.

There are other limitations on cultural diffusion, such as fear and suspicion of outsiders and their ideas. Even more important are the effects of physical isolation. People who have lived in the greatest isolation have had no chance to borrow from others. Extreme examples would be the Greenland Eskimos, who had lost all contact with other human life until their rediscovery in the early eighteenth century. The Australian aborigines were another people living in total isolation from the outside world, in their case, for many thousands of years. Generally speaking, the greater the isolation, the more primitive the society; and the greater the cultural borrowing, the more advanced the society. Naturally, a harsh, unproductive environment, or enervating heat, or impenetrable jungles, or Arctic permafrost, or precipitous mountain terrain can have a negative effect on cultural advancement. Cultural and environmental factors of this kind, and not race or heredity, explain the different levels of advancement of the cultures of the world. Even in advanced modern societies, the most isolated groups tend to advance most slowly: the mountaineers of Appalachia, remote rural communities, and the surprisingly isolated city ghetto areas, for example.

THE FUNCTIONS OF CULTURE   An examination of the functions of culture make it clear why the expression "cultures create men" is not an exaggeration. Culture defines what the proper *family* structure should be, how many wives a man should have, and whether premarital sex relations are a proper preparation for marriage or are grossly immoral. Culture sets rules for the *socialization* and care of children: when they should be weaned, how they should be cared for, and to what extent they should be trained for independence. Culture creates an *educational system* (not always the formal one we know) for teaching the growing child what he must know and how he must behave. Culture provides *values* so that the growing child is taught rights and wrongs and what his aims and goals in life should be. Culture provides *heroes* who exemplify what a good man or woman should be and after whom one can pattern his life.

To a great extent culture molds and channels what we think of as the *human condition*, partly deciding even such biological details as how often we get hungry in the course of a day, at what time we have reached marital age, and whether we express our feelings loudly or with restraint. Even the personality differences that we think of as separating feminine from masculine temperament are interfered with to some extent. Hall tells us that in Iran it is perfectly fitting for a man to burst into tears when overwrought.[5] Since man is the stronger of the two sexes, he should show his feelings strongly. Woman, being the weaker sex, should be able to hide her feelings. This is nearly the opposite of what Americans think of as proper behavior patterns.

[5] Edward T. Hall, *The Silent Language*, Fawcett Publications, Inc., Greenwich, Conn., 1961, p. 50.

Culture also *provides for economic needs*, telling how to earn a living, which jobs should be done by men and which should be done by women. Some occupations are assigned high prestige in one culture and only the most debased status in others, prostitution, for example. Tilling the soil might be considered the only sacred way of life in one culture, and in another culture, it might be thought of as so demeaning as to be done only by women and slaves.

Culture provides a means of *social control*. Not all cultures have complicated legal machinery, but all impose sanctions against those who defy their most sacred customs. Sometimes these sanctions are merely ridicule and ostracism, but these can be powerful forces for control in small, self-contained groups. Imagine the misery of the man rejected by the only people in the world he will ever know! Often primitive cultures can depend upon taboo and fear of the supernatural as a means of control. Modern, secular cultures find the problem of social control more difficult and must depend increasingly on police power and court procedures rather than on family and neighborhood opinion. This is but one illustration of the tendency for cultures to grow more complex and institute more formal and specialized officialdoms as they become more advanced and urbanized.

Culture even *defines reality* and man's relationship to the supernatural. There can be wide variations within such a culture as that of the United States, but even here culture imposes limits, so much so that it would hardly occur to a modern American to worship Quetzalcoatl or to believe in blood sacrifice. In a simpler culture there is little or no variation in sacred belief. In modern cultures, of course, much of existence is defined by science, which greatly enlightens, but takes away much of the mythological wonderment of the past. Even science, however, does not supply answers to the eternal existential questions of man, and he usually looks to the religions and philosophies of his culture for a torch to guide him.

Much of the study of culture is the study of the growth of custom. Sumner used the words "folkways" and "mores" to describe the customs of a people.[6] As originally used by Sumner, *folkways* referred to the old customs whose origins are lost in antiquity but which continue to be followed. The types of food we eat, how many times per day we eat, our customs of dress, how we celebrate traditional holidays, and our burial customs are all examples of folkways. It can be seen that some of these customs change, so that often the term "modern folkways" is used.

Mores are also cultural customs, but they are those that are held with strong feeling and whose observation is insisted upon. Eating with a knife instead of a fork would be a violation of folkways and might cause

[6] William Graham Sumner, *Folkways*, Ginn and Company, Boston, 1940.

raised eyebrows, but to bake and serve a puppy for dinner would bring screams of outrage. Mores would have been violated. In Sumner's analysis the breach of mores constitutes a threat to the group; cannibalism, murder, and treason are extremely good examples. These deviations are easy to understand in Sumner's terms, but it is a little harder to understand why the violation of certain types of food taboos would meet almost as strong opprobrium. The reasoning behind the strong emotions is clear in some cases and less so in others, but always the mores can be thought of as rules whose violation is viewed with great hostility. Obviously there are some customs that are intermediate between these examples of folkways and mores. How does one classify sacrilegious jokes, vile language, or a failure to salute the flag?

Folkways and mores are rules of behavior or *norms*. Some norms are vigorously enforced and written into law; others are frequently avoided. Sometimes mores and laws seem to be one and the same thing, as in the commandment "Thou shalt not kill." The difference is that laws are formalized, legitimately instituted, and carry the threat of punishment by society. Often laws grow out of the mores, but it is important to note that laws sometimes create new mores. For example, when regulations were changed to bring about the racial integration of the Armed Forces of the United States, the decision seemed to be in conflict with the norms of much of the country. Now the idea of integrated Armed Forces is one of the societal norms, with no noticeable movement to turn back the clock to the old days of a segregated army. Laws do not always succeed in changing norms, however, especially if there is great normative conflict over whether the law should be passed; the experience of the United States with Prohibition is an often-cited case.

The norms of society can be thought of as the rules of conduct that flow out of certain *values* or underlying sentiments of right and wrong. A society with strong military values will find it easy to recruit manpower and will probably give high-status awards to the warrior. A society with negative attitudes toward the military service will find recruiting difficult, except in a national emergency, and possibly even then. In our history, Lincoln and Wilson were particularly harassed by this problem, and the Vietnam War gives a modern example of the same difficulty. Our society, on the other hand, has been particularly successful in stressing the values of hard work and success-striving. Leisure has been little admired; hard work has had the greatest value.

CULTURAL ALTERNATIVES AND THE GROWTH OF FREEDOM   The norms of a society are in many cases applied to all of its members equally. No American can be legally forced into slavery or peonage, and, ideally, all should have equal protection of the laws. Laws against theft and murder are also

Culture is a way of life that...	Culture is a functioning system that provides...
Is transmitted from generation to generation	A "proper" family type
Is cumulative	Socialization of the young
Diffuses from place to place	Education
Is selective in what it borrows and retains	Values: rights and wrongs
	Heroes to emulate
Provides specialties and a limited number of alternatives	Ways to channelize human nature
	An economic system
Tends to be integrated around central values	Social control
Can be complicated by subcultures and cultural conflict	Definitions of reality and the supernatural
	Norms for guidance: folkways and mores, group pressures and laws

universal norms, the types that apply to all members of the society equally. There is no such universal law against drinking liquor, and yet any practicing Mormon or Seventh Day Adventist will avoid drink. The minister of another church may be allowed to take an occasional social drink, but his congregation will be horrified if he goes "on a bender," whereas the common laborer might meet much less outrage for the same offense. Physical bravery has always been a norm for Marines or policemen, but only recently has it become so for the college president! In other words, a limited amount of choice is permitted in some norms but not in areas where one's position calls for exemplary conduct.

These examples of differences in the rigidity of the norms are only minor examples of the broader area of cultural alternatives. Durkheim once said of more primitive societies that "one's first duty is to resemble everybody else, not to have anything personal about one's beliefs or actions. In more advanced societies, required likenesses are less numerous; the absence of some likenesses, however, is still a sign of moral failure." [7] An examination of examples will point out the truth of Durkheim's statement.

[7] Émile Durkheim, *The Division of Labor in Society*, The Free Press, Glencoe, Ill., 1947, pp. 396–397.

In the United States today one has many possibilities insofar as occupation is concerned; these possibilities are referred to as *specialties* in sociological literature. Jobs are assigned partly on the basis of sex, but not nearly as much so in modern industrial societies as in traditional ones. Women are not confined to the home but may pursue any job from nurse or school teacher to steeplejack or jockey. The latter jobs can be taken only in the face of much social disapproval, however, for there is still some of the old desire to make people "resemble everybody else." The role of nurse for a man has similar problems, admirable as it is, and other names such as "medical assistant" have been used to avoid the stigma.

Cultural alternatives are the types of choices that allow for differences in ideas and customs and are best illustrated in the fields of religion and politics. One can belong to the Catholic Church, to any of numerous Protestant churches, or to a Jewish temple, or to no church at all. A more unusual person might take up an interest in Buddhism or some other Eastern religion, or might be interested in any of a number of little-known faiths, such as B'hai. In all of these cases he is within his constitutional rights, so that he is really given these cultural alternatives. In another sense, the alternatives are not as open as they seem. The practitioner of a strange religion might be socially shunned. The atheist is looked upon by some as an unredeemed sinner, no matter how good a life he leads.

In the political world, cultural alternatives give one the right to be a Democrat or a Republican or to avoid partisan identification. One can participate greatly or little at all in the political process. The labels "red" or "right-wing extremist" can seriously damage a person's political reputation and public image. To be a Communist or Fascist is legally possible, but can hardly be thought of as a cultural alternative; such philosophies are considered too foreign to the cultural system.

In areas not directly concerned with religious or political philosophy, there are also many examples of cultural alternatives. Styles of dress give considerable freedom, but there are limits. Stern glances of disapproval from some, and ogling from others, greet the girl whose mini skirt is too mini. It would seem to be a reasonable cultural alternative to cut hair any way the individual wishes, but many young men have faced social ostracism for daring to wear long hair. Often this defiance of custom has provoked more wrath than have actual infractions of the law. Such is the compulsive force of culture and its folkways.

CULTURAL INTEGRATION   The opening comments of this chapter imply that culture is patterned in the sense that it has enough consistency to make life meaningful for its members. If a society is cooperative and peaceful and worships gods who are also cooperative and peaceful, the culture will have a religious consistency about it; it will be *integrated* around a set of beliefs. All parts seem to fit together. Anthropologists describe many primitive societies as having been well integrated before the impact of modern civilization disrupted them. Thus, the life of the Great Plains Indians centered around vision quests that brought bravery and magical protection, and this belief was in keeping with a way of life that stressed warfare, hunting, horsemanship, and the adventurous spirit.

Guy F. Swanson has done a fascinating study on the subject of cultural integration as applied to religions, especially of primitive peoples. By careful statistical analysis of fifty societies he demonstrates that advanced groups with various levels of authority over them usually populate the spirit world with various levels of gods. If they have a supreme chief or king, they are very likely to worship a high God above all others. Those groups with strong interests in lineages are likely to worship ancestors. Tribes with strong differences in wealth and position are more likely than others to attribute their moral rules to the gods, thus strengthening the hand of the upper classes over the lower. The author documents even more examples of this correspondence between culture and religious concepts.[8] Years ago Durkheim developed this same idea, but without the documentation that is possible today.

The words "cultural integration" also take on another shade of meaning in the sense that new elements are integrated (fitted) into the culture. The horses of the Great Plains were descended from horses lost by the Spanish explorers, but they quickly became part of the culture of the Indians, making perfect sense in a mobile hunting society.

Many of the white man's cultural traits did not fit in—could not be integrated—into Plains Indian society. Schools, clerical jobs, the idea of saving money, and getting ahead, all seemed unmanly and wrong. Erikson's *Childhood and Society* gives an excellent portrayal of how the customs and values of the Sioux created a character type that could hardly be expected to fit into modern American society.[9] Oliver LaFarge's *The Enemy Gods* tells the tragic story of a young Navaho who takes up Christianity and relates his eventual feelings of guilt, isolation, and remorse for having "followed the Jesus trail," a way incompatible with his kinsmen and their culture.[10]

There are many other illustrations of new and incompatible elements in a culture. Actually, modern societies are always full of new

[8] Guy F. Swanson, *The Birth of the Gods: The Origin of Primitive Beliefs*, The University of Michigan Press, Ann Arbor, 1960.
[9] Erik H. Erikson, *Childhood and Society*, W. W. Norton & Company, Inc., New York, 1950, chap. 2.
[10] Oliver LaFarge, *The Enemy Gods*, Houghton Mifflin Company, Boston, 1937.

elements, only half digested by the culture, so that the concept of cultural integration is hard to illustrate in such cases. In the United States, for example, there are certain basic cultural orientations usually commented upon. Man is seen as the master of nature, the active life is stressed more than the contemplative, and hard work and success-striving continue to be highly regarded. However, even some of these sentiments may not be held as firmly as in the past. As man's attempt to master nature frequently ends in polluting streams, turning lakes into cesspools, and spreading contaminants throughout the world, faith in mastery begins to falter. Americans continue to place great emphasis upon the individual, but as the welfare state becomes a more constant force, the individual's interests often succumb to those of the state. It is still true that all the sentiments mentioned above, plus a strong belief in the democratic process, run strong in America, but it is questionable whether they are consistent enough to give the sense of cultural integration of which the anthropologists speak. Many elements of Christianity stand in opposition to worldly and materialistic success-striving. Although better than 90 percent of Americans claim to be Christians of some type or degree, who would claim that a thorough understanding of Christianity would give a perfect understanding of modern American society?

COMPLEXITIES OF MODERN CULTURES   Modern cultures are complicated by heterogeneous populations made up of people with different interests, different philosophies, different occupations, and different social-class positions. In many modern societies, especially in the United States, many racial and ethnic groups add variety to the culture but also make it difficult to describe the culture in simple terms. The dominant values of the majority are not always the values of various subcultural groups.

Subculture means a smaller culture within the greater one, and a small culture that, despite its distinctive values, is still subsumed under the larger cultural system. The concept is a little tricky. How divergent can a subculture be and still fit the case? Are the extremely isolated old-order Amish a subculture, or are they a distinctive culture? Since they are subject to the laws of the United States and are American citizens and pay taxes, we would probably say that they are a subculture, but the divergence is obviously greater than the meaning implied in such terms as "Midwestern subculture" or "rural subculture."

Much latitude is given in the use of the subcultural concept, and various papers have been written about ethnic subcultures, regional subcultures, youth and age subcultures, deviant subcultures, occupational subcultures, religious subcultures, and many others.

Subcultures can be conveniently divided into three major types. Some are in the process of being assimilated into the general culture and can be called *convergent subcultures*. Many of the ethnic subcultures are of this type, Irish, Italian, Czech, Jewish, for example. Certain religious groups that once seemed very distinctive are no longer as much so, Catholics, Mormons, and Greek Orthodox, for example. They are now moving in the direction of the majority culture and are more completely accepted by it than in the past. Other subcultures converge with the main culture more slowly, if at all. The isolated Amish and Hutterites could be called *persistent subcultures* in contrast to convergent subcultures because they insist on keeping ways of life very different from those who they regard as the ungodly majority. Even they, however, are disturbed by forces, such as the requirements of education, that move them gradually toward modernity and slightly closer to the majority culture. Some of the American Indians on reservations have remained so separate from the culture of the United States as to make an excellent example of persistent subculture. The only problem is that the term "distinctive culture" might fit them better than any subcultural concept could do.

Occasionally a subculture seems to exist mainly as a reaction against the dominant culture. Yinger has coined the word "contraculture" for such groups. Other subcultures may very well have values that conflict with the major culture, but they have not arisen mainly as a reaction against it. The contraculture is primarily a reaction and "can be understood only by reference to the relationships of the group to the surrounding dominant culture."[11] One of Yinger's examples is the delinquent contraculture—the type of culture formed by city boys' gangs, especially if they are dominated more by expressions of hostility than by an interest in theft or other remunerative crimes. The beatniks of the 1950s and the hippies of the 1960s are excellent examples of contracultures, explainable only in terms of reaction against the dominant culture. It should be noted, though, that these groups are not entirely rejecting American norms, but they seem to overstress certain values (equalitarianism and ready tolerance, for example) to the utter exclusion of others, such as middle-class striving and respectability. Such groups, dedicated to opposing the norms of the larger society, can never entirely tear themselves loose. Sometimes they display the very hostilities they oppose; often there is a kind of struggle for status, a status that depends upon just the right degree of rejection of the "square" world, but a struggle for status nevertheless.

[11]J. Milton Yinger, "Contraculture and Subculture," *American Sociological Review*, vol. 25, 1960, pp. 625–635.

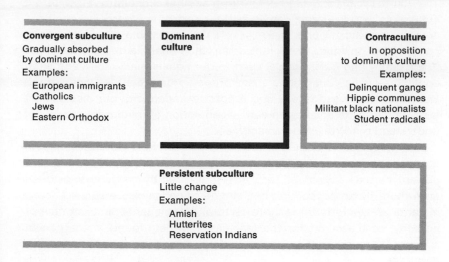

Convergent subculture
Gradually absorbed
by dominant culture
Examples:
    European immigrants
    Catholics
    Jews
    Eastern Orthodox

**Dominant
culture**

Contraculture
In opposition
to dominant culture
Examples:
Delinquent gangs
Hippie communes
Militant black nationalists
Student radicals

Persistent subculture
Little change
Examples:
    Amish
    Hutterites
    Reservation Indians

The distinction between subculture and contraculture can be well illustrated from the experience of the American Negro cultures. Among black Americans, a mother-dominated family, although different from the traditional American model, can be seen as merely part of a subcultural pattern; the Black Panthers' rejection of the whole world of the white man, on the other hand, is contracultural. However, many groups cannot be neatly categorized into one concept or the other. A poor person might express contracultural points of view toward the wealthy or toward "the dirty politicians who run the country" but still be a loyal conformist.

Culture conflict—a conflict over cultural values and norms—exists for all kinds of individuals and subcultural groups, whether they are contracultural or not. Southern blacks moving to northern cities have been enculturated into a different culture from the one they will face in the city. Even some of the rights and wrongs are different. Sons of rural Mexican families grow up in the United States with different cultural values, including attitudes toward *machismo* (manliness, often proved by sexual exploits and fighting) that often get them into trouble. For the last decade much has been written about the "culture of poverty," a culture characterized by feelings of hopelessness and futility, mitigated by hedonistic pleasures on the few occasions when there is money on hand.

The Puerto Ricans of New York City form another subculture with different cultural values. The same can be said for certain southern, mountainous areas where local mores make it virtually impossible for revenuers to collect taxes on liquor. Immigrants from lands where fathers are dominant in the family find it hard to get used to our equalitarian family, and often conflict between generations arises. People from countries where marijuana has been used legally find it hard to understand our inconsistent laws on the matter, just as an earlier generation of immigrants could not understand our Prohibition amendment.

These, then, are some of the complexities of the culture concept in the intricately varied American society, but the concept is just as important here as anywhere. Each man is molded by his culture, or often even more by his subculture; but, simple or complex, the cultural determinants are powerful. It is these cultural determinants, and not race or heredity, that account for the fascinating variety found in the human species. Whoever seeks an understanding of mankind must first study his cultures.

SUMMARY Culture is the total way of life of the people of a society, including their customs, institutions, beliefs, and values. Culture functions as a binding force, holding people together by common attitudes, beliefs, and traditions.

Culture is learned behavior, transmitted through communication, largely in the form of language. Language is so intimately connected with culture that it links its users in common modes of thought and perception. It raises the level of human possibilities far above those of the animal world, since it can relate present to past and future, and the close-at-hand to the faraway. Language (especially when written) makes possible the retention of the learnings of the past and their transmittal to younger generations.

Culture accumulates new traits over a period of time, and it drops many traits that are no longer useful. Sometimes, however, ingrained cultural habits make change difficult. Although culture is a vehicle for man's survival, it is also a trap of habit and custom from which he cannot fully escape.

Cultural traits diffuse from one society to another. Distance is a barrier to cultural diffusion, but sometimes attitudes are even more of a barrier. Cultural traits diffuse if they fit into the needs and values of the receiving culture. Foreign ideas are less likely to be accepted than are products and techniques. Fear of outsiders and extreme physical isolation are very important factors in the prevention of diffusion. Where cultural diffusion is impossible, cultures fail to develop the technologies that the Western world characterizes as advanced. It is difficult to avoid use of the words "primitive" and "advanced," but they should not be taken as descriptive of levels of happiness or psychological well-being.

Some of the functions of culture are those of defining the "right" family type and patterns of rearing the young and "proper" social roles for men and women. Cultures develop values, traditions, and heroes. Cultures help to regulate human nature, even interfering to some extent with such biological matters as age of maturity, how often the individual should eat, and what he should eat. Cultures define reality, influencing one's perception of the world and explaining the supernatural.

Cultures have their values and norms, standards of behavior. Some of the societal norms are enforced equally upon all individuals; others place stronger expectations on people in respected positions than on the common man. Cultures allow certain alternatives, sometimes in such minor matters as style of dress and sometimes in such major matters as religious and political opinions. There are always limits to such alternatives, however. Where laws do not impose limits, the threat of social ostracism does.

Anthropologists describe cultural integration as the condition that exists when all phases of a culture seem to blend together and be intelligible in terms of certain major values and beliefs. Because of the complexities of modern societies and frequent internal contradictions, the idea of cultural integration is harder to illustrate in the modern world than in the "primitive world."

Integration can refer to a process—the integration of new elements into a culture. Frequently the new elements are but poorly understood and are reinterpreted in terms of the more traditional views of the receiving culture. The attempt to integrate new ideas and customs sometimes has a shattering effect on a culture, as when the Great Plains Indian cultures had to integrate large numbers of the white man's ways. Modern societies undergo such rapid change that they are constantly in a state of flux, having the task of integrating new inventions, techniques, and ideas.

Modern societies have so many complexities that variations on the word "culture" must be used for adequate description. Within the culture there are various ethnic, occupational, regional, and religious groups with ways distinctive from the majority. The ways of life of such people are referred to as subcultures, variations on the general culture, but are contained within the same larger society. Some of the subcultures, especially those of ethnic minorities of European descent, can be called convergent in the sense that they gradually lose their distinctiveness as subcultures. Other subcultures are more persistent, trying to cling to distinctive ways, sometimes for reasons of religious conviction.

A special subcultural type arising out of opposition to the prevailing culture is called the contraculture, well exemplified by delinquent gangs, beatniks and hippies, and the Black Panthers. Such subcultures are understandable only as reactions against many of the prevailing societal norms.

Culture conflict is conflict over cultural values and norms. The very discussion of subcultures implies cultural conflict, which is a part of most societies. There are strong differences of opinion as to what the values, norms, and laws should be.

expected behavior
marraige

lady in film in sex Psych

Old woman: It's easy once you begin, like life
and death . . . it's enough to have your mind
made up. It's in speaking that ideas come to
us, words, and then we, in our own words, we
find perhaps everything, the city too, the
garden, and then we are orphans no longer.[1]

EUGENE IONESCO

The Chairs

four

THE PERPETUATION OF SOCIETIES: SOCIALIZATION

Socialization is the process by which people acquire
the beliefs, attitudes, values, and customs of their culture.
It also involves the development of a distinctive
personality for each individual, because the traits of the
group are never absorbed in precisely the same way by all
the people. Cultural and subcultural experience, family
experience, and unique personal experience interact
in complex ways upon individuals whose hereditary
endowments differ. The process, then, creates a
bewildering variety of personalities, but always within
cultural and subcultural frameworks.

THE ESSENTIAL ELEMENTS OF SOCIALIZATION   Human
personality does not develop automatically through
an inevitable unfolding of potentialities. It is true that
a certain level of maturity must be attained before various
possibilities can develop, but whether the human being
develops his full capabilities or not depends upon *human
interaction*, the mastery of *language*, and at least some
measure of *affectionate acceptance*. These three
essentials of socialization usually interact during the
process of social and physical growth.

[1] Eugene Ionesco, "The Chairs," in *Four Plays*, Donald Allen (translator), Grove Press, Inc., New York, 1958,
pp. 111–160.

Through interaction with others one learns appropriate behavior patterns; he learns his rights, duties, and obligations, and he learns which actions are approved and which are forbidden. This learning is accompanied and accelerated by the learning of language. Since people are emotional beings as well as intellectual beings, one must learn to experience love and to give love in return. For the sake of analysis, we will examine human interaction, affection, and language as though they were separate determinants, although in real-life situations these three essentials of socialization are inseparable.

Human contact and interaction are so important that they would seem to need little elaboration, and yet people sometimes assume that real ability can develop without them. The old saying "genius will out" implies that true genius needs no background or training. A little reflection and an examination of the known evidence, however, indicates that even the greatest talent can be wasted if there is no encouragement for its development.

The need for interaction: experimental evidence   We can never be certain that experimental evidence from animal studies is entirely applicable to human affairs, but such evidence deserves consideration. Conclusions from animal studies generally agree quite well with what we know of human development, and, of course, certain types of experiments can be performed on animals but not on human beings. Rat experiments indicate that those rats deprived of companionship and an interesting environment are mentally dull compared with rats "educated" in a stimulating environment. In the case of rats, it is possible to perform autopsies and weigh the brains. The "educated" rats actually have greater brain weight than those from the deprived environment. Apparently both the physical growth of the brain and its functions are influenced by the environment.[2]

Experiments with human beings must of necessity be more limited, but what experimental evidence exists indicates a similar damaging effect from stimulus deprivation. In an experiment performed at McGill University, subjects (volunteer college students) were confined to a small room, isolated, and deprived of anything to stimulate interest; the lights were dimmed and the rooms soundproofed. Feelings of disorientation began within a few hours. Subjects reported that it became increasingly difficult to think clearly. Most of the subjects were having hallucinations within twenty-four hours. Various figures began to appear on the wall in front of them, dancing about erratically. One man was so sure of the reality of his hallucinations that it was hard to convince him they were not real. Measurable differences in brain-wave patterns were also found after a

---

[2]J. T. Tapp and H. Markowitz, "Infant Handling: Effects on Avoidance Learning, Brain Weight, and Cholinesterase Activity," *Science*, vol. 140, May 3, 1963, pp. 486–487.

period of isolation, and emotional responses were described as increasingly childish.[3]

The McGill experiment demonstrated, under controlled conditions, what has often been observed before—the mental and emotional regression that takes place with people long isolated from meaningful contact. In the early nineteenth century attempts were made at prison reform by isolating prisoners from each other. The idea was that as long as the prisoners were isolated, they could not learn criminalistic behavior from each other. Such experiments were eventually abandoned because of the mental deterioration of prisoners long held in isolation. An unusual case of mental isolation occurred among American prisoners of war in Korea, where clever manipulation by the Chinese sowed the seeds of suspicion of man against man until the Americans did not know who they could trust. The result was little communication with anyone for long periods of time and consequent mental depression, apathy, and decline in the will to live.

Cases of very great deprivation of contact among institutionalized people are by no means uncommon. Such cases occur in prisons (both military and civilian), in mental institutions, in homes for the aged, and, in the past, commonly in orphanages.

Isolated children   There have been reports in the past of children (called *feral children*) growing up without human contact. The assumption has been that such children would prove what human nature, unaided by cultural learning, is really like; but the assumption is dubious, and reports of feral children are too unreliable for forming any such conclusions. Although abandoned infants and small children have been found from time to time, there is no way of knowing how long they were abandoned or whether they were normal at the time of abandonment. The closest approach to finding out what happens to the individual who is deprived of contact comes from cases of badly mistreated children, occasionally reported in the news, who have been locked up and given almost no attention. The classic cases of such children are two reported by Kingsley Davis: the cases of Anna and Isabelle.[4]

Anna and Isabelle were two girls found at about the same time, both showing the effects of extreme isolation. Although the two cases are similar, there are also significant differences. Both were illegitimate children, and in both cases grandparents had attempted to hide them away so that their existence would not be known. They were locked in attics, hidden away from society, deprived of adequate sunlight and

[3]Woodburn Heron, "The Pathology of Boredom," *Scientific American*, vol. 196, January, 1957, pp. 52–56.
[4]Kingsley Davis, "Final Note on a Case of Extreme Isolation," *American Journal of Sociology*, vol. 52, March, 1947, pp. 432–437.

nourishment, and deprived of human instruction and the chance to engage in play or other childhood activities. Neither child knew any words; both emitted only animal-like sounds, and both seemed to be severely mentally retarded.

The first significant difference in the two cases was that Anna had been totally isolated while Isabelle had been secluded with her deaf-mute mother. After the girls were found they were given special training, but Anna made only slight progress. She mastered almost no words and continued to be extremely retarded in mental growth. She died four years after her discovery.

By contrast, Isabelle gained command of language. Once she attained her first breakthrough in the grasp of words, her progress became rapid. Eventually she was enrolled in school where she achieved a grade level only slightly below her age and made satisfactory mental and social-emotional adjustment to her classmates. Why did the two girls respond differently to the process of socialization? Of course hereditary differences cannot be entirely ruled out, and Isabelle's training had been better than Anna's, but it seems likely that the greater amount of human contact between Isabelle and her mother was of major importance. There had been at least minimal interaction, more than in the completely empty world in which Anna spent her first six years of life.

Mistreatment of children is frequent enough so that the above case has more than just theoretical importance. We will return to the problem of mistreatment later, but for the next examples we will consider cases involving larger numbers of children, culturally deprived by institutionalization or by subcultural experience.

Deprived subcultural groups   In the early years of mental testing it was hoped that means had been discovered for accurately measuring all children and knowing just what their life potential would be. The reason that such a hope proved unattainable is that intelligence tests actually measure the cultural learnings of children, and children coming from a culture for which the test was not intended, or having had little contact with any culture at all, will naturally test low. The test scores sometimes are so low as to make it seem that the children could not possibly function in life outside of an institution. Actually, what seems to be measured is called *academic intelligence*, as opposed to *practical intelligence*. The former declines much more drastically in cases of cultural deprivation than the latter.[5]

One of the first people to realize the degree to which mental tests reflected the cultural environment was Otto Klineberg, who demonstrated

[5] "Retarded Children Mislabeled," *Science News*, vol. 93, June, 1968, p. 533

that the difference between the test scores of black and white children were to be accounted for by different environmental and educational backgrounds, not by racial difference. He proved his point by showing that both black and white children from backward rural areas scored low on intelligence tests and that if their families moved to areas of better educational opportunity, the intelligence scores of the children went up significantly.

While Klineberg was working on the comparison of rural and urban backgrounds in America, studies were also being conducted in England.[6] English children who lived on canal boats and who had little contact with the cultural environment of the land and virtually no schooling showed a gradual decline in IQ scores from an average of 90 at age five to less than 70 at age eleven. A study of gypsy children (also in England and without schooling) showed an almost identical drop in intelligence-test scores.

In the United States, the English studies were duplicated by a study of Kentucky mountain children, who showed a similar intelligence-score loss. A more encouraging type of study was done on isolated mountain children from Tennessee.[7] By using a longitudinal study covering ten years, the researcher was able to demonstrate a gradual increase in the intelligence-test performance of the children. The reason for the difference was that transportation was improving, there were more schools, and more children were going to school longer.

The importance of such studies for an understanding of socialization into the American culture is obvious. Those who live in a state of isolation from the main currents of life, and especially from good schools, are greatly handicapped. What applies to isolated rural areas applies also to urban ghettos, Indian reservations, isolated ethnic groups in our large cities, and many Mexican American rural communities of the Southwest.

The need for affection   At a 1968 conference of the National Institute for Child Health and Human Development, Dr. Stephen A. Richardson reported an interesting case demonstrating the results of affection in child care.[8] Thirteen orphaned children, less than three years old, had been taken from a state orphanage and were transferred to a home for retarded women. Within two years it was noted that the children showed greater mental ability than the children left behind at the orphanage. A follow-up of the orphans after they reached maturity found them all

[6] Walter S. Neff, "Socioeconomic Status and Intelligence: A Critical Study," The Psychological Bulletin, vol. 35, December, 1938, pp. 727–741.
[7] Lester Rosin Wheeler, "A Comparative Study of the Intelligence of East Tennessee Mountain Children," in Anne Anastasi (ed.), Individual Differences, John Wiley & Sons, Inc., New York, 1965, pp. 203–209.
[8] "Retarded Children," Transaction, vol. 6, September, 1969, pp. 6, 8.

to be normal and functioning well in society. This was not true of all the children who had remained in the orphanage; several of them were mentally retarded and needed institutional care as adults. The conclusion of the study was that the love and attention given the children by the women in the mental institution had made a great difference in their favor. The case is particularly surprising because the women were retarded and could not have given direct mental stimulation.

The problem for the children who remained in the orphanage was not unusual. Orphanages have generally had a record of poor physical and mental health for the children under their care. In a well-known study of a Belgian orphanage, René Spitz gives an account of the extent of the psychological damage and its causes.[9] The orphanage he describes was well run in terms of cleanliness and diet, but the babies were isolated from each other, lacked maternal care and affection, and had nothing to stimulate interest or play activities. A follow-up study after two years found them all to be below average in development, some severely retarded. Not only was mentality affected, but so was health: one-third of the infants died by the age of four. A group of infants in another institution, used as a control group, had no infant deaths whatever. Although the other institution was not as scrupulously clean as the orphanage, the infants' mothers were with them for the first year of life, and the children were given affection and play activities.

Such studies as that of Spitz's on the orphanage are given support in experimental studies. Harry Harlow, in a long series of experiments with rhesus monkeys, found that those raised without mothers showed a high degree of anxiety and did not learn to play with each other as normal monkeys do. Although they matured physically, they did not display normal interest in the opposite sex.[10]

We do not have exactly the same kind of experiment with human subjects to draw from, but the above-cited study of the orphanage and studies of cruelly treated children give evidence of inadequate development for humans as well as monkeys. Many cases of battered children are discovered by doctors and juvenile authorities. Often the authorities are told that the child fell and hurt himself, but sometimes careful investigation proves that the child has been severely and repeatedly beaten. It often develops that the parents of such children were battered children themselves. Nearly always they were starved for affection in childhood. One mother of the affection-starved type admitted to the doctor that she had never been loved. She thought that if she had a baby he would love

[9] Rene A. Spitz, "Hospitalism," in *The Psychoanalytic Study of the Child*, International Universities Press, Inc., New York, 1945, vol. I, pp. 53–72, and "Hospitalism: A Follow-up Report," vol. II, pp. 113–117.
[10] Harry F. Harlow, "Social Deprivation in Monkeys," *Scientific American*, vol. 207, March, 1962, pp. 136–148.

her. "He didn't love me, so I beat him," she said.[11] Just as the emotionally deprived monkey in Harlow's experiment seemed never to achieve emotional normality, so with the emotionally starved human being.

Language and socialization   Language is another essential of socialization. George Herbert Mead was one of the first to recognize the overwhelming importance of language in the socialization process. The individual begins to absorb his culture through the medium of language and other symbolic communication. A *symbol* is anything that stands for something else. All words are symbols, as are gestures, sighs and groans, handshakes, flags, wedding rings, Christian crosses, the Star of David, the Moslem crescent, the Republican elephant, and the Democratic donkey. One has to learn the culture to learn the significance of all such symbols, and the most fundamental of cultural symbols are words. It will be recalled that Isabelle made a breakthrough into the world of people as soon as she began to grasp the meaning of words. Most people know of the famous story of Helen Keller, whose mind was locked away from the world by blindness and deafness until her teacher was able to communicate with her. On a dramatic occasion in her life, Helen grasped the idea that her teacher was writing on her hand a symbol that stood for water. The idea that all things had names (symbols) that she could learn somehow began to waken her mind. Her progress toward education and an outstanding career began at that point.

Anthropological linguists have elaborated further upon the significance of language. In the opinion of Benjamin Lee Whorf and many of his followers, language is not only a means of communication but a means of symbolizing that influences our ways of thinking. We conceptualize the world differently in different languages. Whorf believed this to be true especially of the contrast between Southwestern American Indian languages and the languages of Europe. Whorf's hypothesis has interesting implications for the linguistic problems encountered by the children of minority groups, not just American Indians. It also has wide implications for social-class differences in linguistic ability. The lower-class child often comes to school with a vocabulary and type of grammatical usage that is offensive to his teacher.

Language problems of minority groups   There are serious linguistic problems for the child of the lower-class Negro family. Although American Negroes have always spoken English, their language can be thought of as separate

[11] "The Battering Parent," *Time*, vol. 94, November 7, 1969, p. 77.

in many respects; "A language system unto itself which differs from standard English in everything but vocabulary."[12] Roger Abrahams contends that the original use of English by American Negroes tended simply to fit English words into a framework that was different, often derived from a Portuguese créole tongue picked up from the slave traders.[13] Whatever the origin of the differences in the use of English, they are important from the point of view of education and socialization.

An interesting comment on language differences is provided by a Harlem school teacher, Mrs. Gloria Channon.[14] One of the important problems she notes is that of syntax. *Syntax* (the proper order of words in the formation of sentences) is generally learned unconsciously, just as most of one's spoken language is learned unconsciously by repetition of what is heard at home. In the case of the children from the Harlem school, the syntax learned is very simple, so much so that it cannot become a model for the use or understanding of complex sentences. Sentences are linked together by conjunctions ("An' then I go an' do this, an' then I say to her . . . "). The message is conveyed, but the grammar closes doors to sentences containing many "althoughs," "howevers," and "therefores." Sentence structure (probably reflecting life experiences) tends to be disjointed, and so are reading experiences.

Communication between black and white is also made difficult by ever-changing patterns of slang and habits of speech. Just as teenagers often develop slang that their parents don't understand, blacks often do the same to whites. The habit of "putting on" the white man has been around for centuries. In the old days such language behavior was known as "tomming" or "jeffing"; now, at least in Chicago, the expression is "shucking." Expressions change rapidly, and the ghetto slang is generally unknown to the white observer.[15]

A final illustration of language differences in the socialization process is taken from the case of a Blood Indian who once told an anthropologist about his problems of thinking in his Indian language and translating to English.[16] When thinking of things he considered important— horses, the Sun Dance, or relatives— he always thought in his own language. In thinking of things connected with the school, he thought in English. The English-language world was a world of less clarity and reality than the Indian world, and so was the white man's school.

If the socialization process is to accomplish its aim, the culture must be conveyed to each succeeding generation. Obviously the dif-

[12] Roger D. Abrahams, *Positively Black*, Prentice-Hall, Inc., Englewood Cliffs, N.J., 1970, p. 15.
[13] *Ibid.*, pp. 15–17.
[14] "Teaching Language in a Harlem School," *Transaction*, vol. 6, March, 1969, p. 7.
[15] Thomas Kochman, "'Rapping' in the Black Ghetto," *Transaction*, vol. 6, February, 1969, pp. 26–34.
[16] A. D. Fisher, "White Rites versus Indian Rights," *Transaction*, vol. 7, November, 1969, p. 32.

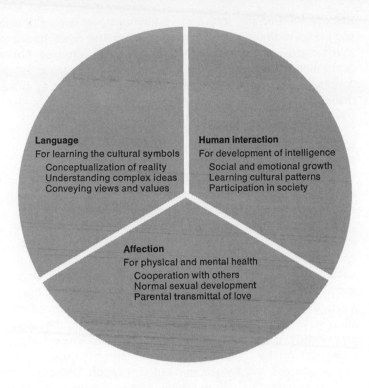

Language
For learning the cultural symbols
Conceptualization of reality
Understanding complex ideas
Conveying views and values

Human interaction
For development of intelligence
Social and emotional growth
Learning cultural patterns
Participation in society

Affection
For physical and mental health
Cooperation with others
Normal sexual development
Parental transmittal of love

ferences in life experiences are such that the culture is conveyed in varying manners and degrees. Because of differences in the types of people with whom one interacts, because of differences in one's experience of acceptance and affection, and because of considerable differences in symbolic communication, great variety in personality types is produced within the same society. There are other differences in the socialization process connected with the degree of persistence and change in socialization patterns.

PERSISTENCE AND CHANGE IN SOCIALIZATION   Since socialization is the process by which people internalize the values of their cultures, it follows that every culture and subculture will make an attempt to socialize children in its own pattern. Many immigrant groups arriving in America made determined efforts to ensure that their children kept some of the values and customs of the old world from which they had come. Many

Chinese children still go to Saturday school to learn the Chinese language, and in the large Chinese community of San Francisco the old tong organizations have only recently begun to lose their influence. For two or three generations Greek children in the United States learned at least some of the Greek language to help retain Greek culture and to make the Greek Orthodox Church services intelligible.

Persistent patterns of socialization   Other examples of the persistence of subcultural socialization are easy to find. Such religious groups as the Amish and the Hutterites have kept their people out of contact with the rest of society as much as possible in order that the old traditional patterns might continue. All people of strong religious conviction try to make sure that their children follow the religion of their fathers.

The persistence of socialization patterns also applies to a considerable degree to social classes. People reared in a middle-class pattern are taught to forego the pleasures of today for the sake of tomorrow, especially in the pursuit of success through education. Upper classes try to train their sons and daughters in the proper pattern, the social graces, styles of living, and the management of family estates. Similarly, lower-class ways of life tend to be self-perpetuating, not because anyone enjoys poverty, but because often there is insufficient knowledge of how to break out of the pattern, and both financial problems and attitudinal values prevent the long-continued education necessary for advance.

There are also different socialization patterns for rural and urban people. In bygone days rural farm life was largely an inherited way of life, and farmers had strongly ethnocentric feelings as to the great worth of the farmer relative to the city dweller. Every attempt was made to instill rural values in the minds of the young. What has been true of the attempt to perpetuate the rural way of life has been equally true of the attempt to perpetuate the Southern way of life, although both are succumbing to the needs of urban-industrial society.

Finally it should be emphasized that the dominant culture tries to perpetuate a general way of life often referred to simply as the "American way." Some conservative Americans like to see American traditions change as little as possible; some liberals are out to promote gradual and limited change, and radicals would like to see fundamental changes in the pattern. The old-fashioned American way of life has stressed rugged individualism, self-reliance, and a strongly competitive ethic.

Many of the subcultural patterns have undergone change with the passing of time and the changing requirements of society. Old ethnic groups begin to lose their distinctiveness to quite a degree. Slight inroads are made in the separatism of some of the fundamentalist churches. The rural pattern of life has undergone a definite transformation so that in many states the distinction between rural and urban has almost disappeared. Even where a definitely rural subculture still socializes people into a distinctive pattern, the impact on the society is less because the rural farm population has declined to only about 6 percent of the total.

Along with the changing socialization patterns for many subcultural groups, has there also been a change underway for the entire society? Nearly everyone would agree that changes have taken place, but there is much difference of opinion as to the direction of the change, and even wider difference of opinion as to the evaluation of the change. Are we losing our old-fashioned values? Are we becoming slavish conformists? Is the old competitive ethic weakening?

Changes in socialization　One of the most influential books to try to analyze the problems of changing personality types and socialization patterns is *The Lonely Crowd* by David Riesman.[17] Riesman maintains that the process of internalization of norms through the influence of others can take place in different ways in different cultures. There are societies in which everyone does the same thing in the same way so automatically that mere imitation of tradition is the mechanism by which the norms are internalized. If we imagine a medieval village or a present-day village in India we can picture a small community in which there is little conflict in point of view or occupation. Everything is learned through tradition. The people of such a society Riesman would call *tradition-directed*.

In the United States, although we have traditions as do all people, there is enough variety so that tradition alone does not direct us. In Riesman's opinion, in earlier America we were of an *inner-directed* type. The inner-directed man, as all men, actually learns his norms from others, but the norms become so strongly internalized that he thinks of them as his own. The inner-directed man develops a strong conscience and sense of righteousness that has been drilled into him by stern parental teaching. A strong case of this type would be the early Puritan model — a Jonathan Edwards or Cotton Mather.

As seen by Riesman, the inner-directed socialization pattern was just right for the development of the dynamic, compulsively driven type of person to develop the nation's resources and conquer a wilderness. Such a man might not have been pleasant to get along with, but he had an inner sense of direction, a "built-in gyroscope," to use Riesman's description.

With the passing of time, the increase of population, urbanization, and massive school systems, the process of learning the norms and the

[17]David Riesman, *The Lonely Crowd*, Doubleday & Company, Inc., Garden City, N.Y., 1953.

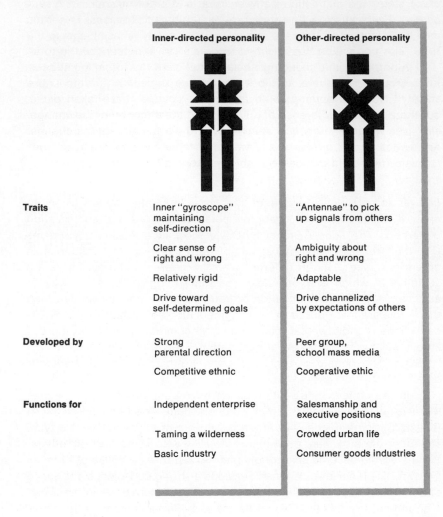

	Inner-directed personality	Other-directed personality
Traits	Inner "gyroscope" maintaining self-direction	"Antennae" to pick up signals from others
	Clear sense of right and wrong	Ambiguity about right and wrong
	Relatively rigid	Adaptable
	Drive toward self-determined goals	Drive channelized by expectations of others
Developed by	Strong parental direction	Peer group, school mass media
	Competitive ethnic	Cooperative ethic
Functions for	Independent enterprise	Salesmanship and executive positions
	Taming a wilderness	Crowded urban life
	Basic industry	Consumer goods industries

resultant personality types have changed. The new type of person can be thought of as having antennae that pick up signals from all the people around him, and these signals take the place of the built-in gyroscope. A new character type is developing, says Riesman, that is better for salesmanship and the demands of a consumer-dominated economy. The new type is reinforced by the teaching methods of modern schools, stressing the ethic of social adjustment and assuring the young that the most important point in worldly success is learning to get along with others. This emerging type of man Riesman characterizes as the *other-directed* personality.

Riesman's work has been widely read and highly praised. As with any work that tries to categorize people Into essential types, it may overstate the case for the sake of clarity. Riesman would not contend that every twentieth-century man is purely other-directed or that every earlier American was purely inner-directed, but he does contend that the emphasis is changing drastically. If he is right we would expect people to follow new fads and fashions more easily than in the past and for children growing up in school to be more responsive to the subcultures of their own generation than to those of their elders.

The old competitive ethic has not vanished entirely, according to Riesman; rather, it shows up in different forms. One once worked hard to succeed by being an independent businessman; he now works hard to learn the ways of the corporation executive, and his future depends on identification with the firm. Once again the new socialization pattern seems to fit the needs of the society, and yet many are unhappy with the picture of the new character type. We would like to think of ourselves as more independent than the other-directed man. Possibly we are. A further examination of socialization and of theorists in the field will show that we can respond to the expectations of others but still retain an independent quality and that something about the human being resists being neatly fitted into a mold.

THEORIES OF SOCIALIZATION   All theories of socialization acceptable to social scientists are based on the premise that the child is not to be regarded as a miniature adult but as the raw material from which a mature personality can be formed. All of these theories also proceed to explain how the child begins to take on adult attitudes and values, how he sees himself as a person, and how he develops a personality distinct from any other. Finally, these theories stress the importance of human interaction, emotions, and symbolic communication.

Mead's theory of socialization   Among the most prominent theorists in the development of social psychology are Mead and Cooley. Mead has been mentioned in relation to symbolic communication. He was also interested in an analysis of how aspects of personality gradually emerge from childhood play and games.[18] In early childhood play, the child observes and attempts to act out adult roles, and in so doing, he is gradually learning some of the attitudes that go with the roles.

[18]George Herbert Mead, *Mind, Self, and Society*, The University of Chicago Press, Chicago, 1934, pp. 68–78.

The process of learning roles by playing at them seems obvious in the play activities of little girls. They take care of dolls and play such realistic roles as mother, nurse, and teacher. For little boys the childhood play is more apt to exist in a never-never land of cowboys and Indians or cops and robbers. Even in this case it could be argued that there is an internalization of the idea of what constitutes "good guys" and "bad guys," and there is definitely a learning of which roles are appropriate for boys and which ones are appropriate for girls.

At the next phase of child play, Mead sees a more important aspect of internalization of society's norms: the development of the concept of the *generalized other*. Children no longer play only at pretend roles; they begin to play games that have definite rules. At first a group of small boys will quarrel angrily over a game of baseball, with cries of "Cheater!" and "Liar!" hurled at each other. The game will break up, until little by little the boys learn that the only way to play is by the rules, the rules that "they" have made up. The indefinite "they" in the statement is close to the meaning of Mead's generalized other. The generalized other represents the rules and judgments of others. There is even the beginning of an understanding of others, a development of empathy, because all players in the game have to learn the roles of the others. Thus Mead explains the beginning of taking the role of others and being socialized by others.

Mead, however, does not make the individual appear as a complete pawn in the hands of others. He uses the simple words "I" and "me" to designate two aspects of personality.[19] The "I" is the subjective side, imaginative, creative, innovative. The "me," an aspect of all personalities, is the objective side of the personality, the part that is largely formed through reaction to others. Obviously, the relative size of the "I" and of the "me" differs for different individuals.

Cooley and the looking-glass process   Cooley, the other great founding father of social psychology, also had some stimulating ideas about the socialization process. He, too, was interested in how the individual takes on the proper attitudes, ideas, sentiments, and habits to make him a cooperative member of his society. Cooley was an extremely perceptive man and a man gifted with empathy, that unusual capacity to feel one's way into the mind and emotions of others. From the study of his own children, Cooley arrived at an idea about socialization that he called the "looking-glass process."[20] As people familiar with infants and small children will have observed, the child at first seems to react to the parent's face more than to the spoken word. When his mother says "No!" the child

[19] *Ibid.*, pp. 152–164.
[20] Charles Horton Cooley, *Human Nature and the Social Order*, Charles Scribner's Sons, New York, 1902.

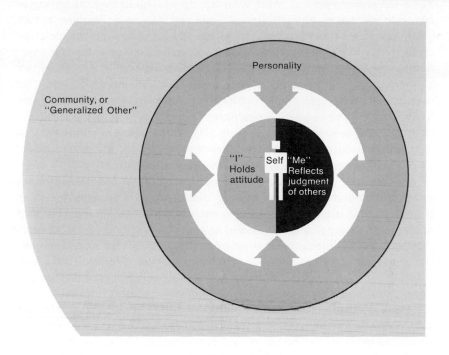

attempts to read her face to see whether she really means it. He looks into her face, Cooley says, for other reasons as well—mainly to see whether he is loved and accepted and whether he is looked upon as good or bad. The essence of Cooley's looking-glass process is that we always look into the faces of others in an attempt to read their attitudes toward us, and that we form our own self-concepts in terms of our imagination of what they think. We literally learn to know ourselves through the eyes of others. There is much wisdom in the old lines from Robert Burns:

> O wad some Power the giftie gie us
> To see oursels as ithers see us!

Cooley does not contend that we always see ourselves as others see us, but what he does say is that we try to do so, and that we see ourselves as we imagine others to see us. Cooley also hypothesized that the looking-glass process begins with the very first days of life.

In the years since Cooley's time there has been considerable argument as to whether the newborn infant perceives much of anything. It has been speculated that sight is so poorly developed that everything is an undifferentiated blur. Evidence from an interesting experiment in infant perception (although not intended as a comment on the looking-glass theory) tends to confirm Cooley's idea. Newly born infants in their first few weeks of life were tested by having a number of objects presented to them, noting which objects they focused their attention upon. The objects included brightly colored balls and balls with various markings on them. One was marked with the outlines of a human face. Without exception, the face was the object preferred by the babies. The other objects with markings on them received very little attention, and the brightly colored balls were completely ignored.[21]

Cooley's looking glass in infancy would reflect the clearest self-image from the glances of the mother and father. In later years, the child becomes more sensitive to his playmates. In the romantic years of early adulthood, the sensitivity is greatest to the object of one's love. Always, however, we are interested in what others think about us, and we adjust our reactions to our perceptions of their attitudes. Often we carry this reaction so far as to pretend interest we do not really feel in order to make the right impression.

The rejected child could be understood in Cooley's analysis as one with a destructive self-concept based on rejection by others. Even the young "tough guy" can be explained as developing a personality that will win him acclaim from the most important members of his peer group. The important people, the ones we look to for our self-image, are the *significant others*. Although the first examples to come to mind are based on childhood experience, there are significant others throughout life. Kin and close friends are always significant; so also are our professional colleagues. The self-image follows us through life, and we will do fantastic jobs of rationalization to preserve a favorable self-image. Think of such expressions as "I was just not myself when I did that," or "That just wasn't like me," or "If they had been decent to me I would have turned out all right." No one likes to abandon a favorable impression of himself. Reckless[22] has done a study supporting the hypothesis that in a neighborhood of high delinquency rates the nondelinquent boys were the ones who had the most favorable self-image. His conclusion is that a self-image of the good boy was a major protection against delinquency.

Criticisms of Cooley and Mead   In spite of these words of praise for Cooley and Mead, it must be admitted that there are criticisms of their concepts and also of the socialization picture developed by sociologists since

[21] Robert L. Fantz, "The Origin of Form Perception," *Scientific American*, vol. 204, May, 1961, pp. 66–72.
[22] Walter C. Reckless and Simon Dinitz, "Self-Concept as an Insulator against Delinquency," *American Sociological Review*, vol. 21, December, 1956, pp. 744–746.

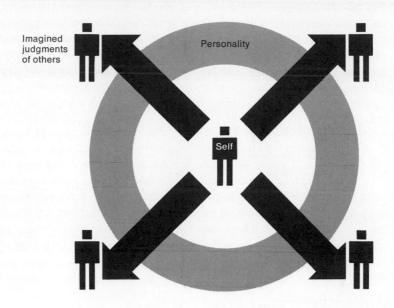

their time. One who is familiar with the works of Sigmund Freud can see that he perceived much of socialization as a struggle between the individual and society. In this respect the view of psychoanalysis has been in opposition to that of Cooley. Whereas Cooley is inclined to picture a harmonious adjustment to society, Freud saw the individual as constantly desiring to throw off the fetters of society's rules and regulations. Rationally, anyone can see that he has much to gain by conforming to the rules, for the very law that prevents him from committing murder or mayhem also protects him from other people of violent intent. Nevertheless, there are always feelings of resentment against rules, routines, customs, time schedules, and the patterns that social life imposes upon us. Even the poetess Amy Lowell ends her famous poem *Patterns* with the line, "Christ! What are patterns for?"

Dennis Wrong[23] has written an excellent article titled "Oversocialized Conception of Man" in which he contends that sociologists have looked a little too much to the harmonious adjustment between individual and society. A great amount of small-group research has been done on how the individual responds to the group; not enough has been done on

[23]Dennis H. Wrong, "The Oversocialized Conception of Man," *American Sociological Review*, vol. 28, 1961, pp. 183–193.

why he often does not respond and why the human being remains a re-calcitrant character. Although there is no definitive answer to the questions raised by Wrong, an examination of the widely conflicting agencies of socialization and pressures upon the growing individual will help to make clear why the socialization process is difficult and fraught with danger.

CONFLICTING AGENCIES OF SOCIALIZATION   Socialization is a complex process. It does not simply consist of fitting men into social and cultural patterns; in modern societies it calls for the development of a type of man who can adjust to changing patterns and who can help to change patterns to fit changing needs. The required personality type is developed against a background of conflicting agencies of socialization. No longer do family, church, and school work harmoniously together without fear of conflicting influences, if, indeed, they ever did. The generally recognized major agencies of socialization face a vast array of contradictory influences, and they are often in disagreement among themselves.

Conflicts within recognized agencies   The major agencies of socialization— family, church, and school—are all discussed in later chapters. For the present we will limit our discussion to pointing out that there are many cases in which one or more of these agencies hardly function at all. Some children are in such constant conflict with the school that enforced schooling becomes purposeless misery; some homes are hopelessly disorganized. The church is often ignored; it seems to be declining as an influence on youth, especially college youth (see Chapter 11). Also, the major agencies of socialization often seem to be working at cross-purposes. A strict, puritanical home may resent a sex-education course given at school, as well as the after-school dances and parties. Parents who are strict disciplinarians may regard the teachers as too weak and permissive; other parents may think the school is tyrannical. There are also indifferent types of parents who do not cooperate with the school even to the extent of encouraging their children to attend. Children reared in a fundamentalist church may be taught that the evolutionary theories mentioned in biology are wicked nonsense. Often conservative parents resent liberal teachers, and liberal parents resent conservative teachers.

The unofficial agencies of socialization   Meanwhile, from outside of school, church, and family, the individual is being influenced by less recognized, but very powerful, agencies of socialization: the movies, magazines, television, advertisements, new types of companions, and the general awareness of a world of bright lights and frivolous pleasures. All kinds of new contradictions come into the teaching of the individual through these agencies. We will elaborate upon one such conflict in values and mention others only briefly.

The violence, nonviolence dilemma   Among the various conflicts that accompany the socialization process is an ambivalence on the part of society toward violence. Although our official doctrine denounces violence, we are aware of violence all around us. The mass media are often held responsible for playing up violence both in news accounts and drama. In the movies the "good guys" always win, but often they win only by being the fastest with a gun. What does this mean to the growing child? Is he being conditioned to violence? Is he building up an immunity to its shock? In *Seduction of the Innocent*, Frederick Wertham maintains that the answer to each question is "Yes." [24] Accordingly, he has long compaigned against violence in comic books and on television. Others have contended that this kind of violence is perceived by the child as existing only in a harmless fantasy world. Some even contend that violent drama might vicariously satisfy the hostile feelings of an individual—feelings that might otherwise be directed against people in the world of reality.

Otto Larsen has edited a well-balanced treatment of the argument concerning violence in the mass media, presenting impressive evidence on both sides. After examining the empirical evidence in the field, he arrives at two important conclusions: (1) Under certain conditions, the observation of mass-media violence can "reduce inhibitions against violent behavior and provide cues that aggression is socially acceptable . . . ." (2) The laboratory evidence, supported by data from the field and clinic, tends to suggest "that exposure to media violence does *not* drain off aggressive tendencies." [25] Larsen reminds us that violence is not just a matter of the mass media.

> . . . The indicators of an abiding fascination
> with violence are all around us, as witness the
> popularity of certain athletic events, such as
> professional football (sometimes referred to as
> "Mayhem on a Sunday afternoon"), the booming
> Christmas sales of toy weapons, ranging from gun-
> shaped teething rings to simulated atom bombs, and
> the continued attraction of both real and fictional
> accounts of war and crime. [26]

[24] Frederick Wertham, *Seduction of the Innocent*, Holt, Rinehart and Winston, Inc., New York, 1954.
[25] Otto N. Larsen (ed.), *Violence and the Mass Media*, Harper & Row, Publishers, Incorporated, New York, 1968, p. 117.
[26] *Ibid.*, p. 19.

Whatever the result of psychological studies and investigations of violence may eventually be, there is no doubt that the young boy, told by his mother that he should not fight, is being bombarded by contradictory stimuli.

A similar analysis of many other types of contradictory stimuli could be made in such areas as the Vietnam War, violence of both demonstrators and police, drug abuse, inconsistencies in court action, hypocrisy in sex norms, and "respectable" alcoholism. The socialization process presents an infinity of confusions and conflicts. As one goes down the road of life, he finds it plastered with billboards carrying conflicting messages. He will be advised to follow the "straight and narrow way," but also to be a sport, take a chance. Members of his own generation may tempt him to try marijuana; when his parents hear of it they will be badly shaken and will need another drink to steady their nerves! He will be confronted with the patriots and superpatriots, and with the radicals and protestors. He will have choices to make about early employment or a college career, whether to follow the Puritan norms in sex or to have his affairs before marriage, whether to adopt a moralistic or a hedonistic philosophy, whether to follow a competitive business orientation or a social-service ethic. And all of these conflicts will be within the range of acceptable behavior as seen by significant segments of society. There are, of course, other possibilities—those that lie along the roads of delinquency and crime and line the path of socialization with more perils.

SOCIALIZATION AND NORMATIVE CONFLICT   The socialization process may be a failure when it does not produce individuals acceptable to the prevailing norms of the society. Occasionally the person seen as a failure today is really an innovator, ahead of his times, possessed of insights that others lack. Such a person may eventually become a hero of society.

The type of failure of the socialization process to be discussed here, however, is the kind of failure that leads to delinquency, crime, alcoholism, addiction, and various other pathologies. These pathologies can be studied from different perspectives. The psychologist might analyze them mainly in terms of particular personality types. A few researchers are reawakening interest in the possibility that certain physical irregularities (the extra Y chromosome, for example) may be a contributing factor in a few cases, but for the vast majority of cases the causes of crime and delinquency must be looked for in the society and the process of socialization of the young.

Social reality and societal expectation   A very influential theory explaining disjunctures between cultural values and social structure was developed

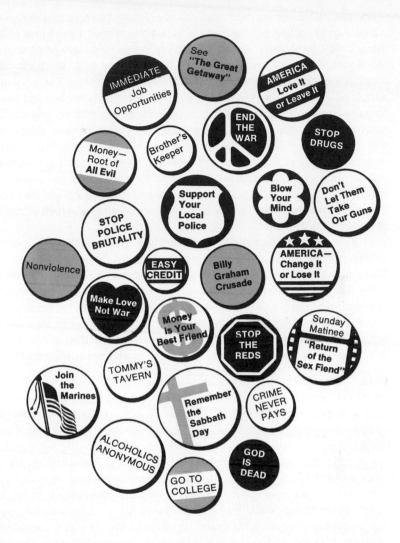

by Robert K. Merton.[27] Merton's explanation of the difficulties of American society with crime and delinquency elaborates on the concept of anomie, a term originally used by Durkheim. *Anomie* refers to a failure to internalize the norms or to conflict within the norms themselves. It is this second meaning of anomie that is used by Merton. He shows that all societies

[27] Robert K. Merton, *Social Theory and Social Structure*, The Free Press, Glencoe, Ill., 1949, pp. 125–149.

make two demands of their people, motivating them to: (1) achieve the success *goals* of the society, and (2) follow the proper *means* for achieving those goals. In modern American society the success goal is often a matter of monetary success. Merton contends that we emphasize the goal of success more strongly than we emphasize honest means. The person who succeeds honestly is most admired, he says, but the second level of acclaim goes to the man who achieves major success by unscrupulous means, as long as he is clever enough not to end up in prison. If we stressed honest means more strongly than success goals, then we would give second honors to the poor but honest. Merton reminds us that we frequently regard the poor but honest as total failures and obviously not very bright. Some people, of course, do not achieve either the goals or the honest means of society, and these are the ones who turn to vagrancy or possibly alcoholism.

The other important point in Merton's theory is that the means for achieving the goals of society are unequally distributed because of racial discrimination, the accidental discrimination of an impoverished home background, and differences in ability. Therefore people from the poor areas of the city will be tempted to try to achieve the goal of money success by illegal means. How strong their temptation in this direction will be depends upon their own values and whether they are surrounded by a community that taunts them if they do not attempt to outsmart the law.

Deviant subcultures   Many other sociologists and criminologists have been influenced by Merton's thought on crime and anomie.[28] Albert Cohen applies the concept in his book *Delinquent Boys,*[29] although he adds an important subcultural explanation that is not in Merton's thesis. Cohen says that lower-class delinquent boys are striving for success in the eyes of their own crowd, and that success is measured by ability to circumvent the school authorities, harass policemen and neighborhoods, and do malicious damage more than in terms of monetary success. Such hoodlumism is especially difficult for the public to countenance; people can understand stealing for practical reasons but do not understand the motivation for delinquency that is malicious and nonutilitarian. The motive behind much lower-class delinquency is an expression of resentment against a society whose success norms seem impossible to achieve.

Cohen, collaborating with Short,[30] also has something important to say about middle-class juvenile delinquency. The middle-class parents unwittingly teach a way of life that is fun loving and hedonistic. The

[28] We are indebted to Leonard Savitz (*Dilemmas in Criminology*, McGraw-Hill Book Company, New York, 1967, pp. 50–65), for the organization of several of these theoretical approaches to delinquency.
[29] Albert K. Cohen, *Delinquent Boys*, The Free Press of Glencoe, Ill., Chicago, 1955.
[30] Albert K. Cohen and James F. Short, Jr., "Research in Delinquent Subcultures," *Journal of Social Issues*, vol. 14, March, 1958, pp. 20–37.

resultant behavior of their offspring is a delinquency pattern centering around sex, automobiles, and liquor (marijuana, more recently). Since the eventual achievement of success goals for this group is likely, the delinquency is not apt to lead to adult crime.

A variation of the theme of the lower-class delinquent subculture is that of the violent gang in the city. As Cohen sees it, the origin of such delinquent gangs is similar to the other lower-class subcultures he has described. A more thorough study of the conflict-centered gang adds that the gang helps to overcome a feeling of inadequacy on the part of boys seemingly born to fail, and it also gives the members a sense of power.[31]

Opportunity for learning crime   Cloward and Ohlin have followed the tradition of Merton in their explanation of delinquency, but they also make important additions to the theory.[32] They are interested in the availability of illegitimate means. The amount of delinquency and its likelihood of turning into adult crime depend to a great extent on whether there is an organized underworld in the area in which the youths grow up, and also on the extent to which legitimate opportunities are lacking.

A word should be said about the work of Clifford Shaw,[33] who makes an important point that should not be neglected in any study of sociology, even though his study is far from recent. A record of the history of certain areas in Chicago demonstrated that the worst sections of the city (as measured by lack of opportunity, dilapidated housing, and the presence of vice) had by far the highest rates of juvenile delinquency, in some cases twenty times as much as the best areas. The high delinquency rate persisted over the thirty-year period investigated by Shaw, in spite of the fact that five different ethnic groups had moved into and out of the area during those years. It makes no difference what the nationality of the people involved; similar conditions produce similar results.

SUMMARY   Socialization is the process by which one internalizes the attitudes, beliefs, and values of his culture. Socialization requires (1) interaction with others, (2) the experience of emotional acceptance, and (3) symbolic communication, mainly through language. There is much evidence, observational and experimental, to prove the necessity of interaction with other people and contact with the culture for mental

[31] Lewis Yablonsky, *The Violent Gang*, Penguin Books, Inc., Baltimore, 1967, pp. 129–139.
[32] Richard A. Cloward and Lloyd E. Ohlin, *Delinquency and Opportunity*, The Free Press of Glencoe, Inc., New York, 1961.
[33] Clifford R. Shaw and Henry D. McKay, *Juvenile Delinquency and Urban Areas*, The University of Chicago Press, Chicago, 1942.

growth. That affection is needed for normal development is demonstrated by studies of isolated children, orphanages, and battering parents who were themselves deprived of affection.

Language is another essential of socialization. Language is not only a means of communication, but to a great degree it is a means of perception and thought. Ethnic groups whose knowledge of the use of the English language is deficient have serious difficulties at school. This applies not just to foreign-language groups but to all groups whose use of English is unusual enough to impair communication.

Although cultural and subcultural groups attempt to preserve their identity by socializing children into their own pattern, patterns of socialization change. Riesman suggests that societies can socialize children into three possible patterns: tradition-directed, inner-directed, or other-directed. America was never very strongly tradition-directed in its socialization pattern, but in the past it was inner-directed; i.e., strong feelings of right and wrong were internalized by growing children as the result of the teachings of stern parents and teachers. The modern pattern, in contrast, is toward an other-directed personality, guided mainly by the expectations of others of his own generation. The new character type is adaptable for salesmanship and working with others, but lacks the independence of decision which was characteristic of the earlier American society, according to Riesman.

The founding fathers of American socialization theory were George Herbert Mead and Charles Horton Cooley. Mead analyzed the process of internalization of the norms through successive stages of childhood play—first at imitating specific roles and later learning generalized rules through the rules of the game. Cooley thought of the socialization process as one of responding to the wishes of others through the looking-glass process. In Cooley's view, we study the faces of others for looks of approval and support, attempting to form a favorable self-image.

Dennis Wrong calls the views of Cooley and Mead "oversocialized conceptions of man." He implies that they overemphasized the tendency of people to conform to expectations. He feels that sociology has not devoted enough attention to why people misbehave and to negative sanctions.

It is obvious that one of the reasons for a failure of the individual to conform to societal expectations is that there is no solid agreement about what those expectations are. Not only do such primary agencies of socialization as family, church, and school sometimes fail to agree, but they find themselves in conflict with unofficial agencies of socialization: the mass media, advertising, exposure to violence, delinquent crowds, conflicting political preachings, propaganda, and demonstrations.

Besides conflicting influences in the media and observed examples of behavior, there are certain societal inconsistencies that pose a problem. Society expects success goals to be achieved, but access to the means of success is uneven. This places pressure on many to "innovate" on the rules by devious means, or to escape from the struggle, or to rebel against the system.

Deviant subcultures of various kinds arise, deviating from social norms in different ways and degrees. Type and degree of deviation depend partly on whether there are out-group resentments against middle-class norms and whether there is an organized underworld giving access to deviant means. Neighborhoods of high delinquency tend to maintain their high delinquency rates regardless of what racial or ethnic group inhabits them.

Then let us pray that come it may,
As come it will for a' that . . . .

That man to man the world o'er
Shall brithers be, for a' that.

ROBERT BURNS
For A'That And A'That

five

DIFFERENTIATION IN SOCIETIES: STATUS, CLASS, AND CASTE

For thousands of years it has been the dream of prophet and sage that men could live together as brothers, not differentiated by social class, free of the arrogance of wealth and of the grubbing misery of poverty. Why is it that this seems to be the impossible dream, even in states dedicated to equality? Only a handful of preliterate hunting and gathering societies remain in a state of complete man-to-man equality. In many societies poverty becomes less acute, but the gulf between poverty and riches is wide enough to create resentment and political and social movements of an equalitarian nature. Yet, ironically, even the communistic societies whose philosophy is most dedicated to classlessness find new class divisions arising, based on power and privilege. Henry George (1839–1897), an interesting and unusual American economic theorist, wrote a book titled *Progress and Poverty* in which he indicated that the two are related. Is there such a connection between progress and poverty or, at least, between progress and the differentiation of social classes? To investigate such a question it will be necessary to attempt a definition of social class, a very difficult task in mobile industrial societies, as will become apparent in the following discussion.

STATUS, ROLE, AND CLASS   In the discussion of socialization it was mentioned that children play at different roles.

We could say also that they become aware of the statuses that accompany particular roles. *Status* can be defined as a position occupied in society, and *role* is the behavior expected of a person occupying such a position. The roles are not played in precisely the same way by all of their occupants, but in an orderly society there is a fair degree of consensus as to what the roles should be. Society can be analyzed as a network of statuses and roles, with various actors occupying statuses and performing roles until the end of their lives and then being replaced by other actors on the stage of life. "All the world's a stage," said Shakespeare in *As You Like It*, "And all the men and women merely players. They have their exits and their entrances; and one man in his time plays many parts."

Shakespeare, in telling us that we play many parts, was commenting on one aspect of status and role, its multifaceted nature. Thus during life we have the statuses and roles of infancy, childhood, youth, adulthood, and old age. We also have the statuses of kinship—son or daughter, husband or wife, mother, father, uncle or aunt, and cousin. Such statuses, together with the status of male and female, are examples of *ascribed* statuses, because they are given to us through no effort of our own. There are other types of statuses and roles, such as king or nobleman, that are also ascribed, although a certain amount of learning should be involved in them—the learning of the manners, bearing, and taste that are supposed to go with aristocratic position.

Status as an overall measurement   When we discuss the status and role of king or nobleman we are really using a somewhat different concept from that of age or kinship status in that the former is an overall measurement of a person's position in society. Nearly anyone can be a husband or wife, but society permits only a few to be of the aristocracy. In societies without aristocracies there are also statuses that more or less summarize a person's position in life. A supreme court justice has a very high status, and when we think of his status we mean only his occupational status. Few are interested in whether he has a large number of children, is adept at cards or golf, or has special ability as an amateur artist or poet. His occupational status is the one by which he is classified, just as the king or nobleman is classified by his hereditary status. An occupational status is called an *achieved* status as opposed to the ascribed status already mentioned. The words "achieved status" are self-explanatory, and can obviously have other applications besides occupational status: athletic competence, college graduation, and skill in art, music, and writing, for example.

Complications in status   So far it seems that a simple definition of class is about to be reached, equating class simply with inherited title in an aristocratic society or with occupational status in a society without titled aristocracy. However, the problem is not that simple. What positions are equivalent to each other in the two systems? Is supreme court justice the equal of an earl? The same person can hold inconsistent statuses, having great wealth and influence, but having such boorish manners as to be unacceptable in elite society. A young man might have high status on the school football team but otherwise be a person of little ability or promise. Another man can finish graduate school, proudly grasp his master's degree, and then be drafted into the Armed Forces as a buck private. What is the overall status of these men? An attempt to define social class in terms of occupational status is helpful but not adequate. Although occupation is a very important measure of class status, it is not the only measure.

Other measures of status include education, income, inherited wealth, family background, reputation, and political power. Some of these measures are difficult to guage with any precision, so occupation is often used as the one measure of social class. Despite the complications, occupation does have the advantage of being fairly easy to determine, and it generally correlates with income and education. However, Weber measured social-class position by the criteria of wealth, power, and esteem.

One further complication in the whole attempt to measure social class by standards of occupation, income, and education is that certain ascribed statuses remain in the picture even in a society that claims to judge people in terms of achievement. Women, for example, often fail to rate as high in prestige in a particular occupation as do men and are much more likely to be passed up for promotion. The junior partner of a law firm does not rank with the senior partners, even though he has the same law degree, because, up to a certain point, age has status. The new college graduate starting business in town will have the advantage of ready-made prestige if he comes from one of the town's distinguished families; otherwise he will have to build his reputation on his own.

Definition of class   With all of these reservations in mind, we can define a *social class* as a collectivity of people sharing similar status or as "a stratum of people who are roughly equal with regard to such factors as family prestige, and occupational-educational-income status, and . . . are accepted by their stratum members as equals."[1] Such a definition may bring to mind a stairstep arrangement of social classes, whereas the American model actually more closely resembles an inclined plane, with one class grading into another almost imperceptibly. Such is by no means

[1] Thomas Ford Hoult, *Dictionary of Modern Sociology*, Littlefield, Adams, and Company, Totowa, N.J., 1969.

always the case with social classes. Social classes can vary from the loose structuring of American society to very great rigidity.

VARIATIONS IN SOCIAL-CLASS SYSTEMS   Social-class systems can be described along a continuum from open class at one extreme to closed class, or caste, at the other. Open class is the ideal type of class system in which movement from one class to another is completely unencumbered. It fulfills the goal of perfect equality of opportunity but exists as an ideal rather than as a reality.

No true "meritocracy"   The British sociologist Michael Young wrote a description of a perfect open-class system which he called the "meritocracy,"[2] the idea being that each individual could rise purely on the basis of merit, and no other way. In this novel about the future he pictured all the changes that England had to make in order to become a perfect meritocracy. Not only was it necessary to do away with all the titles and estates of the nobility, but all inherited wealth had to be confiscated, and no family could give special help to its children. The family, in fact, was depicted as a reactionary institution whose power had to be broken. The school system had to be revised to give special consideration to children from culturally handicapped backgrounds in order to ensure them equality of opportunity. Systems of seniority were eliminated so that the young man could challenge the middle-aged man for his job. Eventually full equality of opportunity was guaranteed. At last the person who failed could no longer blame his failure on "bad breaks"; he had to blame it on his own incompetence. In the last pages of the book, Young boasted that a system had finally been devised that was immune to overthrow, because the people at the bottom of the class system were too stupid for any possible effective organization. A footnote at the end of the book adds that the manuscript was found among the author's possessions after his death in the revolution!

Young is telling us how extremely difficult it would be to establish absolute equality of opportunity. He also implies that no system could make everyone happy and contented. In applying his conclusions to the United States, we could say that our society approaches, but does not achieve, complete open class.

Class in primitive societies   There are, as was suggested in the opening paragraph of this chapter, societies without class—some, but not all, hunting and gathering socieities. If the level of productivity is so low that

[2] Michael Young, *The Rise of the Meritocracy, 1870–2033*, Penguin Books, Inc., Baltimore, 1961.

there is no surplus of goods beyond the minimum for keeping the people alive, there is little chance for class differentiation.[3] In more advanced agrarian societies, social class always comes into existence. Early civilizations had very marked superior classes—military, religious, and governmental—and often very depressed slave and outcast groups. A glance at the progress from simple hunting and gathering societies through the development of agriculture and early urban civilizations would lead to full agreement with the discouraging link between "progress and poverty."

Although many historical systems have become extremely stratified and quite rigid, few have made any upward mobility completely impossible. Vilfredo Pareto, an Italian sociologist, contended that societies have always had a "circulation of elites," either as a result of overthrow or invasion, or as a result of natural changes within.[4] His analysis of circulation within societies was that the clever people (the "foxes") gradually supplement or replace the original conquerors (the "lions") and are eventually themselves replaced by other "lions." Since Pareto had an elitist and antidemocratic bias, he was inclined to exaggerate the lion-fox analogy. Probably the closest approximation of the types of constant changes he had in mind were those of the class system of China.

The Chinese system of class   The ancient class system of China had at least one characteristic of mobility about it; the scholarly bureaucracy attained position by achievement in competitive examinations, not by heredity. Even in the Chinese system, though, there were advantages to wealth, because the studies for the examinations were long and expensive. In theory at least, China, through many centuries, had an interesting class structure headed by the scholarly bureaucrats, with the farmers in the middle and the artisans and traders in lower positions.[5] The scholars held all the important government jobs and helped to centralize the administration and strengthen the hand of the emperor relative to the warlords. The system was very persistent. Although invaders conquered China and new dynasties overthrew the old, the scholarly bureaucracy remained, changing little through 2,000 years of history. There were, however, gaps between real and ideal culture. The number of Manchu officials during the Manchu Dynasty (the last dynasty of China) vastly overrepresented their proportion of the population. Despite Pareto's circulation theory, there always seem to be ways to cheat on the system.

Class in medieval Europe   The system of stratification of medieval Europe had less "circulation of elites" than China, if it can be said to have had

[3] Gerhard Lenski, *Power and Privilege: A Theory of Social Stratification*, McGraw-Hill Book Company, New York, 1966, chap. 4.
[4] T. B. Bottomore, *Elites and Society*, Penguin Books, Inc., Baltimore, 1968, pp. 7–12.
[5] Egon Ernest Bergel, *Social Stratification*, McGraw-Hill Book Company, New York, 1962, pp. 213–221.

any at all. Europe had an *estate system*, a system in which classes had carefully defined legal rights and duties. Most of the rights went to the aristocracy and clergy, and most of the duties went to the peasants, although even the peasants had the right of inalienability from the land. Although they could not legally be driven off the land, the peasants could be sold along with the land. Peasants, or serfs, existed at several levels, all owing labor to a lord; but some were in a state of virtual slavery and others owed him only about one-third of their labor.[6]

The estate system was more rigid than that of ancient China because it lacked a scholarly route to mobility. Occasionally, however, a sturdy peasant's son would be chosen for military training, and occasionally there was an upward route through the clergy. The European system was not the same as caste, although it approached it closely. The estate system waned with the passing of the Middle Ages, but the old upward-mobility routes through military and clergy still seemed at times to be the most promising ones. Stendhal's famous novel *Le Rouge et le Noir* (1831) presents two possible paths to upward mobility for the poor man — *le rouge* (red), the path of the soldier, or *le noir* (black), the robes of the priest. The central character in the novel chooses the priesthood, since military opportunities had declined after the time of Napoleon.

Caste   Caste is a system of social class that precludes any possible upward mobility. Caste is rare in the world, but it is not confined to India. A few characteristics of caste have spread to Ceylon, Burma, parts of Indonesia, and other places in contact with Indian civilization. Caste also has developed in areas remote from India, usually in conquest states. In Africa, one illustration of caste is the relationship between the pastoral Bahima and the gardening Bairu in the old kingdom of Ankole in Uganda. The Hamitic Bahima came from the north, probably southern Ethiopia, and conquered the gardening Bantu people who they call the Bairu. The characteristics of the caste system include occupational differences, the prohibition of intermarriage, the paying of tribute by the Bairu, no military service or right to bear arms by the Bairu, and no holding of public office. There is a denial of any possibility of social equality, as is typical of caste. The total system is complicated by an even lower caste of slaves whose position is also hereditary and precludes any mobility.[7]

The most famous case of caste is in India, of course. The system is too complex to describe in detail, but basically there are four castes: Brahmins (priestly caste), Kshatriya (warriors), Vaisya (merchants and artisans), and Sudra (servants). Caste was imposed, or at least strengthened, in India by the Aryan conquest of about 1400 B.C. A system as rigid as

[6] *Ibid.,* p. 129.
[7] E. Adamson Hoebel, *Anthropology: The Study of Man,* McGraw-Hill Book Company, New York, 1966, pp. 408–409.

caste has also depended upon the internalization of feelings of inequality, the learning of unequal roles, and the development of self-concepts of inferior or superior beings, as the case may be. No system has accomplished this task as thoroughly as the caste system of India, for there the progress of the soul depends upon living out one's appointed destiny in his caste position. The progress of his soul from one earthly incarnation to the next and its ultimate achievement of freedom from the wheel of life by merging with the Eternal depends upon the proper maintenance of caste rules. Modern laws have done away with many of the legal disabilities of caste and have granted the right to vote and the right to an education, but social inequality remains, reinforced by many crippling rules of etiquette and the fear of spiritual pollution.[8]

American caste   Ever since Gunnar Myrdal wrote *An American Dilemma*, containing an analysis of "the white man's theory of color caste," the word "caste" has been used to describe black-white relationships in the United States. Dollard's *Class and Caste in a Southern Town* uses the same definition of the system. Certainly as long as slavery existed, an immobile, endogamous caste existed, supported by law, and even rationalized by religion to some degree. However, the religious underpinnings of caste have been weak in America compared with India. Most of its followers in recent history have thought of Christianity as a religion of equality of man before God. For this reason it took great effort to rationalize the institution of slavery in American society. Strange and conflicting stereotypes had to be created. In one version of racial stereotyping the Negro was pictured as complacent, accepting his status, and loving his white master. In the opposite version he was seen as a savage who must be carefully watched lest he tarnish and defile white womanhood.

There were, however, stirrings of discontent over slavery. The slave image was never completely accepted by the blacks or by all whites. Nevertheless, it cannot be denied that many of the earmarks of caste were present and have remained a century after the abolition of slavery: the dread of intermarriage; segregated schools, restaurants, restrooms, neighborhoods, and sections of town; and inferior images in entertainment, popular jokes, and the often-repeated phrase "I have nothing against Negroes so long as they know their place." Although there are differences between Indian and American caste, it is hard to argue too strongly with those who apply the word "caste" to America's racial history.

There are resemblances to caste in any society in which racial and ethnic groups are so differently treated that being born into any one of them is a distinct advantage or disadvantage. The status of the American

[8] Bergel, *op. cit.*, pp. 35–48.

Indian has proved a distinct handicap in the United States. In Latin America, especially in colonial times, the status of the American Indian was much lower than that of the mestizo (mixed Spanish-Indian), and the mestizo ranked well below the Spaniard.

The phenomena of class and caste have been widespread throughout the world and throughout history. Class distinctions have existed between men in spite of protests, equalitarian ideas, and even revolutions. It is time to look for explanations of social class and ask whether it is functional or dysfunctional to a society.

THEORIES OF SOCIAL CLASS   There have been many theories, some of which have already been mentioned, to support social-class distinctions. Indian caste has been supported on religious grounds as a necessity for the progress of the human soul. A social myth from the Hindu laws of Manu explained that from the mouth of the Resplendent One came forth the Brahmin. The Kshatryia sprang from his arms; the Vaisya from his thighs, and the Sudra from his feet.[9] Slavery in America was rationalized on grounds of "the happiness of the slave with his lot," and of his "need for direction," and sometimes even on religious grounds as God's manifest will.

Modern scholars differ in their interpretations of social class. Lenski[10] shows that for centuries there has been a tendency for conservatives to interpret social class as a functional necessity for the survival of societies. Liberals and radicals, on the other hand, have attacked social-class inequality either as totally unnecessary or as unjustifiably great.

A little reflection on man's inhumanity to man, as seen in the extremes of class, caste, and slavery, is enough to put one's sympathies on the side of the challengers of class. Often rigidly stratified societies have so oppressed the lower classes as to almost exclude them from humanity, thinking of them as beasts of the field, "stolid and stunned, a brother to the ox." "Swine!" Frederick the Great called his Prussian peasants. So great was the gulf between aristocracy and peasantry at one time in France, Carlyle tells us, that returning noblemen, if disappointed in the hunt for game, were allowed to shoot as many as two peasants instead, just for the sport of it.[11] Although much has been made of the idea of *noblesse oblige* (the obligation of the rich and well-born to be good to the "simple folk"), it has often had no impact whatever.

[9] *Laws of Manu*, Book 1, lines 87–89, in G. Bühler (ed.), *Sacred Books of the East*, vol. 25, Oxford University Press, London, 1886.
[10] Lenski, *op. cit.*, chap. 1.
[11] Thomas Carlyle, *The French Revolution*, A. L. Burt, Publisher, New York, 1900, vol. I, p. 11.

The views of the challengers of class   There have been many challengers
to the idea of social class, including some of the early Christians, the
heretical Waldensians, the leaders of peasant uprisings in the sixteenth
century, and the Levellers of seventeenth-century England. Such early
socialistic idealists as Fourrier in France and Owen in Wales were strong
equalitarians, and there were many anticlass sentiments in the romantic
period of English and European literature. Marx, of course, is usually
thought of first as the opponent of social class and the prophet of a
revolutionary movement aimed at ushering in the classless society, but
it is to be emphasized that many others have also called for an end to
class distinctions.

The challengers to social class have generally placed a higher value
on equality than on stability. They have also supported a number of
assumptions about human ability, human societies, and human nature
that contrast sharply with the views of conservatives.[12] The challengers'
view of essential human nature is optimistic, holding that a just social
system can free man from most of his greed for power and wealth. They
see societies as generally unjust and, therefore, as centers of struggle,
rather than as smooth-running systems that should not be fundamentally
shaken. They generally see leadership and high class position as having
been attained originally through conquest and maintained, to a great
degree, through inheritance, fraud, and coercion. Laws are generally
seen as exploitive, favoring the rich. They may seem to be fair, but really
are not. As Anatole France said in *Le Lys Rouge*, "The law, in its majestic
equality, forbids the rich as well as the poor to sleep under bridges, to
beg in the streets, and to steal bread." The opponents of social class
believe inequalities are unnecessary and can be ended, that "Man to man
the world o'er/ Shall brithers be for a' that."

There is little doubt that the constant challenge to gross inequalities
has helped to promote more equitable systems than in the past. In nearly
all the Western world poverty has been greatly alleviated, but the gulf
between rich and poor is still wide. The leading country that claims to
have followed the marxian road to classlessness is the Soviet Union,
but the reality is a long way from the ideal. The present Russian system
can be described as a highly structured class system based more on
power and privilege than on wealth. At the top of the structure are those
in political power. Below them are the military leaders, scientists, recognized intellectuals, managers, and leading professionals. Next are leaders
at various levels: white-collar, skilled, semiskilled, and unskilled laborers,
in layers fairly similar to those of Western Europe or the United States.
Peasants rank lower than most industrial workers. The upper classes

[12]Lenski, *op. cit.*, 441–443.

Supporters of social class say:	Challengers of social class systems reply:
Human nature is in need of strong social control.	Human nature is good; bad social systems corrupt.
Stability is more important than equality.	Equality is more important than stability.
Any system is better than chaos.	Better no system than an unjust system.
Unequal abilities call for unequal rewards.	Abilities are not as unequal as laws and rewards.
High position is usually the reward of hard work.	High position is often based on conquest, fraud, or inheritance.
Class inequality makes societies function.	Inequalities are much greater than needed.

(Adapted from G. H. Lenski, *Power and Privilege:
A Theory of Social Stratification*, McGraw-Hill Book Company, New York, 1966.)

have marked differences in income, live in separate neighborhoods, are socially segregated, and tend to be endogamous (marrying within their own class or social grouping).[13] Upper classes also get such favors as tax breaks and better placement of their children in school. Inequalities of wealth have declined, since there is no private ownership of estates, mills, mines, and banks; but social class persists in pay, power, and prestige. The more conservative social theorists are not surprised; their position is that social class is necessary and inevitable.

Modern defenders of social class   The supporters of social-class systems no longer rely on mythology for an explanation. Social class now is seen as a functional necessity. Lenski sums up a set of conservative views, the converse of those held by the challengers, that support the concept of social class as a necessity.[14] The conservative view is much less trustful of human nature, seeing the need for a strong social system and legal controls. Stability is more important than equality, for stable systems are necessary to keep up the flow of goods and services on which life depends. Even the poorer members of society are much better off than they would be under conditions of anarchy, the view holds, and they generally realize

13 Bergel, *op. cit.*, 230–242.
14 Lenski, *op. cit.*, 441–443.

that fact. Leadership is based to a great extent on merit, not primarily on conquest or fraud.

Mosca and Pareto, two prominent Italian social theorists, went further than simply trying to prove the necessity for social class. They (especially Pareto) tried to show how in modern industrial systems there is enough circulation of elites so that there is no really permanent ruling class. Both theorists were elitists and distrustful of democracy.[15]

Robert Michels also criticized the classless dream, advancing an idea that he called "the iron law of oligarchy." After studying European labor movements, he came to the conclusion that a small clique of leaders was sure to emerge eventually. Because of differences in ability and experience, because of the indifference of the followers, and because men like to exert power, Michels concluded that there could never be real equality.[16]

In the United States, a long argument has been waged over the idea that social class functions to "instill in proper individuals the desire to fill certain positions" and that it rewards in highest rank those positions that "have the greatest importance for society and require the greatest training or talent."[17] Davis and Moore argue that the above statements apply both to achieving societies and to societies with position based on ascription. In the former societies, the major task is to recruit the right people; in ascription-type societies, motivation to perform the duties is given greater stress. The authors wisely avoid a pitfall in their theory by stressing that the theory applies to positions, not necessarily to all persons holding those positions.

Tumin,[18] in reply to Davis and Moore, shows that some extremely important jobs are poorly rewarded, that the magnitude of difference in pay is much more than is necessary for motivation, and that inherited ownership alone—not talent—is the opening to many positions. He also shows that class-structured societies and societies with racial or religious discrimination cut out potential talent rather than promote it. It should also be added that explaining class distinctions as a functional necessity runs into the danger of justifying poverty, social snobbery, and arrogance.

Neither the radical theories calling for the abolition of social class, nor the functional theories explaining its necessity seem entirely satisfactory. Maybe the real question is one of degree of social class, rather than of its existence or nonexistence. Are there characteristics of social

[15]Bottomore, *op. cit.*, 16–20.
[16]*Ibid.*, pp. 18–20.
[17]Kingsley Davis and Wilbert E. Moore, "Some Principles of Stratification," *American Sociological Review*, vol. 10, February, 1945, pp. 242–249.
[18]Melvin M. Tumin, "Some Principles of Stratification: A Critical Analysis," *American Sociological Review*, vol. 18, August, 1953, pp. 387–393.

class in modern industrial societies that make it seem less exploitive than Marx would have expected? Is there a constant circulation of elites?

SOCIAL CLASS IN INDUSTRIAL SOCIETIES In the historical development of societies, the general trend has been toward a strengthening of class as higher levels of productivity are reached. Even the advance from hunting to simple slash-and-burn agriculture increases stratification of society. The advance to plow agriculture increases class differences even more and correlates closely with the institution of slavery.[19]

It would seem rather natural that the trend toward greater differentiation of class, fed by the increase of surplus production, would continue. However, in industrial societies, the first reversal of the trend is encountered.[20] Slavery becomes an inefficient system of labor in societies calling for industrial skills, and so does serfdom. The amount of mechanical power increases overwhelmingly, so that many jobs calling for backbreaking manual labor are replaced by machinery. Education becomes a job requirement of the new society, and there is no longer an upper-class monopoly on learning, as was once the case. The self-image of the common people improves, and equalitarian pressures grow. Labor movements work in the direction of a larger share of production for the worker, and political parties representing the common people work for other benefits. No longer is the worker a cowed and submissive peasant, "the emptiness of ages in his eyes, and on his back the burden of the world." His demands increase, and he is able to make them heard.

Great inequalities still exist, and so does poverty, but the poor become a minority rather than a majority. When Lincoln said, "God must have loved the poor; He made so many of them," he was talking about the common majority of people, not the minority poor of today. The problem of poverty is not to be glossed over, because in some ways it is more agonizing than ever to those who remain behind in an affluent age, but the change from majority to minority status is, nevertheless, a mark of real progress.

Warner's description of class Various attempts have been made to describe the social-class system of the modern United States. The studies of W. Lloyd Warner should be mentioned briefly because they have become a part of our social-class terminology.[21] In community studies Warner identified six classes: upper-upper, lower-upper, upper-middle, lower-middle, upper-lower, and lower-lower. The upper-uppers are the old

[19] Hoebel, *op. cit.*, pp. 402–410.
[20] Lenski, *op. cit.*, p. 308.
[21] W. Lloyd Warner, Marcia Meeker, and Kenneth Eells, *Social Class in America*, Harper & Row Publishers, Incorporated, Torchbooks, New York, 1960, chap. 1. pp. 3–33.

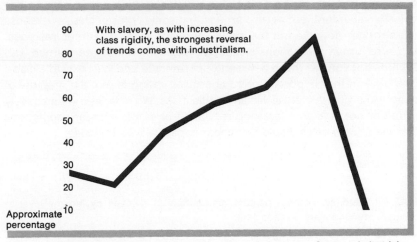

90
80
70
60
50
40
30
20
10

Approximate percentage

With slavery, as with increasing class rigidity, the strongest reversal of trends comes with industrialism.

| Hunting societies | Incipient agriculture | Intermediate agriculture | Plow agriculture | Pastoralism | Greco-Roman world | Industrial society |

Level of development

[Statistics (except for Greco-Roman world) from E. Adamson Hoebel, *Anthropology: The Study of Man*, McGraw-Hill Book Company, 1966, p. 410.]

money class, high in wealth and family name. The lower-uppers are the newly rich. Below them are layers of business and professional people and technical and scientific experts, classified as upper- or lower-middle, depending on how successful their businesses, jobs, or areas of expertise happen to be. The lower-middle also includes large numbers of white-collar workers. The upper-lowers are the respectable poor, employed most of the time at poorly paying jobs. Below them are the people described by many of the middle class as "shiftless and lazy." Warner's descriptions are interesting, especially for describing the community elite, but modern Americans are so geographically mobile that many do not stay in communities long enough to gain the community reputations Warner describes. He admits this is true of the newer areas of the West, especially for the attempt to identify an upper-upper class.

Self-evaluation Another way of studying class in modern America is by self-evaluation. Richard Centers argues that people are very much aware of social class and that self-rating is of great psychological importance. Hodges shows that self-evaluation is quite inaccurate by any objective standard, but he also argues that some types of class awareness are stronger now than in the past.[22] As some types of ethnic, religious, and rural-urban distinctions disappear, we become more concerned with such distinctions as those between upper-middle and lower-middle class. One other rather important point about self-rating is that the majority of people like to rate themselves as middle class. Whether this is objectively sound or not, it is an interesting refutation of earlier marxian predictions that the middle class would disappear in capitalistic societies.

[22]Harold M. Hodges, Jr., *Social Stratification: Class in America*, Schenkman Publishing Co., Inc., Cambridge, Mass., 1964, pp. 14–15, 85–89.

TABLE 5-1   Money income—percent distribution of families by income level in constant (1966) dollars: 1947 to 1966

(Prior to 1960, excludes Alaska and Hawaii. Includes members of the Armed Forces living off post or with their families on post, but excludes all other members of the Armed Forces. Includes small number of families and unrelated individuals with no money income.)

Item and income level	1947	1950	1955	1960	1964	1965	1966
Families, total	100.0	100.0	100.0	100.0	100.0	100.0	100.0
Under $3,000	28.9	28.9	22.8	19.5	16.4	15.5	14.3
$3,000 to $4,999	30.6	29.1	22.5	18.0	16.2	15.2	13.9
$5,000 to $6,999	19.7	20.6	23.3	21.6	18.5	18.0	17.8
$7,000 to $9,999	13.0	13.6	19.7	22.5	23.5	24.4	24.4
$10,000 to $14,999	8.1	7.9	8.8	13.3	18.0	18.7	20.4
$15,000 and over			2.9	5.3	7.4	8.4	9.2
Median income†	$4,401	$4,479	$5,377	$6,174	$6,871	$7,154	$7,436

Source: U.S. Dept. of Commerce, Bureau of the Census; *Current Population Reports*, Series P-60, no. 53.
†*Statistical Abstract of the United States*, 1968, p. 325.

TABLE 5-2   Percent of aggregate income received by each fifth and top percent of families: 1947 to 1966

Item and income rank	1947	1950	1955	1960	1963	1964	1965	1966
Lowest fifth	5.0	4.5	4.8	4.9	5.1	5.2	5.3	5.4
Second fifth	11.8	12.0	12.2	12.0	12.0	12.0	12.2	12.4
Middle fifth	17.0	17.4	17.7	17.6	17.6	17.7	17.6	17.7
Fourth fifth	23.1	23.5	23.7	23.6	23.9	24.0	24.0	23.8
Highest fifth	43.0	42.6	41.6	42.0	41.4	41.1	40.9	40.7
Top 5 percent	17.2	17.0	16.8	16.8	16.0	15.7	15.2	14.8

Source: U.S. Dept. of Commerce, Bureau of the Census; *Current Population Reports*, Series P-60, no. 53.

Objective classifications   An objective classification of people on an income basis is easily obtainable from the Census Bureau. Income distribution is by no means a perfect measure of social class, for reasons we have already mentioned, but it has the advantage of objectivity and of application on a national scale. Table 5-1 shows a steady increase in the number of people in the higher-income brackets and a decline of those in the less-than-$3,000 income bracket, even when the value of the dollar is kept constant. In total income, real progress is being made, but Table 5-2 shows that the poorest fifth of the population has changed very little in relative position, even though its cash earnings have improved.

Diagrammatic representations of class   On the basis of the income statistics just presented, social class could be shown as a simple stairstep arrangement, but such an illustration fails to account for gradations between steps. Warner's community descriptions could be shown in the same way, but the steps would have very different widths. In Warner's analysis, the upper-lower and lower-middle classes make up a majority, "the common-man level." Another possibility is to represent class distribution as an inclined plane, suggesting that classes grade into each other almost imperceptibly.

Another way to represent social class graphically is by a type of panoramic view. Such a scheme has the advantage of showing that people strive for success in their own areas of life and that there are elites in various fields of striving. Our panoramic view shows the highest peaks as those of the leaders of government, industry, and the military; in this respect it places an emphasis on power. There are few completely flat lands, because there are differences in individual prestige at all levels. The submerged area represents people who are really outside the system of competition and of regular employment. The "badlands" remind us that there are levels of prestige and success in the world of crime and that its upper reaches are not too far from the towering heights of power.

Mobility   Although the panoramic view of social class depicts various levels and areas of upward striving, it does not tell how much upward mobility there is. *Upward mobility* is the movement to a higher position. *Career mobility* refers to an upward or downward class status change during one's own life; *generational mobility* is the measurement of a person's achievement in comparison with his parental generation. It is fairly obvious that people are moving up and down the peaks of success and from the lower plains to the higher plains. The real question is whether there is more upward than downward mobility and whether there

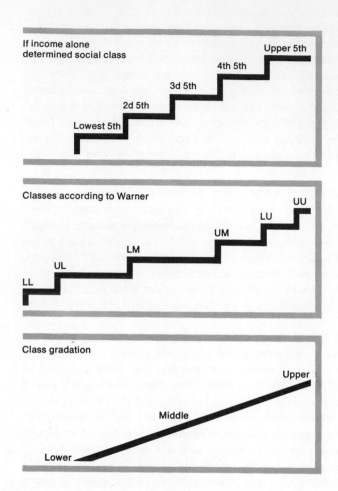

If income alone
determined social class

Upper 5th

4th 5th

3d 5th

2d 5th

Lowest 5th

Classes according to Warner

UU

LU

UM

LM

UL

LL

Class gradation

Upper

Middle

Lower

is as much upward mobility as in the past. America has been a land of opportunity. Is it as much so now as ever?

The occupational demands of industrial systems make it obvious that many of the most rapidly increasing areas of employment are in fields calling for the highly skilled and highly educated, as is shown by the educational statistics from the Department of Labor on page 102. These demands have created much upward mobility in many industrial countries, especially in the United States. A comparison of the United

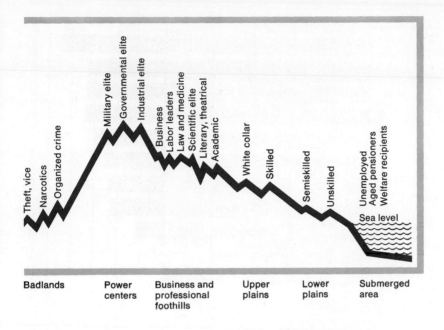

States, Great Britain, the Netherlands, and Japan shows considerable upward mobility in all cases, but the movement into the elite classes (approximately the same as Warner's upper-middle and lower-upper) is greater in the United States than in any of the other countries.[23]

Other evidence of mobility is the disappearance, or near disappearance, of some of the most ill-paying and low-status jobs. Household servants are almost nonexistent. Mining and nonfarm labor show no employment gains. While population and labor supply continue to increase, farm labor declines drastically. Pick-and-shovel crews on highways are replaced by mechanized equipment. Small marginal farms are a rapidly diminishing part of the economy, as is indicated in the table. In 1940, 23 percent of the people lived on farms; by 1968 the figure had declined to 6 percent. The remaining farms are of much higher value, as is indicated by the amount of investment per farm worker—a mere $3,500 in 1940 as compared to $36,000 by 1968.[24] Farming is usually an inherited

[23]Thomas Fox and S. M. Miller, "Intra-Country Variations in Occupational Stratification and Mobility," in Reinhard Bendix and Seymour Martin Lipset (eds.), *Class, Status, and Power,* The Free Press, New York, 1966, pp. 74–87.
[24]*Occupational Outlook Handbook*, U.S. Department of Labor Bulletin No. 1550, 1968, p. 624.

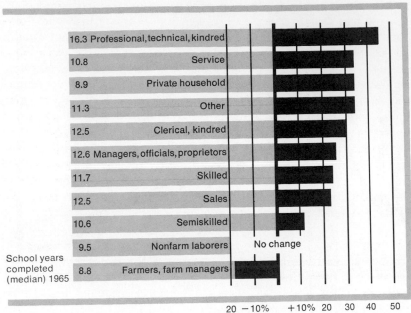

16.3 Professional, technical, kindred

10.8 Service

8.9 Private household

11.3 Other

12.5 Clerical, kindred

12.6 Managers, officials, proprietors

11.7 Skilled

12.5 Sales

10.6 Semiskilled

9.5 Nonfarm laborers   No change

School years
completed
(median) 1965   8.8 Farmers, farm managers

20 −10%   +10% 20   30   40   50

Percent change in employment, 1965-1975

(Adapted from *Occupational Outlook Handbook*,
U.S. Dept. of Labor Bulletin 1550, 1968.)

occupation and has shown less mobility than jobs required in an urban society.[25]

A comparison of occupational distributions over the period 1932 to 1962 shows increasing movement into professional, technical, and managerial jobs and less movement into manual occupations with the passing of each decade. Much of the mobility has been among people moving away from the farms, a process that must necessarily slow down in the future, since so few people remain on farms.[26]

Since different ethnic groups have had different experiences in America, it is interesting to see to what extent they have found it to be the promised land of opportunity. The picture differs considerably de-

[25] Bergel, *op. cit.*, p. 351.
[26] Otis Dudley Duncan, "The Trend of Occupational Mobility in the United States," *American Sociological Review*, vol. 30, August, 1965, pp. 491–498.

pending on which ethnic group is under consideration. The Anglo-Saxons and Scandinavians seem to have a preferred position in job competition. Russians and Czechs have done better than average; Irish and Poles about average, and Italians a little below average. All have shown more upward than downward mobility and, on an occupational basis, have not been the victims of discrimination to the same degree as Negroes, Mexican Americans, or American Indians. "The notion of equal opportunity irrespective of national origin is a near reality," but not when Latin-American and Negro minorities are considered.[27] Even when educational level is held constant, the socioeconomic status of the latter two groups falls short of that of the others, especially for the Negroes.

It would seem, then, that there is much mobility in American life from lower to middle and from middle to upper-middle class and that this mobility holds for most but not all ethnic groups. What about the top? Is there less "circulation of elites," more stability at the top?

Stability at the top   The upper-upper class families of Boston, New York, Philadelphia, and Virginia remain the same over the years. "As for our time, it is safe to say that the upper-upper class is in a state of stability."[28] The tendency for much of the business of the families of old wealth to be handled by expert managers gives a road to upward mobility for the management group, but, at the same time, it ensures that no foolish heir can destroy the accumulated fortunes of one of the old families. We worry little about the possible fall into poverty of the Rockefellers, Mellons, or DuPonts.

Despite considerable stability at the top, the future is never certain. Sometimes new industrial developments can have a profound effect, lifting people rather suddenly to great wealth.

The question of mobility is not one on which all authorities agree. Some are more certain than others that there is more permanence at the top now than in the past. Some also question the degree of upward mobility at middle levels or have doubts about the future. Porter, for example, warns that we may be developing such a complex system, calling for such long and difficult periods of education, that motivation will not be enough to get people to prepare for some of the top scientific, medical, and technical positions.[29] He cites figures, for example, indicating that we have had to import from abroad about 1,500 physicians/year and a total of 63,500 natural scientists, social scientists, and engineers between 1949 and 1964. A more likely explanation for the need to import experts is

[27] Beverly Duncan and Otis Dudley Duncan, "Minorities and the Process of Stratification," *American Sociological Review*, vol. 33, no. 3, June, 1968, pp. 356–364.
[28] Bergel, *op. cit.*, p. 348.
[29] John Porter, "The Future of Upward Mobility," *American Sociological Review*, vol. 33, no. 1, February, 1968, pp. 5–19.

simply that our educational system could not train the needed personnel fast enough. At present we seem to be overcoming such shortages (see Chapter 12).

In summary, it can be said that for the majority groups the upward-mobility rate has been highly favorable in recent years, but problems remain for certain minorities, and there may be more stability at the top than in the past. There is also the possibility that rapidly changing demands might upset the future of mobility in some such way as Porter suggests. There is also another problem very much in the minds of people today because of so much recent comment on poverty in America. Is there an *underclass* that is unaffected by the social mobility we have just discussed?

SOCIAL CLASS AS SUBCULTURE   Elsewhere in this book, considerable comment is made on social-class differences in prospects for education, political attitudes, marital stability, and religious orientation because it is impossible to discuss family, religion, government, education, and racial and ethnic problems without also discussing class differences. In this section, contrasts in class patterns of living will be discussed largely in terms of a lower-class subculture. Let us first sum up what has already been said or implied in previous chapters about class differences and give a brief preview of how social class relates to topics that follow. To quite a degree, social classes can be thought of as subcultures with differences in values, points of view, and expectations. Children are socialized into the various social-class subcultures by home experience and interaction, mainly with people of their own class. The lower class is apt to be more severe in physical punishment of children and less likely to emphasize training for independence and upward mobility than is the middle class.[30] The lower-class child has a greater chance of coming from a broken or unhappy home and of being exposed to attitudes out of keeping with the ethic of success-striving. If he comes from a religious family, he is more apt to experience strong emotionalism in religious services and attitudes somewhat hostile to the leaders of the society around him. He is nowadays likely to see that higher education is desirable, but he may find many obstacles in his way to its attainment. Politically, he will probably learn attitudes that are liberal in the sense of wanting to support labor, graduated income taxes, and welfare measures, but that are illiberal toward the foreigner and the nonconformist.

Other types of life prospects are quite uneven, including the chance of survival itself. The poor have more children than the middle class or well-to-do, and the children are less likely to be planned. They are more

[30]Urie Bronfenbrenner, "Socialization and Social Class through Space and Time," in Reinhard Bendix and Seymour Martin Lipset (eds.), *Class, Status, and Power,* The Free Press, New York, 1966, pp. 362–377.

likely to be born when the mother is too young or when she is too old for healthy delivery. Although only 6 percent of the deaths in the United States are among infants, in the poorest county of the nation 24 percent of the deaths are among infants. Three times as many people are out of work with more chronic ailments among people of incomes of $4,000/year or less than among those with incomes of more than $4,000.[31]

What is true of physical health is also true of mental health. Hollingshead and Redlich, using a five-class analysis, found that the lowest class made up 12.8 percent of the normal population but 36.8 percent of the psychotic population.[32] The more recent Midtown Manhattan Study made similar findings. The higher-income groups showed that 9.9 percent were "impaired" in mental health; the lowest-income group showed that 19.8 percent were "impaired."[33]

The poor are less able to exert influence in the community and in organizational life. The "joiners" in American society are overrepresented by the middle and upper-middle classes and are underrepresented among the poor. The same is true for those who rate themselves high in community leadership.[34]

Work satisfaction differs considerably. In one study, 68 percent of the professionals said that they would continue the same kind of work, even if they had no economic need to work; only 16 percent of the unskilled expressed the same attitude. In another study, from 82 to 91 percent of various professional people stated that they would choose the same line of work if beginning their careers again; only 16 percent of the unskilled workers said the same.[35]

In a number of different success beliefs, the poor contrast sharply with the middle class. More of the middle class believe there is a good chance to succeed and that quality of work is more important than "pull" or "politicking" in order to succeed. More middle class than lower class think well of an occupation that requires a certain amount of risk but has high potential.[36]

Culture of poverty   The term "culture of poverty" has been used to describe the very poor: the unemployed and those in the urban ghettoes and

[31] Robert L. Eichorn and Edward G. Ludwig, "Poverty and Health," in Hanna H. Meissner (ed.), *Poverty in the Affluent Society*, Harper & Row, Publishers, Incorporated, New York, 1966, p. 173.
[32] August B. Hollingshead and Frederick C. Redlich, "Social Stratification and Psychiatric Disorders," *American Sociological Review*, vol. 18, April, 1953, pp. 163–169.
[33] Leo Srole et al., *Mental Health in the Metropolis: The Midtown Manhattan Study*, McGraw-Hill Book Company, New York, 1962, p. 217.
[34] Robert Hagedorn and Sanford Labovitz, "Participation in Community Associations by Occupation: A Test of Three Theories," *American Sociological Review*, vol. 33, no. 2, April, 1968, pp. 267–283.
[35] Both surveys in Robert Blauner, "Work Satisfaction and Industrial Trends in Modern Society," in Reinhard Bendix and Seymour Martin Lipset (eds.), *Class, Status, and Power*, The Free Press, New York, 1966, pp. 473–477.
[36] Herbert H. Hyman, "A Social Psychological Contribution to the Analysis of Stratification," in Reinhard Bendix and Seymour Martin Lipset (eds.), *Class, Status, and Power*, The Free Press, New York, 1966, pp. 488–499.

in such depressed areas as parts of Appalachia. Some of the contrasts between middle and lower class used in this chapter have applied to regularly employed people, above the poverty line. The poverty level is hard to define, but there is certainly merit in Coser's description, "In modern societies the deprived are assigned to the core category of the poor only when they receive assistance. . . ." Poorly paid occupations are not stigmatized, but public assistance is.

Oscar Lewis has described a "culture of poverty" as something existing in fairly similar conditions in many urban societies and most extreme in societies just entering industrialization. He has spoken of the culture as characterized by gregariousness, "lack of privacy, high incidence of alcoholism, early initiation into sex . . . a trend toward mother-centered families." [37]

Elizabeth Herzog reviews this concept with some very interesting and significant reservations.[38] Some of the psychological traits mentioned are simply the necessary adjustments to poverty but not part of a culture. She does not contradict the facts presented by Lewis, but simply the use of the word "culture," for culture implies values. Although the incidence of illegitimacy is high, it is not culturally approved. The mothers of teen-age daughters pray that premature experience with sex will not occur and that their daughters can make a good marriage. Similarly, many drink heavily, but drunkenness is not really approved. Herzog also points out that some of the traits attributed to a culture of poverty are really the result of malnutrition—depression, fatigue, lack of ambition, weakness, and difficulty in concentrating. Similarly, poor school achievement is not advocated by parents; it is simply unavoidable under the circumstances. Herzog and Lewis both agree that a mother-centered family is a phenomenon of extreme poverty and is by no means limited to the Negro poor. In many areas of high employment, adult males fail to function as household heads, regardless of their race.

Decline in poverty   During most of the world's history, poverty for many has been inevitable because of shortages of economic goods. In parts of the modern world that have high productivity and relatively low birth rates, there is no longer any crucial economic scarcity. In such welfare-oriented states as Sweden, poverty is virtually nonexistent. In the United States, it seems safe to predict a continuing decline in the amount of poverty, in spite of a "hard core" of impoverishment and more literature about poverty than usual. A reason for so much discussion of poverty is

[37]Oscar Lewis, Introduction to *The Children of Sanchez*, Random House, Inc., New York, 1961. (Copyright by Oscar Lewis).
[38]Elizabeth Herzog, "Facts and Fictions about the Poor," *Monthly Labor Review*, February, 1969, pp. 42–49. (U.S. Department of Labor, Reprint, *Perspectives on Poverty*.)

that it constitutes an increasing normative strain in a society that claims equalitarian values and produces enough goods to make poverty unnecessary. For this reason, college youth take an active interest in social work and Head Start programs, and politicians find it necessary to at least promise abundance for all.

Poverty was once thought of not only as inevitable but as a necessary goad to force people to work at some of the most dangerous, undesirable, and backbreaking tasks of society. Such jobs are less common than formerly, often having been replaced by machinery. It also appears that there is no shortage of people willing to take whatever jobs are available, provided pay rates are satisfactory. We are not suggesting a disappearance of social class, but it may be that one of the features of social-class systems, grinding poverty for those at the bottom of the heap, will no longer accompany the class systems of prosperous industrial nations.

SUMMARY   Although the desire for a classless society has been expressed frequently in literature and social philosophy, it seems to be an unattainable goal. Societies call for different statuses, some of which have different rank and prestige. Social classes are made up of people of similar status who are conscious of their similarities. Social class is difficult to measure precisely in modern industrial societies, but education, income, wealth, power, and esteem are all suggested as important social-class criteria.

There are great variations in social-class systems. Simple hunting and gathering societies tend to be classless, or nearly so, and the degree of class distinction increases as the development of agriculture makes a leisure class possible. Advanced agricultural societies often form very rigid social systems, such as that of medieval Europe. The most rigid social-class system of all — caste — has developed in a number of conquest states and in India. Although the distinction between position of white and black races in the United States is often compared to caste, there are differences in the amount of mobility and the degree to which the two systems are supported by religious norms.

There are theoretical conflicts over the function of class in societies; conservative writers are a little more inclined to emphasize its functional necessity than liberals or radicals. Among modern social theorists, the argument is more a matter of how great a social-class differentiation is necessary than whether one should exist at all.

Industrial societies show less social-class rigidity than advanced agricultural societies. Since they require many trained people in favorable positions and do not allow an elitist monopoly on learning, industrial societies permit considerable upward mobility. Social class continues to exist, but the lines between social classes are not always clear. Warner describes six social classes in a number of towns in which reputational studies were made. Self-evaluation studies show that a great majority of Americans consider themselves middle class. The objective criteria of education and income are used more easily than self-evaluation or reputational studies, although they are not perfect descriptions of class. A discussion of social-class position also merges into a discussion of elites, people of highest status in various fields. Elites constitute leadership groups but not necessarily classes.

Studies of mobility in the United States and other industrial nations show more upward than downward mobility. Reasons for upward mobility include the appearance of a larger number of high-status jobs and a disappearance of some of the jobs of lowest status and income, farm labor, for example. Although there continues to be much upward mobility, there is some evidence of a stable class of great wealth at the top.

Social classes can be thought of as subcultures, socializing their children into their own customs and values. Viewed this way, lower-class position has the disadvantage of shorter life expectancy, poorer physical and mental health, and less work satisfaction. The various classes have different rationalizations for their position in the system. Wealthy people usually attribute success to effort and ability; lower-class people are more likely to attribute success to luck or pull.

Oscar Lewis has used the expression "culture of poverty" to characterize the way of life of the extremely poor, but there is some objection to the word "culture" in this respect. Many of the life styles of poor people are forced upon them by economic necessity, not by any particular cultural norms that they have developed.

Scarcity of goods once made an impoverished class inevitable, but there is no longer a crucial scarcity in prosperous industrial nations. In spite of the persistence of a "hard core of poverty," there are indications that poverty is on the decline and can be alleviated. Prosperous industrial societies continue to display strong social-class differences, but the tendency is for the condition of those at the bottom of the heap to be less deprived than in the past.

Hath not a Jew eyes? Hath not a Jew hands,
organs, dimensions, senses, affections,
passions? Fed by the same food, hurt with
the same weapons, subject to the same
diseases, healed by the same means, warmed
and cooled by the same winter and summer as
a Christian is? If you wound us, do we not
bleed? If you poison us, do we not die? And
If you wrong us, shall we not revenge?

SHAKESPEARE
Merchant of Venice

six

RACIAL AND ETHNIC GROUPS

Races are the major divisions of mankind; they differ from
each other in color or other inherited physical traits such
as eye form, type of hair, or frequency distributions of
blood types. There are many variations in how experts
classify race, but always they describe race on the basis
of physical type, not cultural type, and always they find
much overlap in racial traits. Not all members of tall races
are really tall; not all members of black races are purely
black, and not all Caucasoids are as white as snow. There
must be, however, average hereditary differences in
physical type before any segment of mankind can be
called a race.

Ethnic groups, on the other hand, consist of people
who are different culturally from the majority of those
among whom they live. The cultural differences may be in
language, religion, or political loyalty, or they may be in
such minor traits as food habits, dress, manners, and
local accents. People can be both racially and ethnically
different from the majority group. For example, American
Indians living on reservations and following their old
customs are different from most Americans in both race
and culture.

Indian people living in town and following the customs of the majority of Americans are racially different but have a similar culture and can be considered a separate ethnic group only if they perceive themselves as such. Jewish people, on the other hand, belong to the white majority race, but if they are orthodox followers of their religious tradition they are somewhat different culturally and can be called an ethnic group.

Both racial and ethnic minorities have suffered persecution in many times and lands. Sometimes they have been treated with inhuman cruelty and nearly exterminated, as was the case of the Jews in Hitler's time, the Armenians in earlier times in Turkey, and many American Indian tribes in American history. Frequently they have been more or less tolerated but not treated as equals; they have been joked about, shut out of social clubs and activities, and even denied desirable jobs, schools, and housing. There are various reasons for the unequal treatment of minorities, but the first one we will study is that of racial and ethnic myth. Unequal treatment has been upheld by various strange beliefs about racial and ethnic groups, often supporting the idea of naturally and divinely intended inequality.

RACIAL AND ETHNIC MYTHS   Many primitives have had myths of an ethnocentric type about themselves and about other people. Often their name for their own tribe means *ourselves*, or *the people*, or *the knowing people,* as opposed to the outsiders, who are thought of as not quite the same as people. Sometimes the myth explains that a great god made *the people*, but a lesser god, of some kind of devil, made the foreigners. More often there is a myth of some great bringer of gifts to *the people* so that they could have a better way of life and be superior to the outsiders.

Modern mythology   Such ideas as these are obviously pure mythology of a primitive type, but the modern civilized world can also hold mythological beliefs about race for the same ethnocentric reasons. Hitler and his followers believed in the superiority of the "Aryan race," although there is no such race, nor is there any such thing as a superior race. The word "Aryan" properly refers to a group of languages, not to a race of people. Americans who believed in slavery made up myths about how God had intended some people to be masters and others slaves. Long after slavery was legally ended in this country, more myths were created to prove that the two races should be kept segregated and unequal. On the opposite side of the racial argument, Elijah Mohammed and his followers propounded a myth explaining how Allah created the black race, and the Devil made the white race, a good example of "reverse snobbery."

Turning to myths about ethnic groups rather than races, one of the best examples is that of medieval mythology about Jews. Jews were accused of worshipping the Devil and of stealing and killing Christian children in order to use their blood at their secret, Satanic rites. Trachenberg[1] tells of the prevailing Christian belief that all Jews, being very clever, could not help but know that the Christian religion was true. The only reason they refused to accept Christianity was that they had sold their souls to the Devil and joined his side. Consequently, the opinion was that no punishment was too severe for Jews, and many cases of torture, murder, and mass exile resulted.

The rise of the Nordic myth   One of the racial myths with the most devastating consequences had a curious beginning. Writing mainly out of resentment against the autocracy of the Roman Empire, the ancient Roman, Tacitus, praised the Germanic people as the repository of virtue and bravery and as lovers of freedom.[2] Many centuries later, the French writer de Boulainvillier, protesting the autocracy of Louis XIV, created the myth that the Latin civilization had always stood for tyranny and the Germanic "race" had stood for freedom. It was in the nineteenth century, however, that the myth of Nordic superiority reached full fruition in the writings of Count Arthur de Gobineau (1816–1882).[3] Although by the end of his life the cosmopolitan and erudite Gobineau had changed his views considerably, his early writings on race had wide impact. He spoke of the horrors of continuous mixing of races and of the impending decline of the Nordic race by blending with Mediterranean types, Eastern types, and Jews. This "bastardization" would lead inevitably to the degeneracy of the Nordic people, just as it had, in his opinion, led to the decline of the ancient Mediterranean civilizations.

Gobineau's racial mythology eventually entered the diseased mind of a fanatical little Austrian painter by the name of Adolph Hitler, and it reached its culmination in the mass murder of 6 million Jews in gas chambers and other death camps.

Reality versus myth   There has been so much mythology about race that we sometimes wonder whether there are any really dependable facts in existence. Physical anthropologists are the most thorough students of human variability and have made some interesting studies on the subject of race. Their classifications do not always agree with each other,

[1] Joshua Trachenberg, *The Devil and the Jews*, Harper & Row, Publishers, Incorporated, Torchbooks, New York, 1966, pp. 124–139.
[2] Jacques Barzun, *Race: A Study in Superstition*, Harper & Row, Publishers, Incorporated, Torchbooks, New York, 1965, pp. 17–18.
[3] *Ibid.*, pp. 54–77.

and none would feel absolutely certain of his explanation of racial differences. They would agree completely on two points, however: (1) race is a matter of physical difference, not mental or cultural, and (2) all human beings belong to one single species, Homo sapiens. In the latter sense we are all brothers, and anthropological science finds itself in agreement with such teachers as Confucius, Buddha, and Jesus.

RACIAL THEORY AND CLASSIFICATION   Few theories are more widely accepted in the scientific world, or more thoroughly substantiated by an impressive alignment of evidence, than the theory of evolution. As more and more bones of ancient man are unearthed, it becomes increasingly clear that he has gradually developed from a small-brained animal of approximately 2 million years ago, generally known as *Australopithecus africanus* (Southern ape-man from Africa), to the large-brained type known as *Homo sapiens* (knowing man).[4] Although there are a few extremely ancient remains from Java, the fossil evidence from Africa is so overwhelming that it seems fairly safe to say that Africa was the place of human origin. At the present state of anthropological knowledge one can tell the racial bigot, "But you, too, are of African descent!"

Special adaptation to climate   Regardless of where man originated, he has always had a way of getting around. Hundreds of thousands of years before the age of jet airplanes, he was migrating from Africa to all parts of Europe and Asia. At least 30,000 years ago he reached the remote continents of North and South America and Australia. Evolutionary theory would assume that during this long period of time certain physical changes came about to help adapt man to his different physical environments. Most people assume that variation in color was one of these adaptive traits, and there is a certain amount of evidence to support the opinion. Studies of American military personnel under varied conditions of heat indicate that the black soldier has greater endurance for hot, moist climates than has the white.[5] Neither of them do particularly well in hot, dry climates; black skin absorbs too much heat, and white skin burns. The preferred type for the great deserts of the world is one with considerable brown or yellowish pigmentation in the skin: the Mongol, Tartar, Tuareg, American Indian, or Mexican, for example.

There are a number of other interesting indications of adaptation to environment. Some people have much greater resistance to the cold than do most members of the human race, and this seems to be especially

[4]John Beuttner-Janusch, *Origins of Man*, John Wiley & Sons, Inc., New York, 1966, p. 146.
[5]Paul T. Baker, "Racial Differences in Heat Tolerance," *American Journal of Physical Anthropology*, vol. 16, September, 1958, pp. 287–305.

true of certain variants of the Mongoloid race. There is evidence that Eskimo have a greater blood supply to face and hands than do most people, helping to protect them against the bitter cold of their environment. Down at the tip of South America, in the frigid land first discovered by Magellan, live the Alacaluf Indians, who in the past wore almost no clothing. Their children have been known to swim in the cold water among the icebergs. Coon[6] reports tests that indicate a much higher rate of basal metabolism for these people than for most other human beings; thus they are able to maintain body temperatures even under Antarctican conditions.

Another case of racial difference is that of the Indians of the high Andes Mountains. Their lung capacities are unusually large, and their red corpuscle count is enough to keep them well supplied with oxygen in the rarified atmosphere in which they live. Other people build up a larger red-corpuscle supply as they adapt to high mountains, but a prominent anthropologist concludes that the natural adaptation of the Andean Indian is greater than it is for other people, and that the trait is hereditary.[7]

Body build and adaptation   A kind of general rule about body build has been suggested, known as *Bergman's rule*: stocky builds are better for cold climates, and long, slender builds are better adapted to hot climates. The Eskimo fit the description for the cold-climate type, and so do many Siberian tribes and Central Asians; they all have short arms and legs in proportion to total body size. There are many exceptions to the rule regarding tall, slender people in hot climates, however (the Nordic, for example), so that the rule remains in some doubt. There are more cases to support Bergman's rule, however, than there are to refute it.[8]

Anthropologists have sought explanations for other racial differences. The Mongoloid eye form is generally believed to represent special adaptation to extreme cold and strong winds, and, as this theory would suggest, the eye form is more pronounced among northern Asians than among southern Asians.

Mentality as adaptation   Regardless of climate or altitude, one physical trait has had survival value for the entire human race in all parts of the world: the development of a superior brain. The evolutionary processes that have led to this development have gone on in all parts of the world. The size of the brain has increased with each successive stage of human

[6] Carleton Coon, *The Origin of Races*, Alfred A. Knopf, Inc., New York, 1962, p. 64.
[7] *Ibid.*, pp. 70–71.
[8] Carleton Coon, "Climate and Race," in Harlow Shapley (ed.), *Climatic Change*, Harvard University Press, Cambridge, Mass., 1954, pp. 13–34.

evolution.[9] It would seem highly illogical to assume that in some parts of the world mental growth has been a favorable and adaptive trait and that in other parts it has been a detriment. The anthropological evidence argues for a great degree of similarity in human capacities, regardless of race or climatic zone.

Perhaps the time will come when we will simply refer to "the human race" without breaking it down into subdivisions. Since we are still strongly race conscious, however, it seems that some type of racial classification should be described.

Racial classification   Mankind was once conveniently divided into precisely three races: Caucasoid (white), Mongoloid (yellow), and Negroid (black). A slight straining of the system included the American Indians as Mongoloid and the Australian aborigines as Negroid. The words "Caucasoid," "Mongoloid," and "Negroid" are still so much a part of common speech that they are hard to drop, but there are suggestions for better systems of classification made by such prominent physical anthropologists as Dobzhansky, Washburn, and Garn. Garn and Coon use the concept of *geographical races*—the races that have developed in major geographical areas of the world.[10] These races include European, Indian, Asian, American Indian, Australian aborigine, Polynesian, Melanesian, and Micronesian. Implied in the classification is the idea that when people have been geographically separated long enough, distinctive types develop. To the list of major races Garn adds local races, such as the subdivision of the European race into Northwestern (formerly Nordic), Alpine, and Mediterranean. He also adds a few *microraces*, small groups hard to classify, such as the Ainu of Hokkaido (northern Japan), often classified as white. This type of classification has the advantage of not trying to force all people into three or four basic types. Garn also notes that the blending of races is gradually producing new types, as in the case of the blending of American Indian and European to create a new Latin American type.

RACIAL AND ETHNIC PREJUDICE   What has been said of physical difference in races is of theoretical interest but is no longer important. In an age of good housing and clothing, climate does not prevent people of any race from living where they choose, even if there are slight differences in resistance to cold or heat. Millions of people of African descent live in the United States, and quite a few are in Canada, experiencing no physical

[9] C. Loring Brace, *The Stages of Human Evolution*, Prentice-Hall, Inc., Englewood Cliffs, N.J., 1967, pp. 59–70.
[10] Stanley M. Garn and Carleton S. Coon, "On the Number of Races of Mankind," *American Anthropologist*, vol. 57, October, 1955, pp. 996–1001.

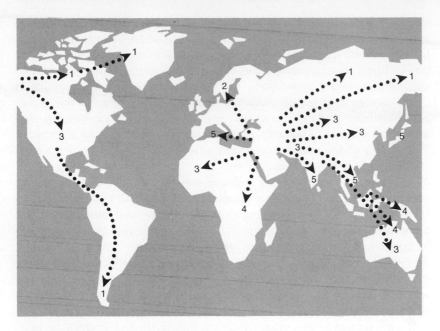

1 Types adapted to the cold; stocky build
2 Blond types in cool, cloudy climates
3 Brown, yellow-brown, reddish-brown in deserts
4 Hot tropics; black
5 Intermediate coloration

difficulty. Members of the white race live in the hot desert of central Australia and manage to survive. Not only do races learn to cope with different climates, but they learn to adopt different cultures. The black American belongs to the culture of America and is as much a stranger to the land of his ancestors as is the member of any other ethnic minority enculturated into this society.

In spite of the above arguments that racial differences are of little importance, they loom large in the thinking of many people. It is the *belief* that race differences are important that *makes* them important. Sociology must deal with the beliefs of people, whether they are true or not, because such beliefs are the basis of action. There are strong beliefs that some races are better than others. Many people become the victims of *racial prejudice*, unfavorable attitudes imposed on entire categories of people.

The origin and maintenance of prejudice   The explanation of prejudice is very complex, but the phenomenon can be explained, in part, as the result of ethnocentric attitudes about one's own group. In order to achieve group solidarity and morale, the in-group has to insist that its cultural ways and even its appearance are better than others. The attitude is usually acceptable to the individual member of the group because his ego is inflated through group identification, and group belonging also gives him a sense of security. Out-groups are thought to be a threat to the security of the culture, especially when its members have a superior status that they would hate to lose. Often one or two foreigners are received as a source of interest and curiosity, but large numbers are perceived as a threat. This was the case with the first Chinese immigrants to California. They were treated as heroes; after large numbers arrived there were anti-Chinese demonstrations. The same principle of the feeling of threat to folkways and status probably accounts, in part, for the fact that school integration in recent years has been slowest in areas where the black population is most nearly equal to the white population. The very expression "white supremacy" implies that whites are under threat unless they keep the upper hand.

Stereotyping—the creation of carelessly formed images of what entire races or nations are like—also helps to perpetuate prejudice. We can stereotype other people as well as racial and ethnic groups, but group stereotyping often bears the most cruel results.

Scapegoating is another method by which prejudices can be created and spread, and often it has become the policy of ruling groups. The word "scapegoating" comes from the ancient practice, described in the Bible, of sacrificing a goat to pay for the sins of the people. It is used in modern times to describe a national policy of finding someone to blame for the nation's ills. For example, in the early days of Communist rule in Russia, the economic system was not working, and millions of people were going hungry. The government made scapegoats of the more prosperous peasants, the kulaks, accusing them of hoarding food and causing famine. Hitler blamed the Jews for the great depression in Germany, and even for Germany's loss of World War I. During the period of heavy immigration into the United States, xenophobic people blamed all the ills of our society on the bad influence of foreigners. Many groups have been scapegoats in many parts of the world.

Prejudice often is strongest in groups that are in declining social or economic status. There are also cases where extremes of prejudice are associated with particular personality types. Some seem to feel more threatened by outsiders than others, and some seem to have a great need to lord it over others.

Prejudice as cultural transmission   In most cases, though, prejudice is more a cultural habit than a symptom of psychological illness. Usually prejudice is simply taught as part of the socialization process. Generations of Englishmen and Irishmen were taught prejudice against each other. Greeks and Turks were long taught by their parents the interminable record of atrocities the out-group had committed. In the United States, prejudice against blacks has been taught generation after generation, sometimes deliberately and sometimes unthinkingly by patronizing actions and attitudes.

Prejudice and discrimination   *Prejudice*, as we have seen, is an attitude. *Discrimination* is a practice, a practice of unequal treatment of groups of people, especially racial, ethnic, or religious groups. It seems clear that prejudice leads to discrimination. It is also true that discrimination leads to prejudice, but the second case is not as clear, and needs a little explaining.

As a general rule, black Americans have been discriminated against in education. At the time of the Supreme Court ruling that schools should be integrated (1954), many school districts spent only about half as much per pupil for Negro schools as for white schools. The result for the blacks was ignorance, poorly paying jobs, and poverty. Whites, then, could see that blacks were generally ignorant, lived in shacks and hovels, and followed only the most lowly occupational pursuits, and this led to prejudice against them. The fact that they were poor and ignorant became a reason for keeping them poor and ignorant.

The same type of connection between discrimination and prejudice has occurred for many other people as well. For centuries, the Irish were poorly educated and poverty-stricken. This condition caused the English to look upon them as stupid. The attitude of Germans toward Poles was very similar, as was that of the Japanese toward the Koreans. People can be backward and ignorant as a result of discrimination, and their backwardness and ignorance can result in prejudice, which leads to further discrimination. The situation can be compared with the old controversy over which came first, the hen or the egg. Myrdal[11] has spoken of the relationship as *cumulative causation*, or a vicious circle, with discrimination barring job opportunities and education, and these shortcomings creating prejudice and renewed discrimination.

Breaking the vicious circle   If prejudice leads to discrimination, then it would seem that a good way to improve conditions would be to educate people out of their prejudices. If, on the other hand, discrimination leads

---

[11] Gunnar Myrdal, *An American Dilemma*, McGraw-Hill Book Company, New York, 1964, vol. I, pp. 75–78.

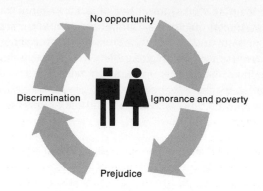

to prejudice, it would seem that making rules and regulations to prevent discrimination would cause prejudice to disappear gradually. Both approaches are helpful, but the second one must be stressed because it produces more rapid results. In an area where everyone is prejudiced, it would be hard to find schools and teachers willing or able to educate people out of their prejudices, but it might be possible to stop the worst forms of discrimination.

One example of officially ending discrimination was the integrating of major-league baseball teams, with Jackie Robinson being the first black player accepted. There were predictions that the baseball fans would boycott the games, but no such thing happened. Once discrimination was ended, people began to accept integrated baseball as a part of the natural order of things. Many members of the present younger generation assume that baseball has always been integrated.

Throughout American history our armed services have usually been segregated into black and white units. Even World War II, fought against the racism of Hitler, was fought by racially segregated American Armed Forces. At the end of the war the Armed Forces were desegregated, as was noted in Chapter 2. The results have generally been favorable and there has been an improvement in morale of the black troops. There are still complaints regarding privileges and promotions, but integration is generally regarded as the natural order of things, and great progress toward racial justice has resulted.

In 1954 the Supreme Court ruled that public schools should be integrated. Later decisions allowed for "deliberate speed," which some districts interpreted to mean "with deliberate delay." In 1969 the Supreme

Court ruled unanimously that integration of the remaining schools should proceed "at once," and integration began in Mississippi in the spring of 1970, against stubborn resistance. Communities in other states have also been resistant, but thousands of schools are now integrated. Resistance tends to be greatest where the percentage of minority students is very large and where strong traditions of inequality exist.

The "Jim Crow laws" that called for separate buses, trains, waiting rooms, and eating facilities are being abolished. Whites see blacks being treated more nearly equal than in the past and the result is to think of them as being more nearly equal; the decline of discrimination is accompanied by a decline of prejudice. There are some members of the older generation whose minds will never change, but the young are much less prejudiced than the old, and even some of the older people change their views. Sometimes there is only a shift in the nature of the prejudice. Whereas nearly four out of five whites now believe Negroes to be as intelligent as whites, less than one out of five believe that the Negroes' economic distress is mainly the result of discrimination. Lack of education is frequently blamed, but large numbers of whites assume that Negroes simply do not care enough to really try.[12]

REACTIONS TO PREJUDICE AND DISCRIMINATION   Many people feel the sting of prejudice occasionally for such dubious offenses as being too young, too old, coming from the wrong part of the country, or belonging to the wrong church or political party. These kinds of prejudice are annoying, but we are generally able to brush them off. What happens to the individual whose whole life is surrounded by prejudice?

Black children become aware of negative attitudes toward their race at a very early age. By the time they are ready to start school, many find communication with whites more difficult than with their own people.[13] In later years, even the good student shows heightened tensity, anxiety, and sensitivity to insult. Since all men—black, brown, or white, Christian, Moslem, or Jew—have feelings, some type of emotional reaction is inevitable. The feeling might be stated as in the quotation from Shakespeare's *The Merchant of Venice*, " . . . and if you wrong us, shall we not revenge?" but, in spite of city riots in recent years, revenge has not been the usual response. Responses have ranged all the way from a destructive self-image and apathy to smoldering rage and rational protest.

The negative self-image   A common adjustment to prejudice and discrimination results in a negative self-image and the loss of confidence.

[12]Howard Schuman, "Sociological Racism," *Transaction*, vol. 7, December, 1969, pp. 46–47.
[13]Thomas F. Pettigrew, *A Profile of the Negro American*, D. Van Nostrand Company, Inc., Princeton, N.J., 1964, pp. 28–29.

If men are always treated as inferior, they have difficulty seeing themselves as bright and capable. When everything about one's position and experiences—miserable homes, poorly paying jobs, frequent resort to welfare, the glances of hostility from others—combine to destroy pride and hope, people often settle into a state of apathy. *Apathy* is the appearance of not caring. Sometimes apathy becomes so much a part of life that it becomes real and not just pretense, at least until some dramatic event changes it into hope or rage.

Apathy sometimes appears to be stupidity. Negroes have often found that the best way to react to the expectations of others is to seem dull. Particularly in the past, making the best of a bad situation called for "knowing their place."[14] The debased self-image has been particularly hard on men of the black race, for men like to be able to assert themselves as the more aggressive of the two sexes and not to be referred to as "boy" all their lives.

Adjusting to discrimination   Sometimes an adjustment to discrimination is made by finding a place that is open in society. In old European cities, Jews often were not allowed to own land or to follow the majority of occupations, but they were allowed to be pawnbrokers and moneylenders. American Indians have been able to weave blankets and make jewelry for tourists, but such occupations fill the needs of only a few. The black people of America have usually had no such possibilities. They have had to compete for the poorest paying jobs and always seemed to be the last hired and the first fired when times became bad.

Sometimes people adjust by making use of prejudice. Prejudice can explain so many failures; why not let it explain them all? The man who fails for other reasons can blame his failure on prejudice and discrimination. It is very easy for the majority group to blame him as an individual, but it must be admitted that he is a product of the kind of society that gives him that type of excuse.

Many victims of prejudice have simply learned to accept their lot, secretly making jokes about the "uppity" people around them. Many have helped to lead their people in the slow climb to better opportunities, and others have grown enraged and violent, setting fire to their rat-infested ghettos. Some have entered the world of crime, and a few, broken in spirit, have become the derelicts of skid row, retreating from the unequal game of life, defeated and no longer trying, closing out the world with alcohol or heroin until their lives, too, are closed out by death.

There is hope, however, for all but the utterly ruined. Increasingly, the voice of protest is being heard at city hall and at the nation's capital.

[14] Roger D. Abrahams, *Positively Black*, Prentice-Hall, Inc., Englewood Cliffs, N.J., pp. 60–69.

The negative self-image
Failure to communicate
Apathetic attitude
Playing the clown
Hatred of self and others

Adjustments
Finding a place (marginal adaptation)
Excusing all failures
Sullen acceptance

Protesting discrimination
Legalistic approach to integration
Mass movements and demonstrations
Political power approach
Violence
Separatism

Urbanization, geographical mobility, military experience, and increased education are among the social changes that have made the Negroes much more openly critical of their lot than in the past. The path of the future will not be smooth, but it seems highly unlikely that second-class citizenship will ever again be the accepted pattern of life.

Protesting discrimination   In the 1960s there were large numbers of riots in American cities, and there were protest movements on the part of the Black Students' Union on many American campuses. These were the most widely noticed forms of protest, but more peaceful movements had started among American Negroes long before.

One of the most important movements for the improvement of conditions for the American Negro is the organization called the *National Association for the Advancement of Colored People (NAACP)*. For more than half a century the NAACP has worked to try to improve opportunities in education and employment. Its methods have always been peaceful, and it has attracted most of the professional leaders of the black community. Lawyers working for the NAACP won the case for desegregation of the schools in 1954, and the legal actions they have pursued in the ensuing years have resulted in declaring large numbers of racial laws unconstitutional—laws for segregated buses and trains, segregated restaurants, and all forms of compulsory segregation.

The efforts to end segregation were aided greatly by the *Southern Christian Leadership Conference*, headed by Dr. Martin Luther King. A dramatic strike against segregated buses in Montgomery was one of the most important events in the protest movement. It attracted wide attention, caused many white liberals to join the civil rights movement, and started a series of attempts (many of them successful) to end segregation.

It was the completely nonviolent approach of Dr. King and other groups supporting him that won the approval of Congress and President Johnson for a strong civil rights law. In a dramatic speech for a civil rights act the President even used the words of the protest marchers: "We shall overcome." He went on to say that we shall overcome second-class citizenship, the Jim Crow laws, and the prejudices that have made them possible. The President also warned that changes must be made peacefully.

Some of the more militant blacks have felt that the new laws are not enough. The fact remains that unemployment among Negroes, especially in the city ghetto areas, is much higher than among whites. Housing conditions are extremely bad, and regardless of the law, segregation remains. These conditions gave the words "black power" strong appeal, and such radical leaders as Eldridge Cleaver and Rap Brown attracted wide attention.

The new movements began to insist on the word "black," rather than "colored" or "Negro," and tried to build a new self-image for the black American. The militant Black Panthers began to take center stage in many of the ghetto areas. The violent side of the protest movement will be discussed in Chapter 7 as an example of collective behavior.

It is impossible to predict the future. Large numbers of moderate leaders are attempting to bring about justice and advancement by peaceful means; it is not yet clear whether their efforts will achieve enough success to dampen the appeal of the more violent spokesmen.

For a considerable segment of the Negro population income has been improving, although the average still lags far behind white income (see Table 6-1). Even a college education does not pay as well for Negroes as for whites. Borland and Yett estimated that the average college graduate of 1949 would receive $86,000 more in lifetime income than would a high-school graduate, but a nonwhite college graduate would receive only $27,000 more. Ten years later, the corresponding figures were

$120,000 and $67,000, respectively. College was paying better returns for the Negro, but a gap still existed. In the authors' admittedly risky projected figures (assuming present rates of improvement for both whites and nonwhites), the differential would not disappear until 2021.[15]

OTHER MINORITY PROBLEMS The problems of racial and ethnic minorities are too many and varied for all to be included in a brief text. Almost all the people of Southern and Eastern Europe and Asia who came to the United States in the period referred to as the *New Immigration*, approximately 1880 to 1920, encountered a number of difficulties. They were often resented by laboring men because of their willingness to work for low wages and by strongly ethnocentric Americans simply because they seemed more foreign culturally than the people coming from Northern and Western Europe. Sudden surges of new people often evoke fear in the majority group, and the New Immigration became massive, mounting to nearly 10 million in the decade 1900 to 1910. Eventually immigration laws were passed to slow the entry of foreigners. The Chinese met great hostility in the late nineteenth century, as did the Japanese in World War II. Even native-born Americans of Japanese ancestry were sent away from their homes on the Pacific Coast to relocation centers in the desert,

[15] Melvin Borland and Donald E. Yett, "The Cash Value of College for Negroes and Whites," *Transaction*, vol. 5, November, 1967, pp. 44–49.

TABLE 6-1 Percent of families with income of $7,000 or more, 1947--1966 (Adjusted for price changes, in 1965 dollars)

Year	Nonwhite	White	Year	Nonwhite	White
1947	6	21	1960	17	41
1948	5	19	1961	17	43
1949	4	19	1962	15	45
1950	5	22	1963	18	47
1951	5	22	1964	21	50
1952	5	24	1965	23	53
1953	9	28	1966	28	55
1954	8	28			
1955	9	31	1966:		
1956	10	35	South	15	46
1957	11	35	Other		
1958	11	35	regions	38	59
1959	13	40			

Source: U.S. Dept. of Commerce, Bureau of the Census, *Social and Economic Conditions of Negroes in the United States*, Bureau of Labor Statistics Report 332, October, 1967, p. 17.

in spite of the fact that their young men fought for America in the struggle against Germany and Italy. There are much larger minority groups that have had their special problems, including the Mexican Americans and the American Indians.

The Mexican Americans   The Mexican Americans are difficult to classify because some are fairly new arrivals from Mexico, and some have lived in the United States for many generations. Some speak English, know little or no Spanish, and do not like to consider themselves a separate ethnic group; others are comfortable only with the Spanish language and retain many ways of the Mexican culture. The Mexican Americans have never been enslaved and have not been the victims of as much ill will and discrimination as the blacks, but as a whole they are a very economically depressed group. Many of their children have trouble in school, largely because of a language problem. Often teachers do not expect them to do well, and teacher expectation of failure is reliably reported to help cause failure.[16]

The Mexican Americans have also been the victims of unfair stereo-typing. They are usually cartooned as people more interested in siestas than in work and more likely to put everything off until tomorrow. As a matter of fact, Mexican Americans do much of the hardest work required on the farms of the Southwest—work that most Anglo-Americans avoid. In the days when many workers, called *braceros*, were allowed to enter from Mexico, they were always anxious to come, and they complained little about hard work, long hours, and low pay. Few stereotypes are further from reality than the stereotype of the indolent Mexican American. Unfortunately, though, horizons have been very limited for many lower-class Mexican Americans, and children have simply followed parents into the ever-shrinking field of agricultural employment.

There are also questions about whether Mexican Americans are really becoming part of the United States. Military-service records would certainly answer this question in the affirmative. Whether motivated by desire for adventure, lack of other opportunities, or patriotism, Mexican Americans have enlisted in the Armed Forces in recent years in larger numbers than other Americans and have died in larger numbers in Vietnam. Whereas people of Spanish surname make up 10 percent of the population of California, they account for 19 percent of the California casualties in Vietnam.[17]

There are, unfortunately, certain Mexican American values, habits, and points of view that have tended to keep many of them in lower-class

[16] Robert Rosenthal and Lenore F. Jacobson, "Teacher Expectations for the Disadvantaged," *Scientific American*, ual. 218, April, 1968, pp. 19-23.
[17] Ralph Guzman, *Mexican-American Casualties in Vietnam* (pamphlet), University of California at Santa Cruz, 1969.

occupations. Manliness has been measured more in terms of success with the women, hard work, and the ignoring of illness than in the pursuit of education.[18] Sometimes the Mexican Americans live in isolated communities that make the learning of American ways difficult. Sometimes they have been characterized as fatalistic and resigned to their present positions. Octavio Paz, a distinguished Mexican poet, says of his own people, including those in the United States, "Yes, we withdraw into ourselves, we deepen and aggravate our awareness of everything that separates or isolates or differentiates us."[19]

Not all would agree with the interpretation given by Paz. Recent years have seen the rise of Mexican American organizations in Los Angeles and elsewhere trying to improve the economic position of their people. The new agricultural labor union led by Cesar Chavez has been very aggressive and certainly is not characterized by people who withdraw into themselves. In New Mexico, Tijerina has led a militant movement for the restoration of lands that once belonged to the Mexican people, again contradicting an attitude of resignation to fate. Chicano organizations on college campuses are working to improve the educational attainments of the Mexican Americans. The aim generally is to participate more fully in the society and economy of the United States. Although their progress toward integration into the society of the United States has often been slow, it has been more rapid than that of many of the original Americans, the American Indians.

The American Indians   A special problem for American Indians is that very large numbers of them wish to continue to be Indians. The official policy of the United States government has usually been one of attempting "rapid integration into American life"—a policy recommended by the Hoover Commission in 1947.[20] The rapid-integration policy has met with resistance from the Indians and their supporters and has not been effectively carried out.

The year 1947 also illustrated another problem of the American Indians: there were severe famines on the reservations of the Hopi and Navaho. The lands assigned to the Indians are generally poor in quality and able to sustain the people only if the seasons are merciful. Blizzards or droughts can be disastrous. Nevertheless, many Indians do not wish to leave the reservations; they feel lost in an alien world if they move away. The reservation Indians are generally accustomed to a communal way of life and have not taken kindly to attempts to break up communal lands into individual holdings.[21]

[18]William Madsen, *The Mexican-Americans of South Texas*, Holt, Rinehart and Winston, Inc., New York, 1964, pp. 20–34. See also Celia Heller, *Mexican-American Youth*, Random House, Inc., New York, 1966.
[19]Octavio Paz, *The Labyrinth of Solitude*, Grove Press, Inc., New York, 1961, p. 19.
[20]Stan Steiner, *The New Indians*, Dell Publishing Co., Inc., New York, 1968, pp. 23–24.
[21]Milton M. Gordon, *Assimilation in American Life*, Oxford University Press, New York, 1964, pp. 11–12.

The American public tends to be sympathetic to the Indians as a people who have been deprived of their land, but not very understanding of their resistance to full integration into the "American way." Warhaftig and Thomas,[22] in a discussion of the Cherokee, conclude that the whites resolve their dilemmas regarding the Indians by simply denying that Indians are really Indians anymore. The white myth says that the Indians are mixing with the whites and losing their old ways, and that they will cease to exist as a people within another twenty years. Actually, about 12,000 pure Cherokees still exist, fairly isolated from the whites. "Seldom had they (the anthropologists) seen people who speak so little English, who are so unshakably traditional in outlook."[23]

The Cherokee divided into two parties at the time of the "Trail of Tears" in the 1830s when they were forced to leave the Southeast and move to Oklahoma, along with the Choctaw, Creek, Chicasaw, and Seminole tribes. The Treaty Party decided that the best policy was to accept the treaty and gradually compromise with the white man's ways. The Ross Party was the party of resistance, and the traditional Cherokees of today are the descendants of the Ross Party.

The Cherokee are not a large nation, but their conflicting attitudes are duplicated by many Indian tribes. Steiner describes a conflict in viewpoint between the young intellectuals and the old "Uncle Tom-ahawks," with the former trying much harder than the older generation to promote education. By far the largest surviving Indian people are the Navaho, now numbering close to 100,000. Of this large population, only 400 Navahos were in college by the 1960s. The chasm that must be bridged on the way to higher education is still broad and deep—all the way from the mud-walled hogan to the university, and all the way from old, sacred traditions to the modern, secular world. The old ways are not going to vanish suddenly but must be recognized as a viable part of a society that places considerable value on cultural pluralism.

AMERICAN CULTURAL PLURALISM   For years the United States has been referred to as a great *melting pot*, with the implication that people from every national background are blending together through intermarriage and cultural assimilation. Blending of this type has taken place with the people of Northwestern Europe and to a lesser degree with the people of Southern and Eastern Europe. Nevertheless, there are many types of Americans who have not "melted." Laws used to prevent, and custom still prevents, many marriages between whites and blacks. Although there

[22]Albert L. Wahrhaftig and Robert K. Thomas, "Renaissance and Repression: The Oklahoma Cherokee," *Transaction*, vol. 6, February, 1969, pp. 42–48.
[23] *Ibid.*

are no laws dealing with the subject, it is obvious that Chinese usually marry within their own ethnic group, and the same is usually true of Mexican Americans. Amalgamation of races is not bringing our racial and ethnic problems to a sudden and happy solution, nor is it necessarily the goal to be sought.

Assimilation   The next possible solution to all racial and ethnic problems would be that of complete assimilation. *Assimilation* refers to a complete blending of cultural traits, but not necessarily intermarriage and racial blending. America has long been noted for her ability to assimilate foreigners who come to her shores, but there is some question as to how total the assimilation should be. Is there not room for continued cultural diversity in America — the ideal of cultural pluralism?

Pluralism   *Pluralism* is the policy of allowing distinct cultural differences to continue on a basis of equality. In Switzerland, for example, French, German, and Italian Swiss all have equal status, with official documents printed in all three languages. Few Americans would advocate carrying pluralism to the extent of using several languages, if for no other reason than the great inconvenience of such a system. Many Americans, however, always have liked a certain amount of cultural diversity. The presence of Chinatown, Jewish delioatessens, Italian bakeries, Mexican restaurants, Greek coffee shops, and Far Eastern import stores add variety to life. New ideas of all types are introduced by people from all parts of the world, and the United States has long profited from this type of cultural diffusion.

The idea of cultural pluralism has never been liked by all people. The most ethnocentric are inclined to say, "Why can't they be more like us?" Nevertheless, it has never been a dominant cultural value of the United States to try to force people to be culturally identical, and there are many minority groups who seek a sense of identity and supportive self-concept by looking to their diverse cultural origins. Many American Indians wish to continue to be identifiably Indian. Many Mexican Americans not only wish to retain some of their customs but even take a measure of interest in Mexico. The people who are presently most interested in a cultural identity are the young black Americans, as evidenced by a growing interest in college courses in black literature, black history, and other phases of Afro-American culture. Recent statements, organizations, literature, and movements among black Americans, Mexican Americans, and American Indians make it seem likely that we can look forward to demands for a degree of cultural pluralism well into the future. For some minority groups, the insistence on at least minor cultural distinctions is important for the maintenance of morale and identity.

SUMMARY   Racial and ethnic divisions are prominent in many parts of the world, especially in such a heterogeneous society as the United States. Race is a matter of hereditary physical difference; it is not a determinant of culture. Ethnic groups are groups that are culturally distinct in such respects as values, customs, religion, and language.

Man has invented many racial and ethnic myths aimed at protecting his ethnocentric feelings about the rightness of his own group. Not only have primitive tribes made such myths, but medieval man made up myths about the Jews, and more modern men have believed in myths about Nordic superiority and white supremacy.

There is much that is difficult to explain about the origin of races, but the most promising theories view racial traits as special adaptations to various geographical conditions. There are probably advantages to black skin color in hot, moist climates and to brown or yellow-brown skin color in hot, dry climates. There are also probably slight variations in the ability of different racial and subracial types to withstand extreme cold. In all cases, however, human mentality has advanced through the two million or more years of man's existence on earth and has been an equally adaptive trait in all climates. Regardless of the slight physical differences of race, all mankind belongs to a single species, Homo sapiens.

Modern racial classifications emphasize such geographical races as European, Indian, Asian, American Indian, and Australian. The implication is that distinctive racial types have arisen in parts of the world that have been isolated from each other. Raciation is also seen as a continuing process, with new types resulting from the process of amalgamation, as in Latin America.

Racial and ethnic prejudices are a common feature of intergroup relations. Prejudice can be explained partly as a result of ethnocentric feelings about the superiority of the in-group and the often imaginary threat of the out-group. Prejudice can also be explained in terms of stereotyping and as a defense mechanism for the person with psychological problems. Often prejudice is reinforced by popular or official policies of scapegoating, blaming misfortunes on the out-group. Prejudice is also very much a matter of cultural tradition. Where particular groups have always been observed in an inferior position, they are thought of as inferior; custom is accepted without reflection.

Prejudice is a matter of unfavorable attitudes; discrimination is uneven treatment. It is commonly stated that people discriminate because of their prejudices. It is equally true that people develop prejudices because they discriminate. For example, long discrimination against Negroes in education equipped them only for inferior jobs, prevented their intellectual development, and led to further prejudice against them.

The vicious circle of prejudice and discrimination is not easily broken, but the best results are accomplished through institutional change. Integration of major-league baseball and other sports has been accepted and has probably also decreased unfavorable feelings. Similar results have been accomplished in the Armed Forces—not that racial strife never develops, but racial integration is successful enough to have become the recognized pattern. Considerable progress has also been made in school integration and in the elimination of Jim Crow laws, although not without a struggle. It is particularly in areas where racial distribution of blacks and whites is fairly even and long traditions of great inequality exist that whites feel most threatened and are most resistant to change.

Minority groups react to prejudice and discrimination in various ways. Treatment as an inferior can result in an unfavorable self-image and/or great hostility. Sometimes minority groups adjust by finding special occupations that are open to them. Sometimes they display the symptoms of retreating from life. In recent years, various factors, including urbanization and more education, have made protest movements common.

The NAACP was long the leading organization for the promotion of rights of black Americans. In the 1950s, Dr. Martin Luther King and his followers turned to massive nonviolent protests, rather than merely to the legal and educational approaches of NAACP. More militant leaders now hold center stage in public attention, but various moderate movements and organizations are still as important as ever.

Other minority groups have experienced discrimination, including the Japanese Americans during World War II, Mexican Americans at various times and places, and American Indians almost constantly.

The old assumption that all minority groups wish complete assimilation is open to considerable doubt. For some groups, a degree of cultural pluralism seems to be strongly desired as a means of identity and group morale.

*. . . (T)he great waves of enthusiasm,
indignation, or pity which sweep through a
crowd do not originate in any one particular
mind. They come to each of us from without
and are liable to carry us away in spite of
ourselves.*

ÉMILE DURKHEIM
The Rules of the Sociological Method

seven

COLLECTIVE BEHAVIOR

Collective behavior encompasses many forms of human
interaction. Included in this general area of study would
be the formation of one's opinion on a public issue, his
presence at the spring formal, and his participation in a
campus riot. The dynamics of human behavior in each
case is the product of the degree of emotional intensity
evoked by the situation and the presence or lack of a
structured social atmosphere. Because the scope of such
behavior is so broad, we shall attempt to present a model
by which it is possible to classify most forms of behavior
which are collective in nature.

COLLECTIVE BEHAVIOR IN EVERYDAY LIFE   Group life and
group activity are inextricably bound to the human
condition. Although it is true that each individual may
have some influence on the group of which he is a
member, it is incontrovertible that the group exercises a
somewhat greater influence on the behavior of its
constituency. In the study of collective behavior, we are
not only interested in the nature of the collectivity, but
we are also interested in the feelings and the actions of
the individual. A quiet collectivity of people listening to a
formal lecture, applauding politely at the conclusion, and
then dispersing illustrates a structured situation.

131

On the other hand, audiences can reach a state of excitement in which members stimulate responses from each other, as in emotionally charged political rallies or in old-fashioned revival meetings. Under other circumstances, an audience may become so emotionally charged that, en masse, it may charge through the streets breaking store windows, hurling bricks, and injuring people.

An illustration of the type of collectivity, familiar to nearly everyone, that is often on the borderline between *structured* and *unstructured* behavior is the college football crowd. Much of the activity in this case is conventional: bands, cheer leaders, song leaders, half-time entertainment, colors, flags, pompons, and all the paraphernalia of the football complex. However, the situation is such that unusual behavior arises; even the quiet person shouts and yells, jumps up and down, throws confetti, and acts in ways that would be difficult to predict from his otherwise constrained behavioral patterns.

To analyze the extremes of collective behavior sociologists often use a tool known as the *ideal-type continuum*, a model or theoretical construct which may or may not exist in reality. This model is composed of polar extremes or theoretical opposites separated by a continuum or line of variation from one extreme to the other. For example, if one extreme were white and the other black, the continuum would include all the possible shades of gray separating the polar opposites. In the case of collective behavior, the polar extremes are represented by the type of collectivities which influence the feelings and activities of the individual.

The crowd and the public   The *crowd* occupies one polar extreme on the continuum of collective behavior; the *public* occupies the other. The activities of the crowd include a number of patterns found in otherwise normal, everyday life. For one thing, as a member of a crowd, one does not cease to be a member of society, bound by many of the general norms of social interaction. For another, even in everyday social interaction, one is strongly influenced by group activities, opinions, and norms. In the crowd, there is *heightened suggestibility*, the feeling that one must go along with the action suggested by the entire group, whether it be laughter, exuberant shouting, or a destructive act of hostility. There is a sense of *loss of individual responsibility*, a feeling of *anonymity*. If the activities in which one participates are those suggested by the crowd as a whole, then how can one be held individually responsible for the outcome of that action? As a member of the crowd, one is also unidentifiable; he is simply a part of the audience, rally, or mob. *Lessened judgment and reflection* are apparent; one does not engage in collective behavior because reflection leads him to think it is wise, but rather because the collectivity has decided it for him. There is a sense of *invulnerability*:

Crowd
Heightened suggestibility
Loss of individual responsibility
Anonymity
Lessened judgment and reflection
Sense of invulnerability
Moral ambivalence

Public
Lessened suggestibility
Individual responsibility
Perceived individuality
Increased sense of individual judgment
Vulnerability
Accountability for one's actions

"No one can get the whole crowd of us!" In some cases, there is a *moral ambivalence* to the crowd. In one sense, the crowd feels a "lofty morality," wrecking vengeance on the wicked and upholding equity and righteousness; but at the same time, the crowd can commit every conceivable outrage and atrocity — stoning, hanging, burning, castrating, and otherwise killing or mutilating its victims.

The activities of the public are, at least theoretically, more rational. As a member of a public, one is not usually in close physical contact with others, and this greatly reduces the possibility of engaging in activities such as those enumerated above. The *public* is a dispersed collectivity. It may think alike or feel alike, but it is not likely, except under extraordinary conditions, to act together, as does the crowd. The *lessened suggestibility* of the public is a function of the fact that a public is composed of individuals who make individual decisions. These decisions, of course, may be influenced by covert or subliminal propaganda, such as is used often through the mass media in advertising, or it may be overtly influenced by a skilled propagandist who openly attempts to convince individuals to accept his viewpoint.

In either case, the individual must accept sole *responsibility* for the decision. He is *not* an *anonymous* part of the crowd; he is a person who can be held accountable for his decision. As an individual, he is *vulnerable* to the philosophical or political attacks of others with whom he disagrees.

Classification of crowds   Even though crowds and publics occupy the polar extremes of the ideal-type continuum of collective behavior, they are not as distinctly oppositional as are black and white. Nor, for that matter, do all crowds occupy the polar extreme; some may approach or approximate the extreme, others may be only barely identifiable as crowds. Therefore, for the purpose of analysis, we present the following typology of crowds, adapted in part from the work of Herbert Blumer:[1]

1.   Casual crowds. A collectivity of people watching a demonstration in a department-store window may be classified as a *casual crowd*. Much of their behavior will not fit the characteristics of the crowd previously presented; but, under certain circumstances, some of the characteristics might emerge. To a certain extent, people who are physically together are also socially together because there is always a degree of social inter-action. If, for example, a department-store employee is demonstrating a high-speed food blender in the store window, people may congregate on the street to observe the effectiveness of the product. If the demon-strator forgets to place the cover on top of the blender, turns the machine to "high," and is then inundated by the contents of the receptacle, the casual crowd is likely to burst into laughter. A lone individual is not likely to stand in the street laughing aloud, although he may find the situation funny.

2.   Conventional crowds. *Conventional crowds* are popularly called *audiences*; but, sociologically, their behavior is conventional in that most of their behavior is defined by the existing norms of the social system. Attendees at political conventions or collegiate dramatic presentations and spectators at football or basketball games typify the conventional crowd. Their behavior generally conforms to norm-role expectations, but circumstances may arise whereby extraordinary demonstrations may occur. If the home team is involved in a crucial game, the applause of the fans may be disproportionate to the achievements of the players. If, by playing only a mediocre game, the home team wins, the spectators are likely to tear down goal posts or carry the coach off the field. This unstructured behavior is built into the system in order that each spec-tator will be sensitive to the emotions of fellow spectators and equally sensitive to the importance of the event.

3.   Expressive crowds. The *expressive crowd* is generally organized in such a way as to permit personal gratification for each of its members. Generally, its activity is viewed as an end in itself, with no objective other than the expression of group emotion. Some expressive crowds are fairly

[1] Herbert Blumer, "Collective Behavior," in Alfred M. Lee (ed.), *New Outline of the Principles of Sociology*, Barnes & Noble, Inc., New York, 1951, pp. 178–185.

well structured—a college dance; others are less structured—a religious revival meeting; and some are fairly unstructured—a campus demonstration. Although it may be argued that a campus demonstration may have objectives other than personal gratification (influencing public opinion or changing administrative decisions), it is true that while the demonstration is in effect the members are congregated for the purpose of expressing their inner emotions.

4. Orgiastic crowds. Although some sociologists may classify the *orgiastic crowd* as one form of expressive crowd, and others would place it in the category of the active crowd, the present text will treat it as an aggregate different from either because it displays characteristics of both. In its structure and dynamics the orgiastic crowd is much like the expressive crowd, but there is a heightened suggestibility, anonymity, sense of invulnerability and moral ambivalence, and a lessened sense of individual judgment, responsibility, and reflection. Under such conditions, the norm-role definitions which are generally maintained may be greatly modified or completely abandoned. New Year's Eve parties and Mardi Gras typify this behavior on a wide scale; on a smaller scale, the orgiastic crowd may take the form of wife-swapping clubs or marijuana smokers.

5. Active crowds. The *active crowd* is self-explanatory; the crowd is in action. Its behavior may be observed as an intergroup fight, act of destruction, or prolonged riot. In any case, the identity of the individual increasingly becomes transformed to an overall identity with the group. When this occurs, all the characteristics of crowd behavior are observable in the most extreme form. For analytical purposes we will examine three manifestations of the active crowd: the mob, the rioting crowd, and the panicking crowd.

The *mob* is a unified crowd with a single objective. Generally, it ignores norm-role definitions and the usual societal restraints. However, group control of the individual is quite strong because mob membership requires absolute conformity from its constituency. The lynch mob is a good example. The individual member shifts his sense of moral responsibility to the group and thus achieves a strange combination of sadism and righteousness. When "respectable" members of the community participate in a lynching without interference by local authorities, the situation almost could be described as *sponsored* by the local mores. The anti-Jewish *pogroms* of czarist Russia were deliberately promoted by the government, as were the attacks on the kulaks in leninist Russia. Long before the program of total extermination developed in Nazi Germany, destructive popular outbursts against the Jews had been promoted.

The United States, as a whole, has deplored such policies, but among local authorities there has been a parallel. A great majority of the lynchings of Negroes (3,408 between 1900 and 1947) that have taken place in this country have been carried out by spontaneous mobs or Klan organizations, with little or no opposition from local officialdom. Erskine Caldwell has characterized the situation in his book *Trouble in July*: the sheriff always manages to be away fishing when a lynch mob forms, even if he has to get up in the middle of the night to be "accidentally" gone.

A *rioting crowd* need not be unified; it may involve several groups of people in different locations. However, these groups will evolve almost simultaneously and engage in almost identical behavior. Riots have been common in the United States, and some of the historical cases should be mentioned so that selective memories do not make us think that the urban disorders of today are entirely new. Antidraft riots in New York City during the Civil War period resulted in over 1,000 deaths. Fights between various immigrant groups and the old Americans have been common, as were fights between Catholics and Protestants. Radical labor organizations such as the Molly Maguires and the IWW have been involved in many acts of violence. The Haymarket Riots of Chicago in 1886, culminating in a bombing, resulted in seven deaths. One of the most destructive riots of all time occurred in Chicago in 1919.

However, the type of disorder most characteristic of recent times is the city riot centering in the black ghetto. Many reports and investigations have been made concerning such riots, including the Report of the President's Commission on Civil Disorders, often referred to as the *Kerner Report*. This commission was originated as a fact-finding body, and its report can be used to substantiate sociological theory.

Neil J. Smelser, a sociologist, provides a most enlightened analysis. He sees the city riot as the product of six conditions which, taken together, constitute "necessary and sufficient" cause for riots; that is, they must be present, or the city riot will not occur; if all six conditions are present, a riot is inevitable. These background conditions for what Smelser calls the *hostile outburst* are as follows: [2]

Structural conduciveness refers to the characteristics of a society that make crowd actions possible—a society of conflicting interests, with some groups unable to make themselves heard through legitimate means, but with easy communication and accessibility to objects of attack. This idea of structural conduciveness is applicable to the labor riots of earlier times and to antiforeign riots and demonstrations. As applied to the city race riots, all the elements of structural conduciveness are present. The dilapidated ghetto dwellings of so many urban Negro neighborhoods

[2] Neil J. Smelser, *The Theory of Collective Behavior*, The Free Press, New York, 1962, pp. 222–269.

lead to demands for new areas of settlement; whites oppose the gradual spread to new areas. The ghetto has its problems that are not handled by officialdom, and traditionally, the group has not been heard very loudly at city hall. There is ready accessibility to the symbols of the power structure: business, rental properties, police, and firemen.

Structural strains are the next ingredient in the explosive situation. On the physical side, these strains consist of such problems as inadequate housing, unemployment, and various forms of discrimination. On the normative level, strains have become especially intense in recent years because of an increasing acceptance of the ideal of equality and a lingering gap between the ideal and the practice. At the same time, greater awareness of the gulf between poverty and wealth heightens the feeling of relative deprivation—a condition whereby the gains of the poor fall further and further behind the greater gains of the middle class.

The spread of *generalized beliefs* is the next step toward a hostile outburst. Such beliefs spread through rumor, scapegoating, or knowledge of a specific incident. In many riots, these beliefs have centered upon the issue of police brutality and/or the economic exploitation of the poor. The ghetto creates an unenviable situation both for its residents and for the police who, because of public sentiment, must be well-trained men, sober in judgment, and cool in performance. No police force completely meets these requirements, and harassment takes place against both black and white lower-class people.[3] Whether such beliefs are true or greatly exaggerated is irrelevant as a background for riot; the important point is that people act on what they *believe* to be true.

Next, *precipitating factors* come into play. Sometimes the precipitating cause is more rumor than actual event, or it may be an insignificant event exaggerated by rumor. In the Los Angeles area Watts riot, for example, the precipitating event was "the arrest of a drunken Negro youth about whose dangerous driving another Negro had complained."[4] While the motorcycle officer who made the arrest waited for a patrol car, an angry crowd began to form, and various versions of what had happened began to spread. A suspicious hate-laden atmosphere needs little to bring on an explosion of emotion. One need only remember that World War I was triggered by a single assassination.

Mobilization for action is also necessary. There is no implication of a vast plot on a national scale in either Smelser's theory or in the Kerner Report. However, there must be at least small organizations and violent leaders to harangue the crowd and spread leaflets. In the big city, mere physical proximity creates a situation in which organization is possible.

[3]Albert J. Reiss, Jr., "Police Brutality: Answers to Key Questions," *Transaction*, July/August, 1968, pp. 10–19.
[4]*Violence in the City: An End or a Beginning?*, Report by the Governor's Commission on the Los Angeles Riots, State Printing Office, Sacramento, Calif., 1965.

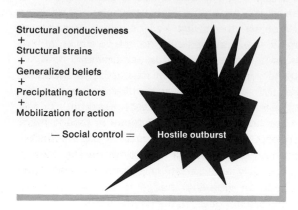

Structural conduciveness
+
Structural strains
+
Generalized beliefs
+
Precipitating factors
+
Mobilization for action

— Social control =   **Hostile outburst**

Earlier in the history of this country, fear—induced by the dominant white group—was so strong in the South that mobilization of the black minority was made impossible.

Finally, there must be a *failure of social control*. If norms of non-violence are strongly internalized they will act as a factor for self-control. Although there were large numbers of counterrioters in all the disturbances of the summer of 1967 urging people to "cool it," there were obviously many who had no such feelings about nonviolence, especially among the more hostile ghetto dwellers. Attitudes toward community leadership were negative. If other agencies of control are adequate, the use of police as a controlling force is unnecessary; when social control breaks down, external controls (police or National Guard) are often brought to the scene.

This, very briefly, is Smelser's theory, with some supportive examples of our own. How does it align with the facts as ascertained by the President's Commission on Civil Disorders?

The terminology is different, but the conclusions are the same. On the subject of structural conduciveness and structural strains, we read "This is our basic conclusion: our nation is moving toward two societies, one black, one white—separate and unequal."[5] In the area of generalized belief, the commission concludes, "The police have come to symbolize white power, white racism, and white repression. And the fact is that many police do reflect and express these white attitudes."[6]

[5] *Report of the National Advisory Commission on Civil Disorders*, New York Times Company, Bantam Books, Inc., New York, 1968, p. 1.
[6] *Ibid.*, p. 11.

On the subject of precipitating causes, the commission reveals case after case in which there were a series of incidents, each intensifying a hostile situation. On the subject of mobilization for action, the conclusion is that the riots of 1967 were "not the consequence of any organized plan or 'conspiracy,' . . . but militant organizations, local and national, and individual agitators, who repeatedly forecast and called for violence, were active in the spring and summer of 1967."[7] Finally, the commission notes the ineffectiveness of social control in several ways: the complaints of inadequate protection for the nonrioters; the hostility of the rioters toward the police, the alienation of rioters from the normative structure, and the lack of training of police, especially National Guard troops, for coping with such emergencies. One of the tragic stories from Detroit illustrates the difficulty in the latter respect:

> Employed as a private guard, 55 year old Julius L. Dorsey, a Negro, was standing in front of a market when accosted by two Negro men and a woman. They demanded he permit them to loot the market. He ignored their demands. They began to berate him. He asked a neighbor to call the police. As the argument grew more heated, Dorsey fired three shots from his pistol into the air.
>   The police radio reported: "Looters, they have rifles." A patrol car driven by a police officer and carrying three National Guardsmen arrived. As the looters fled, the law enforcement personnel opened fire. When the firing ceased, one person lay dead.
>   He was Julius L. Dorsey.[8]

The final manifestation of the active crowd which we will examine is the *panicking crowd*. The panicking crowd is a collectivity whose sole purpose for being is to escape or retreat from something. Generally this occurs in situations where people are trapped or feel that they may be trapped. Ambiguity intensifies the emotions of the individual. Where the total picture of the situation cannot be seen clearly, rumors about what is actually true begin to spread quickly. Panic is more likely in darkness than in daylight because one's feelings of security are more likely to diminish when he does not have clear visual perception. In the dark, noises seem louder, and dimly perceived motion is exaggerated.[9]

Panic is also more likely to occur when the impossible happens, as when a dam suddenly bursts. People can get used to earthquakes,

[7] *Ibid.*, p. 9.
[8] *Ibid.*, p. 98.
[9] Irving L. Janis, *Air War and Emotional Stress*, McGraw-Hill Book Company, New York, 1951, p. 121.

tornadoes, or enemy bombings, at least to some degree.[10] Panic can be avoided by learning exactly what to do under such circumstances. Both institutional and psychological preparations are possible. Psychological preparedness, in some cases, may result from institutional preparations; for example, if people know where to report and to whom they can turn for help during a crisis, it is less likely that they will panic. Other psychological preparations can be rational ones, such as explaining that the odds are definitely in one's favor, or they can be of a more or less magical type. Soldiers in battle often accept a type of superstitious fatalism, specifically, the belief that you are safe until the time the bullet intended for you comes along — the bullet with "your name on it." Among paratroopers, a number of magically protective devices are reported; it is especially important to always keep the pair of wings originally issued."[11]

Mass hysteria is another variable involved in panic situations. One of the amusing and frequently repeated examples of mass hysteria is the incident referred to as "The Invasion from Mars," a radio play produced by Orson Welles in 1938. The play, based on H. G. Wells' novel *The War of the Worlds,* was broadcast as a series of news reports about Martian invaders landing in New Jersey. The report was taken seriously by many people, and panic spread. Some individuals fled to the mountains, one wasn't seen again for two weeks. A group of college coeds locked themselves in the chapel and prayed all night. Frightened crowds gathered in the streets of large Eastern cities demanding action and protection.[12]

There has been no repetition of the "Invasion from Mars" incident. More recently there has been prolonged concern about outer space, but there have been no equivalent panics. In fact, one group which predicted the end of the world based on information received from "saucer people" remained remarkably calm, even eager, when the "end" was to have come. Of course, the leader of the group had been told that she and her faithful followers would be saved by the saucerians.[13]

THE PUBLIC AND PUBLIC OPINION The public, unlike the crowd, is a dispersed collectivity. The individual member of the public is less likely to see himself as a member of a group and is therefore more likely to maintain his own sense of identity. He is interested in making decisions about matters of importance to him, and he tries to make them in a way that seems rational. The summation of all the decisions of individual members of a public is known as *public opinion.*

[10] Kurt Lang and Gladys Engyl Lang, *Collective Dynamics,* Thomas Y. Crowell Company, New York, 1962, p. 84.
[11] Melford S. Weiss, "Rebirth in the Airborne," *Transaction,* May, 1967, pp. 23–26.
[12] John Houseman, "The Men From Mars." *Harper's Magazine,* vol. 197, no. 1183, December, 1948, pp. 74–82.
[13] L. Festinger, H. W. Riecken, and S. Schachter, *When Prophesy Fails,* The University of Minnesota Press, Minneapolis, 1956.

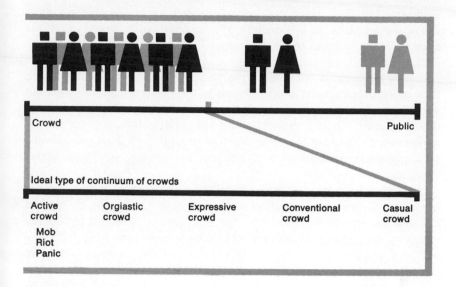

Crowd   Public

Ideal type of continuum of crowds

Active crowd	Orgiastic crowd	Expressive crowd	Conventional crowd	Casual crowd

Mob
Riot
Panic

In some ways public opinion seems more organized than some of the types of crowds we have been discussing, but it also has a large element of spontaneity and unpredictability about it. Some communities allow urban deterioration to proceed to the point of no return before public opinion becomes aroused. Local graft and corruption become important issues sometimes, and sometimes they are bypassed. Nearly everyone is familiar with contemporary attempts to sound out public opinion relative to elections, and although methods have been carefully developed over many years, there is still an element of guesswork involved in predicting the winner.

There is even some difference in point of view as to the degree to which public opinion is spontaneous and the degree to which it is manipulated. Often the words "mass society" and "mass media" conjure up pictures of a public that is ruled and regulated by forces behind the scenes. In this case, public opinion becomes only that which the leaders desire it to be. C. Wright Mills was prone to this type of analysis. He believed that contemporary public opinion is formed by a flow of information from the leadership downward to the people, whereas at some previous time opinion was formed at the "grass-roots" level and communicated upward.[14] However, he admitted that in our present society there are countervailing powers in the leadership, but he feared that counter-vailing forces were on the decline in a world in which major decisions must be made in areas where the public is in a poor position to judge—military affairs, for example.

The process of public-opinion manipulation is always of interest, both to the propagandist whose job it is to form or change public opinion and to the sociologist who studies the methods of the propagandist and the effect on the public. How effective are public-relations firms (propaganda firms)? They are certainly effective enough to be used increasingly by industrial organizations and political candidates; yet, they sometimes fail.

Robert Heilbroner tells an interesting story of a United Nations campaign in one city. Industrial firms and community opinion leaders decided to interest the public in the organization. Preliminary polling indicated that about 75 percent of the people already held favorable attitudes toward the United Nations. After the big campaign, surveys showed a decrease in support for the UN. Why? The only conclusion seemed to be that the public resented having the idea "sold" to them by public-relations firms. Sales resistance appears in the political sphere as well as in the commercial.[15]

Lang and Lang give two similar examples of the unpredictability of the public. In 1958 several states placed right-to-work bills on their ballots for the public to vote on. In the majority of cases the right-to-work bills were defeated, and yet Lou Harris' analysis was that a majority of the voters were actually in favor of the bills. The Harris Poll is a respec-table one, and in this case its prediction was based upon a sampling of opinion which indicated that a majority of the people opposed the idea of a "closed shop" where only union members are allowed to work. The right-to-work bill would have allowed a worker to hold a job in a unionized plant without having to join the union.

The same authors cite a study clearly indicating that community leaders were more tolerant of differences of opinion than was the "average person" in the days of Senator Joseph McCarthy. However, leadership opinion during the McCarthy era was largely silent. "Prudence doth make cowards of us all," and hence opinion leaders do not always lead.[16]

This very brief discussion is enough to demonstrate the complexi-ties of public-opinion formation and public-opinion research. It is an oversimplification to say at the end of each election campaign, "The

[14] C. Wright Mills, "The Mass Society," in Eric Josephson and Mary Josephson (eds.), Man Alone: Alienation in Modern Society, Dell Publishing Co., Inc., New York, 1962, pp. 505–516.
[15] Robert L. Heilbroner, "Public Relations: The Invisible Sell," Harper's Magazine, vol. 214, no. 1285, June, 1957, pp. 23–31.
[16] Both examples from Lang and Lang, op. cit., pp. 377–378.

public has clearly spoken." It is also erroneous to assume that the public is always putty in the hands of the "mass media," "the establishment," or whatever term is used to designate the supposed controller of opinion.

SOCIAL MOVEMENTS   The last form of collective behavior that we will examine is that of social movements. Social movements do not really fit onto any of the ideal-type continuums that have been introduced; they are not the result of crowd behavior, and they are not necessarily the product of public opinion. Favorable public opinion regarding a social movement, however, will help to further its cause. *Social movements* are those engaged in by a collectivity of people whose goals are generally long range. The collectivity need not be in close physical proximity, but the members must see themselves as part of a group.

Social movements encompass many different forms, but we will concern ourselves with three types of movement that seem to be of current interest: reactionary, reform, and revolutionary.

Reactionary movements   Like all social movements, the reactionary type has a background in structural strain. Those who join a reactionary movement see the ills of modern society and desperately desire to improve the social fiber. To some people, the way to improve society is to return to the "good old days" when America was truly American and not a land of foreign and "un-American" influences. Looking nostalgically to an idyllic past that is more an imaginative construct than a true reality, the John Birch Society is one of the best-known modern examples of this sentiment.

It is also common for reactionary movements to oversimplify the solutions to social problems. The Prohibition party, campaigning vigorously against "demon rum," and the Women's Christian Temperance Union may also be classified as reactionary movements, although their goals may be different from those of the "Birchers."

Reform movements   In general, reform movements are aimed at accomplishing the announced values and ideals of the society which, according to the members, are not being practiced. In the past we have witnessed such movements as the anti-slavery movement, aimed at guaranteeing freedom to all those who were not in prisons and yet were not free, and the suffragette movement, initially aimed at gaining for women the right to vote. It should be added that many members of the Suffragettes (along with the Anti-saloon League) campaigned for child-labor reform, labor laws for women, and educational reform.

Crowd

Short-range group goals

Individual sees himself
as member of group

Physical proximity necessary

Public

Short- or long-range
individual goals

Individual does not see
himself as member of group

Physical proximity unlikely
and unnecessary

Social movement

Long-range group goals

Individual sees
himself as member of group

Physical proximity unnecessary

The most prominent movement of recent years has been the civil
rights movement that has achieved great advances toward ending the
second-class citizenship of black America. Actually, the civil rights movement can be thought of as a series of movements involving many groups,
such as the National Association for the Advancement of Colored People,
the Southern Christian Leadership Conference, and the Urban League.

In another sense, it is all one movement aimed at bringing about equal status for all races. In some cases, the civil rights movement has influenced and joined forces with other prominent movements, notably the peace movement and the student rights movement (see Chapter 12). All are aimed at social reform, all see some kind of "power structure" blocking their way, and all have displayed violence at times.

As of this writing, the women's liberation movement has not been linked to the civil rights movement, although a number of the goals of each group overlap. Women are now pointing to discriminatory and preferential hiring practices in industry, wage discrepancies that tend to award more money to men who do the same work as women, and exclusion of women from certain trade and professional schools.

In a different area, two closely related movements have taken on greatly added momentum as we enter the decade of the seventies — the environmentalist movement and the Zero Population Growth movement (ZPG). Both movements begin with the premise that "the right to the pursuit of liberty and happiness" is being denied to individuals by a society which, through overpopulation and certain governmental, industrial, and personal practices, makes its water undrinkable and its air unbreathable.

Generally, reform movements tend to create deep feelings among the public by presenting their cases as matters of extreme urgency. In reference to civil rights, Dr. King focused our attention on the problem by pointing out that we had created "a situation that cannot be ignored"; environmentalists and ZPG point to a "clear and present danger." It seems, however, that such rhetoric is necessitated by the fact that, if society waits too long to act, the course that it is taking may be irreversible.

Revolutionary movements Revolutionary movements usually aim at attaining utopian ideals. These movements attempt to build worlds of their own that reflect a particular philosophy or exhibit "perfect" social systems. In the past, such attempts have included Brook Farm and the Oneida Colony. In a sense, the Black Muslim movement may also be classified here. At one time, Muslim advocates of black nationalism proposed that a separate black state be set up within the United States and that this state be inhabited and administered solely by members and sympathizers of the movement.

The Third World movement is one which involves certain groups within the United States, but it also has a strong international appeal and following. The movement is aimed at all oppressed peoples or people who feel that they are being oppressed. It has a strong bent toward socialist philosophy and a real, but unsystematized, goal of social revolution.

Social movements and cultural relativity   Before ending this section and this chapter we must point out that any description of a social movement is related to and meaningful in terms of only that country for which the movement is being described. The typology of movements used in this text is written with reference to the social system of the United States of America. Remember that in Russia our description of a revolutionary movement would illustrate a reactionary movement, and in Cuba "our" reactionary movement would be considered an attempt at social revolution.

SUMMARY   Collective behavior is the behavior of an aggregate of people. It may take the form of a crowd wherein one might observe physical proximity, loss of individual responsibility, anonymity, lessened sense of judgment and reflection, a sense of invulnerability, heightened suggestibility, moral ambivalence, and increasing group identity. An aggregate of people may take the form of a public—a dispersed collectivity representing the polar extreme opposite that of the crowd and displaying all the opposite characteristics. Finally, it may take the form of a social movement with long-range goals and elaborate organization.

Crowds may be analyzed according to where they "fit" on a continuum. The continuum is a line of variation, but along the line we may observe certain points which are descriptive of distinct types of crowds— casual, conventional, expressive, orgiastic, and active. Active crowds may also be classified according to the patterns they display and the structure they assume—mobs, riots, or panics.

As a member of a public, one is interested in making private decisions, although his decisions may be subject to manipulation by others. The collective product of all private decisions is called public opinion, and the manipulation of public opinion is referred to as propaganda. Although propaganda is effective in some situations, it may also have a boomerang effect and achieve the opposite results in other situations.

Public opinion which is favorable to a particular social movement may help to further the cause of that movement. All social movements have a background in structural strain, but different movements react differently in attempting to relieve the strain. Reactionary movements generally aim at returning to a previous and more "sane" social order. Reform movements try to improve the existing system. Revolutionary movements would like to change the system to one that is more ideal or utopian.

*A settlement of the moon may be of some
military advantage to the nation that does the
settling. But it will do nothing whatever to
make life more tolerable, during the fifty years
that it will take our present population to
double, for the earth's undernourished and
proliferating billions.*[1]

ALDOUS HUXLEY

Brave New World Revisited

THE GROWTH OF THE HUMAN GROUP: POPULATION

When Aldous Huxley issued that statement there were
about 3 billion people living, and space exploration was
just beginning. He predicted that there would be a world
population of 6 billion around the year 2010 and warned
that we could not survive if we did not curb the growth
of the human group. Today, the footprint of man on the
surface of the moon is not a projected possibility, it is a
reality. At the same time, the prospect of an overpopulated
world in the near future is accepted by even the most
optimistic sociologists. In fact, most population experts
are inclined to trim ten years from Huxley's prediction.
The overriding question asked by people concerned
about the future of mankind is: "Do we still have enough
time to save ourselves from the effects of population
explosion?"

**THE DEMOGRAPHIC TRANSITION AND THE POPULATION
EXPLOSION** If we could turn our clocks backward about
50,000 years we would find a rather sparsely populated
world.

[1] Aldous Huxley, *Brave New World Revisited*, Bantam Books, Inc., New York, 1958, pp. 7–8.

147

People would be gathering food or hunting other animals to provide themselves with enough nutrition to survive their rather short life-spans. Population density might be as low as 200 square miles/person, and the possibilities of overpopulation would be extremely remote. What then has happened to mankind to bring him to his present predicament? There may be no definite answer, but there are a number of theories supported by a fund of statistical data that can give us some insight into the problem.

One fact is certain: population increase is intricately bound with the availability of food and the state of technology within a society. In his "Essay on the Principles of Population" the Rev. Thomas Malthus, an early nineteenth-century economist, states that population is necessarily limited by the means of subsistence, and when the means of subsistence increase, population likewise increases.[2] However, food production is not likely to increase until certain technological changes have occurred. The hunter or food gatherer of an earlier era followed a migratory way of life. He was a nomad who traveled the land in a constant search for food, never settling in any one place for any significant length of time. As his population grew at a slow but steady rate it gradually became apparent that man was crowding the territory from which he eked out his subsistence.

About 10,000 years ago, in some obscure fashion, the life style of the species underwent a marked metamorphosis. At that time the first great technological innovations occurred. Specifically, mankind achieved the invention of agriculture and the domestication of animals. His nomadic past was abandoned in favor of forming permanent settlements. These early villages continued to grow until they began to take on the shape and characteristics of a *city*. This urban revolution probably occurred about 4000 B.C. in the fertile valleys of the Tigris-Euphrates, the Nile, the Hwang Ho, and the Indus Rivers.

The formation of these early cities was as important as the invention of agriculture in determining the future of man's development. In terms of population and food production, the character of the city is important because it dictates that some men become farmers to supply the food, while others become nonagricultural consumers to "keep the farmers in business." As agricultural technology advanced, greater surpluses of food enabled an increasing number of people to free themselves from the land. Once this trend was set, it continued to perpetuate itself. Throughout modern history, we have witnessed an accelerated exodus from rural to urban areas.

The urban trend was hastened by the Industrial Revolution—the third great technological advancement in the history of man. The net effect of industrialization has been to increase the density of population

[2] An excellent brief adaptation of Thomas Malthus, "An Essay on the Principles of Population," can be found in Louise B. Young (ed.), *Population in Perspective*, Oxford University Press, New York, 1968, pp. 8–29.

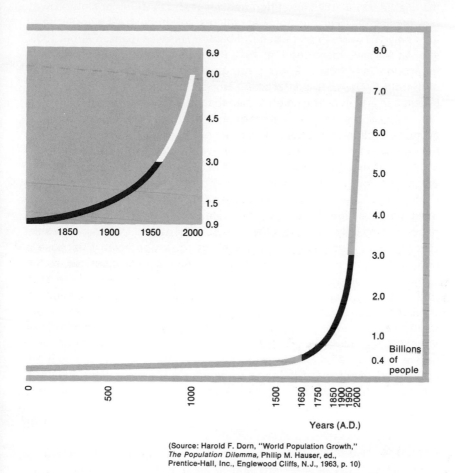

(Source: Harold F. Dorn, "World Population Growth,"
The Population Dilemma, Philip M. Hauser, ed.,
Prentice-Hall, Inc., Englewood Cliffs, N.J., 1963, p. 10)

in the cities. Mass production and rapid transportation have transformed the Western world into an urban world. But the "creature comforts" of the city have not developed without demanding some sacrifice from the individual.

Davis notes that " . . . the growth of the earth's population has been like a long, thin powder fuse that burns slowly and haltingly until it finally reaches the charge and then explodes."[3] It is becoming increasingly evident that, viewed in world perspective, we are now reaching

[3] Kingsley Davis, *Human Society,* The Macmillan Company, New York, 1949, p. 595.

the charge. About 1830, after hundreds of centuries of rather slow growth, our species reached the point at which 1 billion persons were living. It took only 100 years to add a second billion. This was realized about 1930; and, as we have mentioned, in 1960 there were 3 billion people living in the world. This fantastic spurt in our growth rate is graphically illustrated by Harold F. Dorn.[4] It is interesting to note that his projection of future population is significantly higher than that predicted by Huxley.

The peoples of the nineteenth and twentieth centuries are certainly no more prolific than those of the preceding eras. The great change in the complexion of the world's population, therefore, cannot be explained in terms of natural reproduction. Again, we must turn our attention to the relationship between population growth and food production and technology. In remote and isolated parts of the world we find that birth rates are quite high, but so are death rates. The people who inhabit these regions enjoy only the lowest level of technology and live on a bare subsistence level. Their population does not grow appreciably because a lack of food and modern medicine (a technological advance) causes the people to be susceptible to the spread of morbid diseases. If the birth rate is unsually high (50 births/1,000 population/year), it is counterbalanced by an equally high death rate. Let us suppose that an industrialized nation introduces the people of this area to new methods of agricultural production and the use of modern medicine. We can expect several outcomes on the basis of past experience: death rates will fall drastically, life-spans will increase significantly, and unless the birth rate is arrested, population will explode. In a less dramatic sense, this is basically what has accounted for the rise in world population.

POPULATION CHARACTERISTICS   Population characteristics are studied by a specialized field of sociology known as *demography*. A demographer is one who attempts to describe and analyze living groups of people, and the major reason that demography falls within the realm of sociology, rather than that of some other science, is that the main causes of population trends are social. In pursuing knowledge of these social trends the demographer has employed three basic concepts known as the *demographic processes*: fertility, mortality, and migration. By analyzing each of these processes, he can obtain a fundamental knowledge of the nature of the group.

Fertility refers to the actual number of children born within a given population. Usually this is expressed as a birth rate. There are many different ways of determining the birth rate of a group, but the simplest is

[4]Harold F. Dorn, "World Population Growth," in Philip M. Hauser (ed.), *The Population Dilemma*, Prentice-Hall, Inc., Englewood Cliffs, N.J., 1963, p. 10.

called the *crude birth rate*, which is obtained by dividing the total number of births per year by the total population (according to midyear estimate) and multiplying the quotient by 1,000.

$$\text{Crude birth rate} = \frac{\text{total number of births/year}}{\text{total population}} \times 1{,}000$$

Often, fertility is expressed in terms of the number of births per year per thousand of population; but whether expressed as a percentage or as a mathematical ratio, fertility should not be confused with fecundity. *Fecundity*, a concept related to but not synonymous with fertility, refers to the reproductive potential of a population. Social factors always keep the fertility rate well below the biological capacity for reproduction in all groups.

A few examples will illustrate the difference between fecundity and fertility. Let us hypothesize that a woman with normal reproductive potential could produce as many as twenty children, ruling out the possibility of multiple births. Yet, in most societies, and particularly in Western society, the woman who bears twenty children is far above the norm, even if multiple births do occur. Moreover, basic values often dictate the ultimate family size. In 1944 the Supreme Soviet passed legislation designed to stimulate the birth rate in Russia. Beginning with her third child, the Russian mother was paid a lump sum of 200 rubles/child. Additionally, she received 40 rubles/month for each child beginning with her fourth offspring. With the arrival of her eleventh child, and for all subsequent children, she received an initial payment of 2,500 rubles plus 150 rubles/month. These economic rewards seem more than sufficient when we consider that the average monthly income in Russia was about 650 rubles.[5] However, a study conducted by Strumilin published in 1961 points out that the average size of the Russian family is nearly identical to that in the United States, approximately 3.7 members.[6]

Mortality or death rates are calculated the same way as birth rates and are also influenced by social factors. Recently the question has been posed as to how much we value life and to what extent we shall go to preserve it. In Western society we have transplanted vital organs to individuals who most certainly would have died without such operations. Artificial hearts and kidneys have been devised to prolong life, and even after death a person's body may be preserved through the new methods of cryonics, or "freezing," to await the day when the course of the terminal disease that ended his life may be reversed. Among certain other

[5] All statistics are cited in E. W. Burgess, H. J. Locke, and M. M. Thomes, *The Family*, American Book Company, New York, 1963, chap. 6. Also see Gerald R. Leslie, *The Family in Social Context*, Oxford University Press, New York, 1967, chap. 5.
[6] S. Strumilin, "Family and Community in the Society of the Future," *The Soviet Review: A Journal of Translations*, vol. 2, no. 2, 1961, p. 7, cited in Burgess et al., *loc. cit.*

cultures, the attitude might be such that death is a natural occurrence that must take its normal course. Man's interference with the "plan of cosmos" may not be permitted. A strong belief in reincarnation may not be conducive to an excessive or artificial lengthening of one's present life.

The third demographic process is *migration*. Although this process refers to the movement of people into or out of a given geographic area, demographers often prefer to specify the direction of the movement. *Immigration* signifies the movement of people *into* a geographical location from some external source; *emigration* denotes the movement of population *out of* a given area. The choice of which concept is used depends upon one's point of reference. If a native of Great Britain moves to the United States he is an immigrant in this country and an emigrant according to Great Britain.

Sociologists tend to emphasize the importance of birth and death rates in determining the course of population growth because migration does not affect the statistics if we take a world perspective. This, of course, would not be true if we were colonizing the moon or other planets. However, migration has been a very important factor in the growth of many regional populations. Its effect on the United States is obvious; we have received 30 million immigrants since 1800. What is not nearly so obvious is the effect that the Great Irish Emigration had on Ireland, reducing its population from 8 million to 4 million. Likewise, the significance and repercussions of the forced immigration of Africans to the New World has been overlooked by the white American population until recently.

All three demographic processes are profoundly influenced by two fundamental factors: age and sex. Dennis Wrong points out that age and sex "are the most important population characteristics from the formal demographic standpoint, because they are directly related to fertility and mortality."[7] We must add that they are also highly correlated with migration patterns. Wrong goes on to explain that only women "within a certain age span are capable of producing children, and people die more frequently at some ages than at others."[8] The relationship of age and sex to migration is not as clear. Yet we can devise some reasonably accurate generalizations based upon past observations. First, people on the move are likely to be young. Petersen notes that over two-thirds of the immigrants to the United States in the nineteenth century were between fifteen and forty years old.[9] Sometimes areas have been partially depopulated of their young until they have begun to look like colonies for the aged. During the period of heavy migration out of Ireland, some rural villages looked as though an evil pied piper had lured away their

[7] Dennis H. Wrong, *Population and Society*, Random House, Inc., New York, 1967, p. 6.
[8] *Ibid*, p. 6.
[9] William Petersen, *Population*, The Macmillan Company, New York, 1961, p. 593.

young. The pied piper, of course, was the hope for economic opportunity in the New World. Within the United States, migrants are also likely to be young. It seems that as we get older we are less likely to search for new horizons, and we are less apt to adjust to new demographic conditions. However, there are many noteworthy exceptions to such generalizations.

Sex is not as highly correlated with migration as is age, but some significant findings have been reported. Generally, we have observed that "internal migrants are predominantly female and international ones predominantly male. . . ."[10] Although this has certainly been true in the past, it would seem that the continuing emancipation of women, increased opportunities for female employment, and weakened parental bonds are gradually changing the composition of international movement. Moreover, within the United States, the pattern of internal migration has undergone a change. It is now common for a family to move its permanent residence across state boundaries. The farm boy who once lacked the skills appropriate for city life is now gaining these skills through our expanding system of public education, thus enabling him to move to the city. The net effect of these changes might well bring about a leveling of the significance of sex in internal and international migration. Nevertheless, as late as the 1960 census, Washington D.C. had an excess of females, and Alaska had an equally great excess of males.

Actually, an uneven sex ratio can develop regardless of any migration. In countries where medical care is good, women have a lower mortality rate than men, and there are considerably more women in the population, especially in the later years of life. Occasionally this ratio is reversed, but mainly in countries where medical care is almost non-existent and many women die in childbirth. People often attribute the greater number of women in the population to the effects of war on the fighting men, but this accounts for only a fraction of the difference in most cases. The main difference is a higher male death rate from heart disease, accidents, and many other aspects of ordinary civilian life.

FAMILY PLANNING AND BIRTH CONTROL   We have previously noted that technological advances in medicine have led to a drastic reduction in the death rate of the human group. In industrialized countries we have also witnessed a gradual drop in the birth rate, but this has not been the case in those countries that are presently industrializing. For example, the countries of Latin America have benefited from the introduction of pesticides, disease control, and modern sanitation. These countries are now approaching rather stable, low death rates, but they are not experiencing a corresponding decline in fertility. The widened gap between

[10] *Ibid.*, p. 593.

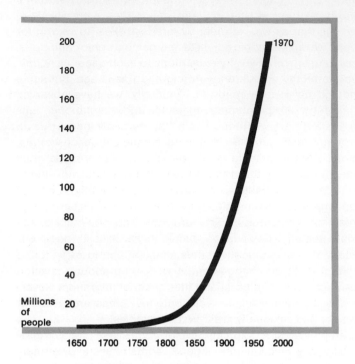

these two crucial rates has produced a population explosion which has probably been unparalleled in the history of man. Most industrialized nations have succeeded in cutting their birth rates to a greater or lesser extent. In the United States we must now face the question, "Have we done enough to curb population growth?" The accompanying illustration shows the course of growth we have exhibited.

In 1963, Donald J. Bogue pointed out that if the population of the United States continued to grow at its present rate, it would take only one century before we reached the figure of 1 billion people. He emphasized that this is "equivalent to one-third of the world's present inhabitants, and would be roughly equivalent to moving all of the population of Europe, Latin America and Africa into the territory of the fifty states."[11] If this prospect seems frightening to those who worry about population, the situation faced by underdeveloped countries is little short

[11] Donald J. Bogue, "Population Growth in the United States," *The Population Dilemma*, Philip M. Hauser (ed.), Prentice-Hall, Inc., Englewood Cliffs, N.J., 1963, pp. 71–72.

of terrifying. Asia, Africa, and Latin America will undoubtedly show the most rapidly rising growth rates in the world in the next decade. The reason is clear: death rates are showing significant declines, but birth rates are not changing appreciably (see Table 8-1).

In view of the problem of overpopulation faced by the United States and the world as a whole, William Vogt has raised some soul-searching questions: "What right have you to have a child?" "Does the world need more babies at the present time? Does the United States? Does any particular family?" "Will the world, the United States, and any particular family be in a better state after the birth of that last child than it was before?"[12] Not all will agree with the vehemence of Vogt's questions; some may rightfully resent being made to feel guilty over each child, but even in our affluent society we must realize that there are limits beyond which human crowding cannot go. The only possible means of avoiding the catastrophe of the future is population control. Mark Twain once commented that everybody talks about the weather, but nobody ever does anything about it. Today we could say the same about population control. The time is swiftly approaching when man will exercise some control over the weather, but will he do the same about his own breeding habits? There are a number of methods available to us at this time to ensure that we will not overcrowd the planet. Infanticide, genocide, and war are three of the simplest means of reducing population, but few of us would like to resort to such measures. Through legalized abortion and birth control Japan has cut its birth rate in half within a decade. Scandinavian countries are nearing a stabilization of population through effective family planning. Australia may well be experiencing a negative growth rate because it has adopted widespread use of contraceptive devices.

However, North Americans who are experiencing a rather prolonged period of affluence tend to ignore the potential population pressure of

[12]William Vogt, *People! Challenge to Survival*, William Sloane Associates, New York, 1960, chap. 7.

TABLE 8-1 Falling death rates in the hungry world
(per thousand)

	1935	1950	1965	1980†
World	25	19	16	12.7
Asia	33	23	20	13
Africa	33	27	23	18
Latin America	22	19	12	8.2

Source: *Population Bulletin of the United Nations*, no. 5, 1962, p. 17, and Population Reference Bureau, *World Population Data Sheet*, December, 1965, in William Paddock and Paul Paddock (eds.), *Famine: 1975! America's Decision: Who will Survive*, Little, Brown and Company, Boston, 1967, p. 16.
†Projected

the future. "Sure," we say, "I've got five kids, but I can afford them. They've never wanted for anything." Even though such statements may be descriptively true, they tend to ignore the possibility that these "kids" may someday have children who cannot be adequately fed, housed, and clothed as the population continues to increase and natural resources continue to be depleted. Population specialists caution that we must act today to secure tomorrow for our children. William and Paul Paddock assure us that failure to act will surely result in a collision course with famine.[13]

A more serious problem is facing Latin America where food is still a scarce commodity. Birth control practices are meeting with some success in the United States, but they are exhibiting marked failure among our neighbors to the south. In predominantly Catholic countries we tend to place the blame for high birth rates on the premise that artificial contraception is not condoned by the religious values of the people. Although this has some relevance, it is probably true that the Church has less affect on family size than does the attitude of *machismo*: one shows his manliness and status by the number of children he can produce. Another reason is that, although mortality rates have declined, the fear persists that some children will not live and that several are needed as a guarantee of family survival. The children are even seen as an economic asset in some areas, as they were in the earlier years in the United States.

Coupled with these values is the undeniable fact that, regardless of the culture in which we have been raised, human beings love children. In a peasant society, where there is little excitement or outside interest, children fill lives that would otherwise be lonely and empty, probably much more so than in a busy urban society. Even in urban society our love of and need for children is such that we may sometimes feel guilty about the possibility of preventing the birth of a child. The philosophical significance of this idea cannot be ignored, but as William Vogt aptly states:

> Until the ovum is fertilized by the sperm there is no life,
> no sentience, no possibility of deprivation.
> By failing to have a child we do it no harm. It is not.
> So far as the *child* is concerned any qualms, conscious
> or subconscious, we may feel about not having it are
> baseless. We are not depriving "it" of anything.
> There is no "it." Had I never been born, it would
> not have made the least difference to me.[14]

13William Paddock and Paul Paddock (eds.), *Famine: 1975! America's Decision: Who Will Survive*, Little, Brown and Company, Boston, 1967, p. 16.
14Vogt, *op. cit.*, pp. 151–152.

The question now arises as to what incentives can be given people to limit the ultimate size of their families. Several attempts have been made in different parts of the world. India, with an extremely high rate of illiteracy, has posted billboards containing a visual message only. On one side a large family dressed in rags is portrayed; on the other side is shown a small family who are well clad and appear to be well fed. Vasectomy (male sterilization) camps have also been set up throughout the country-side, and "agents" are given a commission for each man they deliver. The operation which is performed is simple; it takes only minutes, ensures infertility with a rather high degree of confidence, and does not interfere with normal sexual performance. Many of these clinics offer some monetary reward and, perhaps, a transistor radio.

In Korea, government employees travel from village to village distributing information on family planning and birth control. Women are encouraged to sign up for the "program," and the effort is meeting with some success. In fact, Korea may become the first nation to significantly reduce its birth rate before industrializing. In industrialized countries with low rates of illiteracy, our main hope for population control lies in education. The seriousness of the problem can be made known to the people if we effectively utilize our systems of mass media and public ecucation.

POPULATION QUALITY   Throughout most of man's history, only the fit survived. The defective child seldom reached maturity: the mentally ill were tortured or shut off from society, and the physically weak were left to their own inept devices. Today the social conscience of most societies dictates, and science ensures, that the survival of the "unfit" be as equal as that of the "fit." Certainly we would have it no other way. Along with the medical knowledge we have acquired to sustain and prolong life, we are now developing technology that can ensure the procreation of a population nearly devoid of physical and mental defects. The deteriorating effects of syphillis and its resultant mental illness, general paresis, have been nearly eliminated. Physical and mental inadequacies such as cretinism or acromegaly are now nearly extinct because of thyroid and pituitary treatments that prevent or reverse their development. Polio is rapidly becoming a disease of the past, and its possibility of occurrence among children born today is as remote as the possibility of smallpox. At one time diabetics simply died; now insulin injections or tablets allow them normal life-spans and normal life experiences.

The net result is that we are not simply permitting the unfit to survive, but we are actually closing the gap between the "strong" and the "weak." As the gap closes and as more individuals enter into and live through their reproductive years, we can expect population to increase to larger and larger proportions. Although the rate of *increase* is diminishing, we are increasing the population base. The implication is clear: a lowered rate of growth does not necessitate a decline in the absolute number of people added to our population each year.

How does this affect the quality of our population? It has been stated time and again by many social scientists that as we solve one social problem we tend to create others. In this case, an increased quality of population, coupled with an increased number of people within societies, might result in deleterious side effects.

John B. Calhoun created an artificial, overcrowded slum. The residents were not human beings; they were rats. As the density of population increased several uncommon phenomena were observed. Many of the females were unable to carry pregnancy to full term. If they did, some failed to survive delivery of their litters. Males became sexual deviants or cannibals. Neurotic tendencies were manifest in symptoms of overactivity or total withdrawal. Offspring were overprotected or abandoned; in either case, most of them died.[15]

Although we cannot accurately generalize the observation of the behavior of rats to that of human beings, we can speculate about the effects of the quality of population that a "standing-room-only" world would produce. *Population quality* refers to the physical and mental characteristics displayed by the human group. Even though many physical handicaps and certain psychological disturbances have been solved, a number of secondary problems have arisen.

First, as birth and death rates decrease, we can observe a definite aging of the population. This means that the percentage of elderly persons is growing proportionately larger. As this trend continues, the occurrence of senility is likely to become more widespread. To prepare ourselves for this possibility, the new field of *social gerontology*, a sociological attempt to understand the problems of the aged, is receiving more and more attention.

Second, as the density of population becomes more pronounced, it is likely that it will become increasingly difficult to maintain a strong sense of individuality and identity. Our era has been called the *age of anxiety* by many psychologists, denoting that there may be some validity to the predictions of Thomas Malthus that the continued growth of the population would result in only vice and misery.[16] Calhoun's rats seem

---

[15]John B. Calhoun, "Population Density and Social Pathology," in Louise B. Young (ed.), *Population in Perspective*, Oxford University Press, New York, 1968, pp. 375–389.
[16]Malthus, *op. cit.*

to bear out this morbid prognostication, but, so far, human beings in overcrowded circumstances have not been so drastically affected.

Finally, we must ask, "Can we maintain a high quality of population as our growing number of people deplete our resources of food, water, and minerals?" Some social scientists will argue that we are not now able to ensure a high population quality because so many of the earth's inhabitants are undernourished. This may be true, but the problem does not lie in our inability to produce food for the masses. Rather, the problem is one of inequality of production in the various countries of the world. Some of the most crowded areas are also areas of the least efficient agriculture and they produce a low per-capita yield that barely sustains life. Now, even in affluent societies, we must face the question of whether or not our production of food and supply of resources will be able to keep pace with the extent of our reproduction. It is becoming increasingly evident that population control and population quality are intricately linked. How well we manipulate these two variables will determine the course of the future of our species.

SUMMARY   Fifty thousand years ago the world was rather sparsely populated when hunting and food gathering societies predominated. However, as surpluses of food were built up in early villages (and later in the first cities), population began to increase. By 1960, an overpopulated world of 3 billion people existed.

The study of population is known as demography, a field of sociology that describes and analyzes living groups of people. The major demographic processes are (1) fertility, the actual number of children born within a given population, (2) mortality, the actual number of deaths that occur within a society or region, and (3) migration, the physical movement of people into or out of a given geographic area.

Because of a decrease in mortality rates, many areas of the world are undergoing a period of tremendous population increase. Nonindustrialized countries seem to be growing faster than industrialized nations. However, even industrial nations are now facing the problems caused by too large a population.

Population control has benefited several countries whose methods of birth limitation, legalized abortion, and voluntary sterilization have been observed. Some nonindustrialized or industrilizing countries, such as Korea, have already instigated massive programs to limit the size of their populations. As birth rates continue to decline, the population as a whole ages. The field of social gerontology is becoming increasingly important because it is concerned with the problems of the aged.

Population quality refers to the physical and mental characteristics displayed by the human group. In the past, only the most fit individuals survived, but now it is possible for a large proportion of the "unfit" to survive. This adds to the problem of overpopulation, but not significantly. The major problem encountered by overpopulation is the effect that over-crowding may have on the population of an entire society. Population contol and population quality seem to be intricately linked.

The houses were never high enough to satisfy
them; they kept on making them still higher
and built them thirty or forty storeys with
offices, shops, banks, . . . one above another;
they dug cellars and tunnels ever deeper
downwards. . . .

No light of heaven pierced through the smoke
of the factories with which the town was girt,
but sometimes the red disk of a rayless sun
might be seen riding in the black firmament
through which iron bridges plowed their way,
and from which there descended a continual
shower of soot and cinders.[1]

ANATOLE FRANCE
Penguin Island

nine

CONGESTION OF THE HUMAN GROUP: THE URBAN TREND

Mankind has gathered into groups, not only to protect life
and ensure its propagation, but to enrich life through
meaningful contacts with other human beings. People
come together to exchange ideologies, to stimulate the
process of innovation, to stabilize a set of values, and to
establish an orderly pattern of existence. Yet, when we
look at the sprawling cities of our modern industrial
nations, we find that the congestion of the human group
may often interfere with the attainment of those goals for
which we have adopted the city as our habitat. Exactly
what has happened to bring about the crises of urbanism
is not easily explained, but a consideration of the trend
which has led to the contemporary condition can shed
some light on the development of our urban predicament.

[1]Anatole France, *Penguin Island*, Modern Library, Inc., New York, 1933, p. 279.

URBAN GROWTH AND URBAN CRISES   The growth of cities was not rapid in the early periods of urban development. Large numbers of peasant and pastoral people had to supply the food and other commodities needed by urbanites, and the yields of farmland were not great enough to support more than a small minority of nonfarming people.

Ancient cities   The ancient cities faced many problems that would be with man in one form or another throughout the remainder of history. Not only was the problem of the production of an agricultural surplus with which to feed the town a formidable task, but the problems of transportation of goods to the city created another barrier to urban growth. The great cities of antiquity had to be small compared with the metropolis of today because of the problems of food production and supply. Ur of the Chaldees attained a population of only about 34,000 during its first 2,000 years of existence, but eventually it numbered over 200,000. The latter estimate, however, included populations living outside the city walls.[2]

In ancient times, as well as in modern, there was normative conflict between city and countryside, as recorded in Biblical maledictions upon Sodom and Gomorrah, Babylon, Neneveh, and Tyre. The ancient city also had its problems of sanitation. Many cities were located along rivers which acted as open sewers and garbage disposals, and fluctuations in the population of Imperial Rome may have been caused in part by problems of sanitation.

The word "polis," applied to the cities of the Greeks, is related to the word "politics," implying that the city was the center of government. In this respect, many cities had a greater importance than do cities of today, in spite of the smaller size of earlier cities. They developed as independent entities, dominated a hinterland around them, and occasionally became the centers of empires. The city of antiquity was thus a place of pride and power, demanding a loyalty of its citizens that is now claimed by the nation-state.

The medieval city   Many of the cities of Southern Europe in the medieval period were the shrunken remains of the cities of the Roman Empre, but they often had much of the independence of the ancient polis. They maintained garrisons and carried on diplomacy. The Hanseatic cities of Northern Europe were formed more exclusively for trade and commerce and, in this respect, resembled the cities of today. They also attained a degree of independence and allowed much greater freedom for their citizens than was permitted the serfs of the medieval estates.[3] There was

[2] Lewis Mumford, *The City in History*, Harcourt, Brace, & World, Inc., New York, 1961, p. 62.
[3] Max Weber, *The City*, Don Martindale and Gertrude Neuwirth (translators and eds.), The Free Press of Glencoe, Inc., New York, 1958, p. 182.

a saying, "city air is free air"—in the city, one could shed the shackles of serfdom. In a sense, the statement remains true throughout history, not in relation to serfdom, but in relation to the crippling bonds of traditionalism and provincialism that are common in small towns and villages.

The problems of health and sanitation were met only in very crude ways during that period. Sometimes open streams carried off the sewage of the city, but often there were virtually no disposal facilities. Mumford points out that in Cambridge piles of dung were allowed to accumulate in public places for a week, and in many towns corpses were buried in the city centers where, by decay and seepage, they contaminated the water supply.[4] In spite of this, he concludes that the medieval town or city was not as bad as it is sometimes pictured. It had the advantage of little crowding so that people could usually dispose of their wastes in the ample garden plots behind their houses. The problem of wastes was to become worse in some respects in the modern world.

The modern city   The modern city is an industrial city. Much more than the ancient or medieval city, the modern city is an outgrowth of trade and industry. As it grew in size and affluence, it also became more enmeshed in both the economy and polity of the larger society. Sjoberg has done a study of the preindustrial city, including modern cities of a nonindustrial type, as well as cities of the past. Although such cities differ from case to case, a generalized summary shows both contrasts and similarities when compared with the industrial city.[5]

Contrasts.   By comparison with the modern industrial city, the preindustrial city is small, numbering only 10,000 in population in most cases, and numbering 100,000 only rarely. The extended family tends to dominate the way of life in some respects, although the city, in general, is characterized by habitation of smaller, nuclear, families. The city itself, as previously noted, tends to be an independent political entity with a centralized and oligarchic government. Education is only for the privileged class in the preindustrial setting; under conditions of industrialization, it is provided for all classes.

The preindustrial city was more sacred than secular, because it was often the center of religious life. Religious norms were enforced by custom and sometimes even by law. Political and religious unity, along with the influence of the extended family system, gave it more a sense of community than is generally observed in the industrial city of this era.

The production of an agricultural surplus has always been a requirement of city life, but here again a contrast in life styles can be noted. In the preindustrial city, a majority had to till the soil so that a minority could live in the city. Today, a majority live in the city. Even by the time

[4] Mumford, *op. cit.*, p. 288.
[5] Gideon Sjoberb, *The Preindustrial City*, The Free Press, New York, 1964, pp. 323–332.

The contrasts

The preindustrial city
  Small, usually 10,000-100,000

  Politically independent

  Extended (consanguineal) family

  Education upper class

  Religious unity,
  approaches "sacred society"

  Sanitation problems:
  mainly human and animal wastes

  City walls, limited suburbs

The contrasts

The industrial city
  Large, usually 100,000-8,000,000

  Subordinate to nation

  Restricted (conjugal) family

  General education

  Religious diversity, and secular

  Sanitation problems:
  industrial waste, air contamination

  "Exploding metropolis," suburbs

The similarities

The growth of class differences

Segregation of minorities

Economic and ecological segregation

Heterogeneity: all walks of life, many kinds of people

Mass entertainment

Development of intellectual life, arts and sciences

---

of the Civil War only one-third of the people in the United States had to work the land. By the end of World War II only one person in twelve farmed for a living. By 1970, the agricultural product of the United States was increasing more rapidly than ever before. This observation takes on special significance when we consider the fact that now only one man in forty-three is occupied with farming![6]

Similarities. Although a number of contrasts have been cited, many similarities appear to exist when industrial and preindustrial cities are compared. Class differentiation, for example, is very much in evidence in both types of city. Minority groups are segregated into particular quarters today, as they were in preindustrial cities. The modern industrial city also is segregated into various economic categories in much the same

[6]Jules B. Billard, "The Revolution in American Agriculture," *National Geographic*, vol. 137, February, 1970, pp. 147–151.

way as the ancient city was segregated into specialized areas for various crafts, shops, and types of labor. New forms of entertainment exist today, but they are reminiscent of the Roman circus maximus, the Byzantine hippodrome, the Olympic Games, or the Greek theater.

Urban crises   As the industrial era proceeded, cities began to expand by extending their boundaries and crowding more and more people within the urban complex. Factory systems were developed to provide for the increasing numbers of people, and the rudiments of mass production came into existence. The city also needed people in order to operate effectively. For some time, the mutual dependency established between population and cities worked well. However, by 1960, Manhattan had an average population density of 75,000 persons/square mile, and more than 23,550,000 inhabitants lived within a 10-mile radius of the city.[7] This is just part of a larger urban complex, Megalopolis, that will be discussed shortly.

Arensberg and Kimball point out that the human community is a minimal unit of population whose members must coexist to insure the continuance of the species.[8] As communities continued to grow in size and population they became cities. In the United States, there were twenty-four urban places, only two of which had populations in excess of 25,000, when the first national census was taken in 1790.[9] By 1960, 5,400 urban areas had absorbed 92 percent of the total population growth.[10] In time, and with further expansion, some of these urban places began to merge so that one could not tell where one city ended and the next began. On the northeastern seaboard of this nation, such an area is described by Jean Gottmann as *Megalopolis*. It is "an almost continuous stretch of urban and suburban areas from southern New Hampshire to northern Virginia and from the Atlantic shore to the Appalachian foothills."[11] By the time this book goes to the printer over 40 million people will be living on this rather small land space. Some experts, including Lewis Mumford, believe that under such conditions community may become anticommunity, contributing not to the enhancement of human life, but, perhaps, to its demise.

This statement may seem somewhat alarmist; however, there is some evidence to justify its inclusion in a sociology text. It is not the intent of the authors to predict the doom of urban areas, but rather to

[7] Estimated population statistics based on Philip M. Hauser and Leo F. Schnore, *The Study of Urbanization*, John Wiley & Sons, Inc., New York, 1965, p. 11.
[8] Conrad M. Arensberg and Solon T. Kimball, *Culture and Community*, Harcourt, Brace, & World, Inc., New York, 1965, pp. 16–17.
[9] Hauser and Schnore, *op. cit.*, p. 7.
[10] *Ibid.*, pp. 7–8.
[11] Jean Gottman, *Megalopolis*, The Twentieth Century Fund, New York, 1961, p. 3.

point out that such conditions may not be beneficial to the inhabitants of these supercities. Aside from the asthetic needs which draw people into close association, such as the need to identify with a group and the need for security which comes from acceptance by others, human beings also have physical needs. Water and air are the most basic of these.

Laurence M. Gould reports that at least sixty underdeveloped nations already face water-shortage problems, and in America, New York City dumps 200 million gallons of raw sewage into the Hudson River every day, thus threatening the water supply.[12] On the other side of the continent, San Francisco is facing the problem of losing its famous bay to land-fill operations, most of which has been directly or indirectly caused by covering former garbage dumps. In November, 1969, reacting to the cries of the citizenry to "save our bay," the San Francisco Board of Supervisors' Health Committee recommended that the city ship its garbage by rail to Lassen County. Although this increases the economic problems of San Francisco, it is an economic boon to Lassen County, which hopes to become the "garbage dump of America."[13]

The problem of clean air was nearly nonexistent so long as most of the people lived at "home on the range . . ." where the skies were not only free of clouds but free of smog and pollutants. As living patterns changed, so did the condition of the atmosphere. In 1900, only 40 percent of this country's 75 million population lived in urban areas. By 1960, with a population of 180 million, 70 percent of the people were urban dwellers. Edward Edelson points out that now "more than half the American people live on just 1 percent of the nation's land mass. It is in these relatively small and crowded areas where most of the country's air pollution is created."[14]

When people mass together in great numbers extensive services must be devised to meet their needs. In the process other problems may be caused. Operating industrial plants and heating houses and apartments through the use of fossil fuels adds pollutants to the environment. Every day, chimneys in the United States pour out 100,000 tons of sulphur dioxide, and motor vehicles add 230,000 tons of carbon monoxide.[15] It is no mere coincidence that the growth of urban areas has been accompanied by problems of air and water pollution; the pattern has been continuous throughout history. It is only the technology of the industrial city that adds to the problems started in medieval times.

[12]Laurence M. Gould, "While There Is Still Time," *Bell Telephone Magazine*, American Telephone and Telegraph Company, New York, January/February, 1969, p. 6.
[13]Charles Hillinger, "The Garbage Dump of America," *Los Angeles Times*, Friday, July 4, 1969, p. 3.
[14]Edward Edelson, "The Battle for Clean Air," *Public Affairs Pamphlet No. 403*, Public Affairs Committee, Newark, N.J., 1968, p. 3.
[15]Gould, *loc. cit.*

ECOLOGICAL CHARACTERISTICS OF THE CITY   In a sociological sense, *ecology* refers to the relationship between man and his *social* environment. The ecological pattern of a neolithic village was quite different from that of the modern metropolis. Such a village was relatively uncomplicated; it was composed of people from like backgrounds who had similar interests, a condition known as *homogeneity*. The members of the village enjoyed a primary relationship with each other and a strong feeling of community. Tönnies described such a social organization as one which was oriented toward the achievement of group goals. Each individual took part in the activities of the community. His actions were prescribed by tradition, and his attitudes were based upon sentiment. Tönnies called this pattern of group life *gemeinschaft*, a community in which the relationships among members were valuable in and of themselves.[16]

However, as population increased the need for a different kind of living arrangement developed. The gemeinschaft type of society did not have the distinct authoritive body that is necessary to govern large numbers of people. Because it was tradition oriented, it lacked the cultural perspective necessary for change; its emphasis on close personal relationships hampered its ability to expedite matters quickly. As a result, early communities, villages, and tribes began to take on the shape and characteristics of the modern city. Unfortunately, these characteristics had some undesirable side effects.

To administer a large population is to divest the individual of some of his autonomy; to maintain the population is to mass produce; to specialize parts of the population for the performance of different activities is to separate individuals from other parts of the total culture. As the city developed and grew, it needed greater centralization of power, mass production (and eventually automation), and produced increasing alienation among its members. In Tönnies' terminology, this represents a movement away from gemeinschaft toward gesellschaft. The *gesellschaft* pattern is more impersonal, and the goals of the individual take precedence over the goals of the group. Rather than depend upon tradition and custom for guidance, man is controlled through a formalized system of laws. This is an *associational* society with superficial and transitory relationships based upon the rational pursuit of self-interest through business and commerce. Although gesellschaft society exists only in the imagination, many sectors of the modern world are rapidly approaching its realization.

In industrialized countries, the trend toward gesellschaft orientation is exemplified in the cities. The characteristics of gesellschaft have

---

[16]Ferdinand Tönnies, *Community and Society*, The Michigan State University Press, East Lansing, 1957.

Gemeinschaft

Homogeneity: sameness, likeness

Group-oriented

Tradition dominates patterns

Individual guided by sentiment

Each man part of
the overall culture

Each man a jack-of-all-trades

Relationships among people
valuable in and of themselves

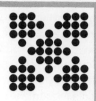

Gesellschaft

Heterogeneity: mixed
background and interests

Individual-oriented

Business and commerce dominate

Man guided by rational pursuit
of his own interests

Specialization

Relationships transistory
and superficial

resulted in the segregation of cities into special-interest areas. In 1925 Ernest Burgess attempted to describe this pattern by introducing a model of city development known as the *Concentric Zone Theory*. His idea was that at the core of a city, using Chicago as a specific example, a central business district would be located. As one journeyed toward the outer band of the circle he would encounter a zone of transition, a workingman's residential area, a middle-class residential area, and finally, the commuter's zone. Chicago, of course, cannot serve as a model for all cities, and Burgess' theory has been criticized on this count, despite the fact that it was not his intention to propose that such a theory would explain the development of all urban areas. Nevertheless, because of limited application of the Concentric Zone Theory, other theorists devised other models, none of which have universal validity. Hoyt's *Sector Theory* is illustrated in the accompanying figure.

The sector of the city that was once the highest priced residential area eventually declines, but high-value areas extend beyond it in the same part of town. There are many areas where this is true, especially if natural beauty or other advantages give particular areas of the city a high residential value. Often, though, other factors also affect the pattern of growth — railroads, industrial developments, hills, or other natural barriers. Often in rapidly growing Western communities the most impoverished area is a rural-urban fringe at the outskirts of town (often stretching out along railroad tracks) rather than the zone in transition near city hall.

Other new patterns are emerging, the major one being an outward explosion in all directions, resulting in urban areas with many centers. Some cities, notably Los Angeles, originally grew by combining several communities. Other cities, once compact, now resemble Los Angeles, reaching out tentacles in all directions and establishing new suburban centers at the ends of each.

The nature of the city and man's attraction to urban living can be summed up by reviewing the theory of Robert E. Park, a leading University of Chicago sociologist. "In the freedom of the city," he wrote, "every individual, no matter how eccentric, finds somewhere an environment in which he can expand and bring what is peculiar in his nature to some sort of expression."[17] Basing his ideas on this premise, Park concluded that each city was made up of "natural areas," subcommunities which have characteristics attractive to those whose special needs or interests are matched to the ecological conditions of the areas. Therefore, in some unplanned fashion, every city will evolve a central business district, exclusive residential areas or suburbs, areas of light or heavy industry, a labor mart, slums, ghettos, bohemias, and hobohemias. As the appeal of cities began to spread to wider and wider factions of the population, the city per se became indistinguishable from contiguous areas outside its political boundaries. The *metropolis* had been formed!

"Today, metropolitan areas spill beyond their central cities, embracing smaller cities and towns, and surrounding numerous semirural patches."[18] Within the metropolitan area, the central city politically, socially, and economically dominates most areas outside its own politico-geographic boundaries. In order to classify properly the residential patterns of the United States' population, a new concept was devised by

[17] Robert E. Park, *Human Communities*, The Free Press, Glencoe, Ill., 1952, p. 86.
[18] Edgar M. Hoover and Raymond Vernon, *Anatomy of a Metropolis*, Doubleday & Company, Inc., Garden City, N.Y., 1959, p. 2.

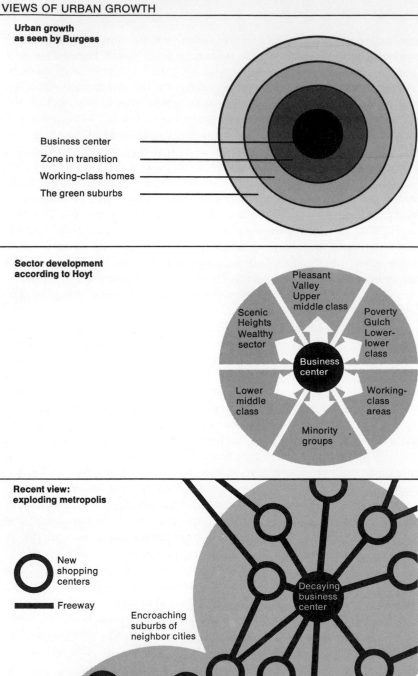

**Urban growth
as seen by Burgess**

Business center
Zone in transition
Working-class homes
The green suburbs

**Sector development
according to Hoyt**

Scenic
Heights
Wealthy
sector

Pleasant
Valley
Upper
middle class

Poverty
Gulch
Lower-
lower
class

Business
center

Lower
middle
class

Working-
class
areas

Minority
groups

**Recent view:
exploding metropolis**

New
shopping
centers

Freeway

Encroaching
suburbs of
neighbor cities

Decaying
business
center

the Census Bureau and put into effect in 1950. As of that date, much of the nation's population was counted as inhabitants of *Standard Metropolitan Statistical Areas* (SMSA). The SMSA is a largely nonagricultural area containing a "mother city" or a pair of twin cities of at least 50,000 population. In the SMSA, unincorporated areas are strongly influenced by the general characteristics of the central city or cities.

However, by 1960 a new category was needed. Some metropolitan areas had continued to grow to the extent that the end of one SMSA could not be distinguished from the beginning of another. To eliminate an artificial separation of residential areas, the concept of the *Standard Consolidated Area* was added to the list of classifications used by the Census Bureau. The Standard Consolidated Areas (SCA) are contiguous Standard Metropolitan Statistical Areas. At the introduction of this new classification only two SCA's were reported: New York—northeastern New Jersey (the largest) and Chicago—northwestern Indiana. The first is only part of Megalopolis.

THE GHETTO IN AMERICAN CITIES   As the problems of the city began to enter the consciousness of the American public, a new word was added to its vocabulary—"ghetto." However, the word is not a new one, nor is the ghetto a phenomenon in recent American history. A *ghetto* is a segregated area (or neighborhood) within a city whose inhabitants are largely confined to a single ethnic or racial category. This ecological pattern may well be as old as the city itself. Certainly it was a principal living arrangement for Jewish people in the medieval cities of Europe, and it has been a consistent pattern in America. Usually it emerges in the oldest parts of the city and houses the most recent group of immigrants. As any specific group becomes more "acceptable" to the dominant group of society, it usually experiences gains in prestige, economics, and power. When an immigrant group becomes economically successful, it is likely to move out of the ghetto, leaving the neighborhood to less successful or more recent neophytes. Peter I. Rose gives the following description: "In the metropolitan centers of the North the pattern was often repeated: the areas of original settlement successively became the ghetto-communities of the older settlers, the Irish and Germans, East Europeans, Jews, Italians and most recently, Negroes from the South, and Puerto Ricans."[19]

However, after World War II the nature of the urban ghetto began to change. Immigrants still came to the shores of the New World but not in massive ethnic or national units. The migration of greatest significance was an internal migration. Southern and rural Negroes came in increasing

[19] Peter I. Rose, *They and We*, Random House, Inc., New York, 1964, p. 33.

**Ecological segregation:
natural areas**

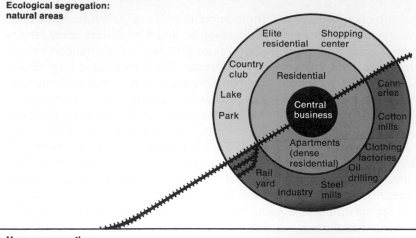

**Human segregation:
the ghetto**

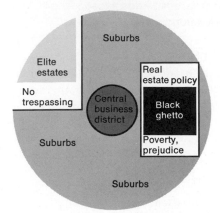

numbers to the Northern cities and settled in the deteriorated neighborhoods vacated by the Jews and Italians. Of course, Negroes were here
long before any of the other groups, but they were among the last to
urbanize. Once the process started, however, it moved rapidly. Broom and
Glenn have observed that in the "twelve most populous metropolitan
areas in 1960, 55 percent of the whites lived outside the central cities,
compared with only 19 percent of the Negroes."[20] This phenomenon
has changed popular usage of the word "ghetto."

[20]Leonard Broom and Norval D. Glenn, *Transformation of the Negro American*, Harper & Row, Publishers,
Incorporated, New York, 1965, p. 163.

Traditionally, the ghetto communities of large cities represented urban areas distinct from one another in terms of cultural heritage, language, and customs. In traversing New York City, for example, one might pass through a neighborhood with an unmistakable Polish characteristic, enter a neighborhood where Italian and English languages are used interchangeably, and end in an area where Chinese characters identify the different business establishments. Today the word "ghetto" means "black."

It is quite significant that the inflow of Negroes to the cities has been paralleled by an outflow of whites. In a real sense, the development of suburban areas has been a major contributor to the growth of urban ghettos and a major cause of the decay of core cities. It is no secret that the majority of urban blacks are poor and that the majority of suburban whites are at least economically comfortable according to national standards. As whites leave the city they take most of their taxable income with them, but still whites tend to control the power structure of the metropolis. The meaning of this chain of events is aptly conveyed by Kenneth E. Boulding:

> The reason why cities are ugly and sad
> Is not that the people who live there are bad;
> It's that most of the people who really decide
> What goes on in the city live somewhere outside.[21]

The suburb is intricately linked to the city. Were it not for the city's business and merchandising districts, it is unlikely that the suburb could support itself. Most suburban dwellers work in the core or inner city; it is their primary source of subsistence. It would seem that if a suburbanite were insensitive to the city's needs, he would also be unconcerned about the source of his own livelihood. As the ghetto continues to expand and decay, the city increasingly takes on its characteristics, becoming less attractive to the middle-class suburbanite.

Norman Hill points out that in many states the rural and suburban vote tends to ignore the problems of the city.[22] Somehow the ghetto becomes unreal; ghetto life becomes a horror story intended to scare people in the same fashion as did Frankenstein's monster. Pure fiction! However, if it is not fiction, if such things do exist, it is better not to talk about them. The suburbanite is likely to go to the polls, vote "no" on state aid to the cities because it will increase his property tax, return home, turn on his stereo, and listen to a rendition by Peter, Paul, and Mary of "Where Have All the Flowers Gone."

[21] Kenneth E. Boulding, "Ecology & Environment," *Transaction*, vol. 7, no. 5, March, 1970, p. 40.
[22] Norman Hill, "The Crisis in the Cities," *Agenda*, vol. 4, no. 5, May, 1968, p. 6.

MENTAL LIFE AND THE CITY   The city has been the focus of much criticism in American history, long before our current worries over water and air, traffic congestion, and racial segregation. Some of the criticism was merely that of a romantic love for nature, nostalgia for an old way of life close to the good earth, or the old man's warning against the temptations of the city. Rural life was seen as better than city life, closer to nature and to God. The Populists and followers of other farm movements argued against the interests of the urban East not merely in economic terms, but in moralistic terms. The Eastern interests that William Jennings Bryan saw "pressing down upon the brow of labor this crown of thorns" were represented by city men—for the most part, New Yorkers and bankers.

Criticism by the American intellectual   More intellectual men than Bryan were also unhappy about the city. Jefferson worried about urban mobs and hoped for a nation that would forever preserve a rural orientation. Emerson echoed a similar theme. Morton and Lucia White[23] did a study of the anti-city bias of large numbers of American intellectuals—Jefferson, Emerson, Melville, Hawthorne, Henry James, William James, Dreiser, Dewey, Park, and many more. We shall return to the views of Dewey and Park after first studying the perspectives of Georg Simmel, a German sociologist and a teacher of Robert Park.

Georg Simmel   Although Simmel (1858–1918) did not belong to the modern period of Megalopolis, his writings on the subject of interaction in the city and the effects of city life on intellectual and emotional life sound contemporary and have influenced sociological thinking up to the present day.

According to Simmel, the city calls for increased alertness on the part of the individual. More stimuli impinge upon the senses and nerves at all times, intensifying awareness and stimulating the mentality of the individual. At the same time, the emotional side of life begins to decline. People do not relate to each other as closely as in the less crowded areas of the country and village. People are seen more as competitors than as friends: ". . . city life has transformed the struggle with nature for livelihood into an interhuman struggle for gain. . . ."[24]

Simmel calls the essence of the city personality the *blasé attitude*, the feeling that one can take anything in his stride without becoming ruffled. The contrast is clear in the reaction to the tragedies that constantly occur in life. If a fatal accident occurs in a small town, everyone

[23] Morton White and Lucia White, *The Intellectual Versus the City*, Mentor Books, New American Library, Inc., New York, 1964.
[24] Georg Simmel, "The Metropolis and Mental Life," in Eric Josephson and Mary Josephson (eds.), *Man Alone*, Dell Publishing Co., Inc., New York, 1962, p. 162.

is concerned, there is common grief, and the incident lingers as a subject of conversation. In the big city, fatalities attract almost no notice. One listens to a recitation of traffic accidents on the local radio station, becomes bored with it, and turns to the latest hit songs.

The big-city dweller must dismiss many things from his mind, or he would face constant neurotic worry. The field of perception is narrowed to that part of the cityscape that concerns us—that and no more. This causes us to wall out other people. In apartment living it is not unusual to wall out the next-door neighbors. They are so close physically that social distance must be maintained for the sake of preservation of privacy. The walling-out process becomes a habit of mind and emotion. We do not see people whom we prefer not to see, nor do we see "the other side of the tracks." Our view is limited and exclusive.

Park and Dewey   Simmel's point of view is similar to that of Park's.[25] Because of a background in journalism, Park was particularly interested in the city from the viewpoint of communication. In the great city, he observed, communication between regions, social classes, and ethnic groups tends to break down. The major human problem of the city was that of preservation of a sense of community through mutual understanding and through awareness of common interests and issues. John Dewey[26] saw the problem in a similar way. He feared that the reduction in primary-group interaction was a threat to democracy and that the city was too cold and impersonal for the interchange of opinions and ideas so necessary to the democratic process.

The evidence pro and con   The criticisms of the city's effect on the mental and emotional life of man cannot be dismissed lightly. There is much evidence that tends to support the critics. Crime rates are higher in the city and so are rates of narcotics addiction, alcoholism, mental disorders, and suicide. The most deteriorated areas of our cities abound with people who seem to have been crushed by the urban struggle. Such facts seem to argue strongly against the city, but some reservations must be made. Are these unfavorable traits characteristic of all urban areas or only of certain urban areas? Do they exist of necessity just because of the urban way of life, or are they amenable to improvement even under urban conditions?

Leo Srole and his colleagues, in their study of mental health in midtown Manhattan,[27] use descriptions reminiscent of Simmel—"city of strangers," "anomic," "loneliness in the crowd." They are describing a

[25] White and White, *op. cit.*, pp. 160–170.
[26] *Ibid.*, pp. 171–180.
[27] Leo Srole et al., *Mental Health in the Metropolis*, McGraw-Hill Book Company, New York, 1962, chaps. 7–8.

city of high competition, rapid pace, and considerable opportunity for the striver. They quote various people who like the area because it does not intrude on privacy or interest itself in small-town gossip. But the mental-health statistics are not encouraging; they show a rate of psychological impairment about three times higher than those found in a similar study of the smaller city of New Haven. There are, however, differences within midtown Manhattan, with the poor having considerably higher rates of psychological impairment than the middle class. It is also interesting to note that impairment rates were not as high in other parts of Manhattan as in its central section. Three areas in Manhattan were found that were almost perfect models of community concern, with self-help associations, recreational facilities, a jobs-for-youth service, and even open-air art shows and concerts. It seems that alienation is not an inevitability of the big city.

Whatever its psychological problems, the city environment is not as insistent on tradition and conformity as the rural area. It is the city that protects and encourages the unusual artist or musician; there he finds kindred spirits to encourage him, people who form little subcultural groups interested in the very things that interest him. It is in the city that he will find the schools and libraries and art galleries and museums that help to liberate the human mind. (The very word "civilization" derives from the Latin word for city.)

THE FUTURE OF THE CITY   Lewis Mumford asks, "If the places where we live and work were really fit for permanent human habitation, why should we spend so much of our time getting away from them?"[28] The dream of nearly every urban man is to have someplace—a cabin in the mountains, a bungalow at the beach, a cottage in the countryside—to "get away from it all." Of course, we like to go to the city for cultural activities and to do our shopping, but the truth is that few people really want to live there. This is the real urban crisis: when the city can no longer satisfy its inhabitants, the people no longer care about the maintenance of the city.

The cities will survive, but the question which we now are asking ourselves, both public citizens and elected officials, is how shall they survive and in what condition will we find them twenty years from now. Will the cities continue to deteriorate, or can they be revitalized? The answer lies in the extent and types of fiscal policy, political action, and social reform that develop. Hill[29] has proposed a threefold plan:

1.   Creation of a national job pool. This first strategy for easing the frus-

[28] Lewis Mumford, *The Urban Prospect*, Harcourt, Brace & World, Inc., New York, 1968, p. 9.
[29] Norman Hill, *loc. cit.*

tration and decay of the cities would involve organization and planning by the federal government to move people to where jobs are available. It would mean moving people out of the ghetto, or out of the city. People would have to be relocated near new employment centers, and they would have to be provided with integrated housing units, services of every nature, and schooling.

2. A national land policy. The creation of a national land policy would enable the federal government to buy up idle land held by speculators or to utilize land now in its possession in order to build new towns and communities. Such communities might be developed as "satellite cities" — smaller, self-sustaining cities located near large metropolitan areas. Such communities would draw their populations from presently over-crowded urban areas, thereby not only contributing attractive living space but easing the population pressure of the metropolis.

3. A national migration policy. In America, people are free to migrate wherever they desire, but some cities seem to repel migration because they do not match the expectations of potential immigrants. There are wide disparities, for example, in health and welfare facilities from city to city and state to state. Eliminating such disparities might serve to level off population densities by redistributing the people who now crowd into some cities and shy away from others.

The future of the ghetto within the city may well be as complex a problem as the future of the city itself. Jane Jacobs has reported that the slum ghetto is as much an organized way of life for its residents as is the suburb.[30] In some cases attempts at urban renewal may break down the cohesiveness and "sense of community" that separate the ghetto from the total culture of the city. Even though life in this part of the city may look bleak to the outside observer, it may well be meaningful and important to the inhabitant. Ghetto dwellers often resist the relocation programs that sometimes accompany urban-renewal projects because these programs destroy a way of life that is familiar.

Stanley Milgram concludes that people respond adaptively to the city and its patterns.[31] If this is the case, we may assume that such an adaptation might occur in such specialized areas of the metropolis as the ghetto and suburbia. These characteristics only complicate the matter of trying to understand the future of the city.

SUMMARY   Although the city is relatively new in the history of man, it has gone through a number of interesting transformations. The ancient

[30]Jane Jacobs, *The Death and Life of Great American Cities*, Random House, Inc., New York, 1961.
[31] Stanley Milgram, "The Experience of Living in Cities," *Science*, vol. 167, no. 3924, March, 1970, pp. 1461–1468.

cities were independent entities which sometimes became centers of empires. Medieval cities also attained a degree of independence but usually encountered many of the same problems faced by the modern metropolis. The modern city is industrialized, larger in scope, and more involved in the economy and polity of the larger society.

Cities and population generally have been mutually dependent upon one another. Some cities have expanded, incorporating more territory and larger populations. Megalopolis now represents hundreds of cities and tens of millions of people merged together on the Northeast coast of the United States. Under such conditions, problems of air and water pollution (among others) are magnified.

In a sociological sense, ecology refers to the relationship of man to his social environment. In an ecological sense, the history of man has been the history of progression from gemeinschaft (village community) to gesellschaft (closely represented by Megalopolis). As cities' influences began to spread beyond their geopolitical boundaries, populations had to be counted in units referred to as Standard Metropolitan Statistical Areas, and in 1960 two Standard Consolidated Areas were delineated by the Census Bureau.

The ghetto is part of a city's ecological pattern. It is a segregated area within a city whose inhabitants are largely confined to a single ethnic or racial category. Although the ghetto may be a "normal" development within cities, and ghetto life may be meaningful to its residents, it is generally viewed by outsiders as a substandard part of the city.

According to Simmel, the city has a dual effect on the mind of man, increasing his mental perception but interfering with emotional response. Whatever its faults, the city provides a mental freedom unknown in the small town.

Today the city faces many problems, and a number of proposals have been examined as possible solutions. Among them is a threefold proposal to create a national job pool, establish a national land policy, and institute a national migration policy. Despite the proposals, the problems remain with us, and the future of the city is unclear.

A man must be with his family to amount to anything with us. . . . In the white ways of doing things the family is not so important. The police and soldiers take care of protecting you, the courts give you justice, the post office carries messages for you, the school teaches you. Everything is taken care of, even your children if you die; but with us the family must do all of that.[1]

Pomo Indian quoted by permission of Burt Aginsky
"An Indian's Soliloquy"

ten

THE FAMILY IN THE MODERN WORLD

The sage Confucius spoke of the family as the foundation of the state. Comte said that the family, not the individual, should be thought of as the social unit for study in the developing science of society. Cooley called the family the first and most ideal example of primary groups, those groups that are a "nursery of human nature" and the creators of the finest sentiments known to man. Every politician running for office keeps up the family image with a smiling picture of himself, his wife, and his children. The family would seem to be the most secure of all institutions.

    Yet there is much concern about the family in modern society because of slowly rising divorce rates, the "generation gap," difficult children and harassed parents, and the gradual absorption of more family duties by the school and other institutions. Has something suddenly gone wrong in the "nursery of human nature," or have there always been problems?

[1] Burt Aginsky, "An Indian's Soliloquy," *American Journal of Sociology*, vol. 46, 1940, pp. 43–44.

In the midst of our troubles, do we sometimes look upon family life of older societies with a nostalgia that it does not entirely deserve?

CONTRASTING FAMILY TYPES   A comparative view of family types may help to answer this question. The types of families found in the world are interesting and greatly varied. Some are polygynous, with one man to several wives; a few are polyandrous, with one wife for several husbands. In a few cases marriage ties are of minimal importance, and the real care of the children is vested in the mother and her brother. This has been true of some of the Pueblo Indians of the Southwest and of the Nayars of the Malabar Coast of India. Sometimes the married couple moves to the man's village (*patrilocal residence*) and sometimes to the woman's village (*matrilocal residence*). Lineage is sometimes traced through the mother's line but more frequently through the father's line. All of these and many other variations are of interest and theoretical importance in the development of social systems but are of less importance for the present study than another underlying difference in family arrangements. Does the family include large numbers of relatives, held closely together by the kinship bond, or is it a small, isolated unit? How powerful an institution a family is depends to quite an extent upon the answer. Two contrasting family models will be described to illustrate the difference in structure and function and the consequent differences in the strength of the family organization.

The consanguineal family   The first family model, the one particularly typical of China in the days before the Communist Revolution, consists of a large number of kinsmen living under one roof or in close proximity to one another—often the grandparents, their sons, their sons' wives and children, and even their sons' children's children. The word "consanguineal" is applied to this type of family, meaning literally "of one blood," but in this case applied only to relatives of the father's line. There is a strong allegiance to the family elders, and even deceased ancestors are held in high respect. Rules of status and etiquette make the family a well-regulated system in which each member knows his proper place. The family as an entity is far more important than the individual; consequently marriages are usually arranged by "wise old parents" rather than depending on the whims of young lovers. Males are dominant, and the young bride is responsible to her husband and his parents. A famous statement in the writings of the ancient Chinese philosopher Mencius gives an interesting idea of the length to which female inequality was carried:

It does not belong to a woman to determine anything
of herself, but she is subject to the rule of the
three obediences. When young she has to obey her
parents; when married she has to obey her husband;
when a widow she has to obey her son.[2]

The basic link in the consanguineal family is between father and son, and it takes precedence over the husband-wife bond. This family has an eternal quality about it: members die but are replaced by other members, and the family as an entity goes on forever. There is a well-defined division of labor between man and woman. Although the formal rules give the advantage to men, women often gain status and prestige with the passing of years. The young are subordinated to the old so that the family has a conservative, unchanging character about it. This family is well adapted to an agricultural society where tradition is strong and change is slow and where all members must work together to survive. It gives a sense of belonging and security although the individual must subordinate his desires to the good of the family group. Even before the Communist Revolution the old type of family was gradually changing, especially in the urban parts of China under the impact of modern technology.[3] In rural areas, family structure is still strong.

The nuclear family   The opposite type of family can be called the *nuclear* or *conjugal family*, consisting of a married couple and their children. This family is fairly well separated from other relatives, visiting only occasionally if at all. "Conjugal" refers to the marriage tie, and "nuclear" means that the family includes no outside relatives. The basic unit is that of a husband and wife who have married for love, with or without the approval of anyone else, often on short acquaintance. As parents, the man and wife do not have the secure feeling that goes with well-defined status and role, but they read the current literature on care of children and try to remember what they have learned in their psychology classes. They have their moments of doubt but congratulate themselves on being modern, democratic, and unrepressive. Above all, individual happiness is the goal, and neither parents nor children must be too greatly subordinated to the good of the whole. Husband and wife are equal and have the right to equal gratification in marriage; otherwise it is not worthwhile. This family can be thought of as a temporary entity, coming into being at the time of marriage, and ending with the death of the last marriage

[2] Will Durant, *Our Oriental Heritage, Story of Civilization*, vol. I, Simon & Schuster, Inc., New York, 1954, p. 683.
[3] Ch'ing-k'un Yang, *The Chinese Family in the Communist Revolution*, The M.I.T. Press, Cambridge, Mass., 1959. For description of consanguineal family, see also Francis L. K. Hsu, *Under the Ancestors' Shadow: Chinese Culture and Personality*, Columbia University Press, New York, 1948. See also David Mace and Vera Mace, *Marriage East and West*, Doubleday & Company, Inc., New York, 1959.

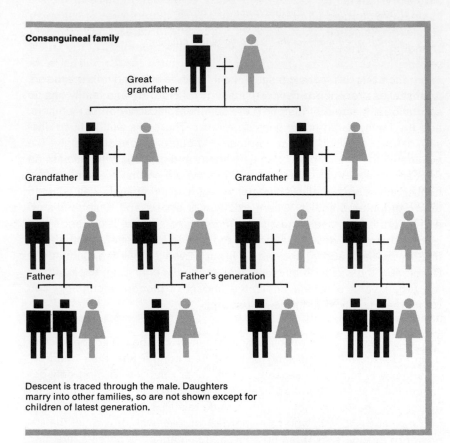

Consanguineal family

Great grandfather

Grandfather

Grandfather

Father

Father's generation

Descent is traced through the male. Daughters marry into other families, so are not shown except for children of latest generation.

Nuclear family

partner. Whatever its problems, it tends to free the individual for the competitive struggle of modern society with its requirement of changing places of residence, pursuit of education and a career, and constant changing of acquaintances and associates. Although many of the family sentiments remain, this type of institution is much less familistic in its orientation than the consanguineal family. The American family presented is most typical of suburban middle class, but American families in general approximate this model more than the consanguineal model.

THE CHANGING FUNCTIONS OF THE FAMILY The consanguineal family is, obviously, the type of family with the largest number of functions, sometimes being almost a government and social-security system of its own. In modern societies families have tended to lose some of their traditional functions as other social institutions grow in importance. The family functions that show sufficient change to require discussion are sexual regulation and procreation, status ascription, economic interdependence, education, recreation, and care of the aged.

Sex regulation and procreation At first glance the functions of sex regulation and procreation might seem to be constants in a society. All societies impose certain restraints on sex (an incest taboo as a bare minimum), although few have attempted to impose the absolute rule that no sexual relations can be tolerated outside of marriage. This puritanical standard has long been thought of as the ideal norm in America, although it has been violated by a large part of the male population. Violation of the sexual norms by many males, but only a few females, was once made possible by prostitution. In recent decades more women also have sexual relations outside of marriage, although usually with men they love and hope to marry. The change is gradual, however, and not the sudden "sex revolution" played up in the popular press. A collection of statistical surveys, in spite of a few inconsistencies, generally indicates the gradual nature of the change in sexual behavior.[4] A poll of college students in late 1969 found 61 percent of the men and 35 percent of the women students reporting premarital or extramarital relations.[5] It is noteworthy that those majoring in business—in many respects a conservative group—rated highest in premarital affairs. Apparently political and sexual conservativism do not go hand in hand. The uneven rates reported by the two sexes indicate that at least a few of the women must have a permissive philosophy.

[4] Erwin O. Smigel and Rita Seiden, "Decline and Fall of the Double Standard," *The Annals of the American Academy of Political and Social Science*, vol. 376, March, 1968, pp. 7–17.
[5] "The New Mood on Campus," *Newsweek*, vol. 74, December, 1969, pp. 42–45.

Statistics on premarital relations do not imply that pressure for marriage has declined, but they do indicate that the romantic ideal of the "woman on the pedestal" has declined. Men and women are more nearly equal in sin as well as in politics. This so-called new morality is by no means universal, and its impact on marital success is not clear, but the point is that sexual relations are less restricted to marriage than in the past, and the modern family is less able to teach strict sexual norms to its children.

Procreation is still considered legitimate only within the context of marriage and family, but it is estimated that one-fourth of all brides are pregnant at the time of marriage.[6] This means that many couples start marriage with a child on the way, and this is only an extreme case of a very important trend regarding procreation, the tendency for nearly all children to be born while the parents are still young. In 1890 the average age of the father at the time of birth of his last child was 36; by 1959 the age was 27.9. For the mother the corresponding ages were 32 and 25.8 (see Table 10-1). Since life expectancy for the wife had increased by ten years in the same length of time, and for the husband by more than five years, the conclusion can be drawn that the responsibilities of parenthood occupy a small portion of the total lifetime of the family. Much of the work of the family is completed while the parents are still fairly youthful; the dependence of member on member does not last as long as it once did.

[6]"Middle-Class Litters," *Nation*, vol. 200, June 28, 1965, p. 687.

TABLE 10-1   Median age at first marriage, 1890–1967

Year	Male	Female
1890	26.1	22.0
1920	24.6	21.2
1930	24.3	21.3
1940	24.3	21.5
1950	22.9	20.3
1955	22.6	20.2
1960	22.8	20.3
1965	22.8	20.6
1967	23.1	20.6

Source: U.S. Dept. of Commerce, Bureau of the Census, *Statistical Abstract of the United States*, 1968, p. 61.

Family status   Looking next at the concept of *ascribed status*, it can be shown that awareness of family status is less acute than in the past. Admittedly, the family still tries to give the children all the advantages it can (in this respect it is one of our antiequalitarian institutions), and in the case of "old money" families, these advantages are very considerable and persistent. For the average middle-class family, there is a strong contrast. Formerly, such a family lived in a small town and was well known by reputation. Everyone knew about the Van Bluebloods in their mansion and about the Joads in their shack. Family status persisted. Now, on the other hand, the children of each family go to a large, anonymous school in a big, anonymous city and will eventually hold positions working for an equally anonymous corporation. Also, the achieved status of the individual is no longer expected to be that of his parents. In the days of an agricultural society occupations were much more apt to be inherited than they are now. All of these changes weaken the family's ability to give the children a permanent ascribed status.

Economic change   By far the most important area of function loss for family is in the field of economics. This applies to economic interdependence of family members and to family cooperation in economic production. The eminent French anthropologist Claude Lévi-Strauss[7] provides an interesting insight into the first of these economic factors in family. He concludes that the institution of marriage is most compulsive in a society in which the division of labor between men and women is clear cut and absolute so that the single or divorced person finds existence almost unbearable. This, he goes on to say, is much more important than sexual attraction in many societies where extramarital relations are easily tolerated. Shaw's famous witticism that the popularity of marriage derives from its combining the maximum temptation with the maximum opportunity hardly applies in such cases. The dependence of man and woman on each other for survival does apply. In the Western societies of today, with women achieving greater and greater economic equality and independence, this reason for remaining married is far less compelling than in the past.

The other economic change, which is even more important, is in the role of the family as a unit. Once the average family was a collective enterprise, running a farm, blacksmith shop, grocery store, or other small business. Boys learned their occupational roles from their fathers and girls from their mothers. Children were in constant contact with the

[7] Claude Levi-Strauss, "The Family," in Harry Shapiro (ed.), *Man, Culture, and Society*, Oxford University Press, New York, 1960, pp. 261–285.

parents, absorbing their knowledge, their views, their mores, and also their old wives' tales, superstitions, and prejudices. Now children spend far more time at school, and the father has a job that keeps him away from home. The family no longer earns its living together—a strongly integrative function—but is more inclined to compete in the spending of the income, a somewhat divisive function.

Education, recreation, and protection   Education and recreation remain, to some degree, family functions. Certainly the family is concerned with them, but family members learn different specialties in school. The teaching changes with each generation, and increasingly, the methods and content of education are thought of as the business of the school. Since families are extremely uneven in their ability to give mental stimulation to young children, there are increasing attempts to get children from slum homes into preschool programs to give them a better start in life. For many other families, including the affluent middle class, there is a slow trend toward more nursery schools to ease the burden of child care for working mothers. Even the old family function of discipline is, to a great degree, turned over to the school. The family carries on certain recreational activities together, especially when the children are young, but commercialized facilities now make an age grading of recreation more and more possible, with family members going their own separate ways.

The family role of protection and care for the aged has almost disappeared. Social security and welfare services represent institutional efforts to care for the aged in other ways, and private enterprise is now opening beautiful retirement communities for those aged who are sufficiently affluent to afford them. Convalescent homes are a booming business, providing for the less affluent and for the senile among the elderly, but often are poorly run and provide only minimal custodial care. Despite much sentimentality over such institutions as Mothers' Day, the aged, as a class, tend to be poor and increasingly separated from the main currents of life.

Shortcomings of families of the past   Lest the above description sound like nostalgia for the past, it should be pointed out that there were also strains in older types of families. Dire economic necessity undoubtedly forced many women to tolerate mistreatment. Children were often thought of as an economic investment and were overworked. Many times families were rendered miserable taking care of ancient, tyrannical grandparents. We shall examine various possibilities for evaluating changes in family function; the main point until now is that the changes have had the cumulative effect of making the family an institution with fewer functions

The old farm family

The modern urban family

Procreation: many children, long period of childbearing	Procreation: few children, planned, close together in age
Status: strong community awareness of ascribed status	Status: less awareness of family status
Livelihood: all share in family work at home	Livelihood: father works away from home, often mother does too
Education: largely a family function	Education: specialized task of the school
Recreation: largely a family function	Recreation: specialized and commercialized
Care of aged: family responsibility	Care of aged: public responsibility

than it had once and not as strongly compelled by economic or other necessity to remain together.

INTERPRETING CHANGES IN THE FAMILY   The family, once an institution that asserted its primary position in many of the basic tasks of society, now is more limited. It still has the important roles of early socialization into societal customs and values and of providing companionship, affection, and psychological security. However, when people express a desire to "put father back at the helm," or to return to "the good old days," they fail to realize the necessity for a correspondence between family type and societal need. The young must be prepared for the world of today and tomorrow, not for the "good old days." The family must produce children capable of adjusting to a rapidly changing society. Does the modern family accomplish this task?

Optimistic interpretations of the modern family   The most encouraging interpretations of the modern American family are from those that see it in terms of adaptive transformation to meet societal and individual needs.

A famous essay by Talcott Parsons[8] analyzes the family in terms of function and concludes that the middle-class American family is precisely the kind of family required by an urban, mobile society. The individual is freed from most kinship responsibilities, creates his own achieved status, and is free to form his associations among his status equals. Parents do not stand in the way of children if their best opportunities lie in moving away to a distant city, and hopefully a personality type is created by the new family that makes the continuous adjustment to new places, people, and circumstances relatively easy. Davis expresses a similar view, seeing the reasons for change in the family as basically economic and generally functional to the society. " . . . it (the family) achieves more companionship and democracy than its predecessor. On the whole it is far better than the patriarchal mode of peasant-agricultural countries, far better than the *mariage de convenance* [literally "marriage of convenience," but actually meaning an economically wise marriage] of the European upper classes. . . . "[9] Both Parsons and Davis look upon occasional break-up of marriage and some isolation in old age as simply the price that must be paid for an individual-oriented family in a society placing a high value on freedom and individual happiness. No family system can combine the best of all possibilities.

A pessimistic evaluation   Not all sociologists are as sanguine as Parsons and Davis about the family. Arnold Green, in his essay "Why Americans Feel Insecure,"[10] pictures an upwardly mobile middle-class family in which parental attitudes toward the children are strongly ambivalent. Children get in the way of parental career ambitions and hedonistic enjoyment of life. A decline in respect for parental status makes the children harder to manage, resulting in the use of love and the threatened withdrawal of love as weapons of control. The threat of love withdrawal, plus many conflicting expectations on the part of parents and society, make for neurotic tendencies in many. Criticisms of this type appear often in sociological and psychological literature as well as in popular magazines. They may help to explain the phenomenon called *generation gap*, but changes in family roles undoubtedly also contribute to the gap.

Changing roles of family members: children and mothers   Such terms as "matriarchal" (mother rule) and "filiocentric" (child centered) have been

[8] Talcott Parsons, "The Social Structure of the Family," in Ruth S. Cavan (ed.), *The Family: Its Function and Destiny*, Harper & Row, Publishers, Incorporated, New York, 1959, pp. 241–274.
[9] Kingsley Davis, "The American Family, What It Is and Isn't," *New York Times Magazine*, September 30, 1951, pp. 18, 41–42.
[10] Arnold W. Green, "Why Americans Feel Insecure," *Commentary*, vol. 6, July, 1948, pp. 18–28.

used to describe the present American family. The implication is that father has lost much of his role and that "mom" reigns supreme or that the children have taken over. Before making too many hasty judgments about the sudden emergence of dominant wives and uncontrollable children, however, it is well to recall that folk literature is full of tales of nagging wives and undutiful sons. What was really the typical situation in the American past? Furstenberg has researched this question historically with a study of large numbers of commentators on American society of the period 1800 to 1850. For those who blame Dr. Spock for the permissive pattern of rearing our children today, there is a rude shock. "The most significant observation about American children was the permissive child-rearing patterns that were apparently widespread at this time." [11] One of the observers he cites (Harriet Martineau) comments on the connection between this pattern and preparation for democracy:

> Freedom of manners of children of which so much
> complaint has been made by observers . . . is a
> necessary fact. Till the American states cease to
> be republican the children there will continue as
> free and easy and as important as they are. [12]

Just how permissive the people of earlier America were, compared with today, is a little harder to assess, but it is significant that our ancestors also were seen as permissive parents. Such cultural patterns usually develop over a long period.

On the subject of woman's role, Furstenberg's studies tend to bear out the popular view of its gradual growth and increasing complexity. Foreign observers of the early eighteenth century expressed surprise that the married woman was so severely restricted by home duties. After marriage her freedom was gone; she was "laid on a shelf," as a woman of the time stated the matter, although in many ways she was treated with great politeness and respect.

What seems to be true now is more or less the opposite. The modern woman might complain that chivalry is gone, but she certainly cannot complain of being put away on a shelf, out of sight of the social world. Today over half the married women work outside the home for at least part of their married years, and the family is interested in educating girls as well as boys for a job. Pay and opportunities for promotion are grossly unequal for women, however, and are becoming the focus of a new women's rights movement. Woman's social participation has increased greatly, however, and the "right" type of marriage is a companionate

[11] Frank F. Furstenberg, Jr., "Industrialization and the American Family," *American Sociological Review*, vol. 31, June, 1966, pp. 326–337.
[12] *Ibid.*, p. 332.

type. Woman has gained status, but her role is a more complicated one than formerly.

Problems of the male ego   An important consideration of the woman's role is how it interacts with those of other members of the family. Spindler did a study that compared American and German servicemen in the World War II period. He attributed the contrast partially to the difference between the male-dominated German family and the American family with "matriarchal tendencies." Besides the German's greater respect for orderliness and authority, there were well-marked ways to show manliness—harsh discipline and physical strength, "an iron heart in an iron body." These measurements of manhood were not stressed by the American, and his respect for order was much weaker. That he should emphasize freedom and individual initiative was a reflection of many of the values of his culture. Spindler attributes the contrast between the German male-dominated family and the American family mainly to the contrast in ways of expressing manliness. The American was more likely to show insubordinate attitudes and "tough-guy" aggressiveness, use foul language, and boast about sex exploits. The "hard-guy" image is attributed by Spindler to the attempt to rescue the male ego from too much early dominance by the mother.[13] Whether Spindler is correct or not in his analysis of consequences of the mother-dominated family, it would be unfair to assume that some mothers have taken a dominant role through intent. If their family roles have become dominant, it has often become so largely through default.

The father's role   The role of the father has changed as a result of changing job requirements. For several generations more and more fathers have worked away from home; now the pattern is almost universal. This fact has left more of the responsibility of the children and their disciplining to the mother. Ideally, the father should be in a position to set a role-model in more ways than merely as breadwinner. A good relationship between father and daughter is closely connected with later marital happiness for the daughter. For the son, a good relationship with the father helps the learning of proper masculine roles. This task is rendered difficult when television and motion-picture stories show true masculinity as gunning down badmen or bombing enemy cities, while the father is quietly at work as a bank teller. The Wild West definition of masculinity is not in keeping with the current period of cultural development and is consequently dysfunctional. Another problem is that too many jobs of the adult world have no appeal for growing boys. This creates many

[13]George D. Spindler, "American Character as Revealed in the Military," *Psychiatry*, vol. 11, August, 1948, pp. 275–281.

problems for youth and is a major theme of Paul Goodman's book *Growing Up Absurd*. Many fathers find it easier to relate to their sons through the athletic and recreational worlds than through the world of work or intellectual training. Youth advisors would certainly agree that this situation is better than having no common interests whatever and that anything that keeps communications open between parents and offspring is helpful, but is it a little too superficial? The disillusioned youths of today, often coming from families of high socioeducational background, make it seem that something of the kind is amiss. Are fathers and mothers able to convey the kind of message that will make the future of the family secure?

Children and the family future   As previously stated, children do not have the role in the economic maintenance of the family that they once had, except occasionally in the impoverished family. They are not needed for tilling the soil, clearing land, or taking care of their parents in their old age. It is in this respect that the family depends more upon affection for its center of being and is closer to the norms of today than many older families would have been. In the typical middle-class family there are from two to four children, they have been wanted and planned for, and there is no intent to exploit them economically. The family has a vested interest in its children, nevertheless, wanting them to be a credit to the family, maintain its status, save the parents from a lonely old age, and possibly even fulfill the dreams that the parents were not able to fulfill. Are the family and other institutions of society socializing the children in a way that will permit them to fulfill this future?

Many writers have dealt with the problem of new socialization patterns for children. Martha Wolfenstein writes about the "fun morality" that requires making fun out of all the duties of parenthood so that infants and children will be joyous and unfettered by guilt feelings.[14] She sees that the attempt at merging work and fun results in diffused impulses and insufficient drive. Riesman wrote in a similar vein, seeing the emerging other-directed personality as a type with less drive and less courage of his convictions than the older inner-directed type. Years ago Parsons wrote an analysis of the role of youth, especially high-school youth, as primarily an irresponsible one, in no way preparing practically for later duties in society.[15] Goodman perceives the position of youth as one that is ignored and not taken seriously by society and one that has especially ominous problems for the young man who is not academically gifted.

[14] Martha Wolfenstein, "The Emergence of the Fun Morality," *Journal of Social Issues*, vol. 7, no. 4, 1951, pp. 15–25.
[15] Talcott Parsons, "Age and Sex in the Social Structure of the United States," *American Sociological Review*, vol. 7, no. 5, 1942, pp. 604–614.

What worthwhile occupation beckons him? What hope does he have? Goodman sees youth as envied, advertised, and glamorized but not assigned an important role or even treated as though an important role is possible.

One can still question whether any of these studies really demonstrates that youth is not, in the long run, preparing for societal roles and for family roles. In a marital system based on free choice, dating and popularity pursuits in high school (part of the "irresponsible" role) might be precisely the right preparation. In a society calling for more white-collar workers and professionals than businessmen of an aggressive type, the other-directed pattern might be fairly satisfactory. Miller and Swanson did a study of two Detroit family types that they refer to as *entrepreneurial* and *bureaucratic* families. The older entrepreneurial family conditions children to enter the competitive world of business, emphasizing the old virtues of independence, thrift, and an aggressive approach to life. This type of family is still in evidence but on the wane. The bureaucratic family (so called because it equips a person to take a position in a bureaucracy), the growing type, tends to stress getting along with others, but places less emphasis on independence, thrift, and business values.[16] Whether one grieves over the decline of the entrepreneurial family or not is a matter of values, but a functional interpretation of culture would maintain that family training is functioning to create the personality type needed for saleswork, meeting the public, and fitting into the organization.

Independence training   The foregoing discussion seems to imply an indoctrination into either a pattern of bureaucratic conformity or of entrepreneurial success-striving. Actually many young people seem to turn their backs on the entrepreneurial values and to resist bureaucratic conformity as well. The separation between generations seems to be wider today than previously, but youth's search for independence is, in many ways, a familiar story. A restricted conjugal-family system must allow youth to achieve a measure of independence from the family home. Such freedom, to a degree, is acceptable to parents, but a distinction must be made between sponsored and unsponsored independence.[17] If young people are trained to take care of their own money, hold part-time jobs, assume the care and maintenance of their cars, and so forth, they are attaining an independence sponsored by their parents. If they run off from home to join a hippy commune, they are asserting an unsponsored independence. The type of relationship that exists between

[16]Daniel R. Miller and Guy E. Swanson, *The Changing American Parent*, John Wiley & Sons, Inc., New York, 1958.
[17]Bernard Farber, *Family: Organization and Interaction*, Chandler Publishing Company, San Francisco, 1964.

generations will help to determine which kind of independence is followed.

There is a strong correlation between social-class position and the training of children for independence. Bernard Farber says of the social-class contrast:

> Ordinarily, for middle-class children, independence
> from the family has the meaning of maturing into
> adulthood while for lower-class children independence
> from the family means deviance from conventional
> standards through committing delinquent acts.[18]

The lower-class family pattern aims more at trying to enforce obedience to rules than at training for sponsored independence. Ethnic background, too, shows considerable influence on the independence-training pattern. Bernard Rosen[19] made a study of independence and achievement training among several ethnic groups in a New England community. He concluded that Jewish and Greek families stressed achievement and independence training more strongly than the other groups in the study: Italian, French Canadian, and Negro. He sees this difference as part of the reason for the more rapid achievement of middle-class status by the former two groups.

FAMILY STABILITY   It would seem reasonable to suppose that the family that performs a large number of functions and exists in a society that is strongly kinship oriented would tend to have considerable marital stability. Yang and Hsu describe the old Chinese family as having these characteristics and as being a family system in which divorce was very uncommon. The fact that marriage was arranged rather than carried out on a basis of free choice would seem to the Westerner to spell less marital happiness, but Yang concludes that marriage was, generally, at least as happy as in the West.[20] There was a tendency for people to marry and then fall in love; here people fall in love and then marry.

Western romantic expectation   Western marriage places a high premium on romance, which does not always result in permanence of attachment. The lyrics to such songs as "Some Enchanted Evening," implying eternal attachment at a moment's glance, make beautiful poetry but constitute an unrealistic basis for marriage. The sudden glow of passion and marriage based on short acquaintance undoubtedly help to explain why our highest divorce rate to date came immediately after World War II when many wartime romances proved not to have the necessary stability.

---

[18] Ibid., p. 370.
[19] Bernard Rosen, "Race, Ethnicity, and the Achievement Syndrome," American Sociological Review, vol. 24, February, 1959, pp. 47–60.
[20] Yang, op. cit.

Success factors in marriage   Since the American marriage system is not strongly bolstered by economic necessity, and since law and public opinion more readily accept divorce, the road to marital stability would seem to lie in the careful selection of compatible mates. As a matter of fact, love is not entirely blind. A large percentage of dates are between people of the same social class, and a large majority of marriages link people of the same social class, same locality, same race, and same religion.[21] Similarities of background, interests, and values are stressed in college courses in family and marriage as predictive of marriage success, as are long acquaintance and sufficient maturity. The idea of complementary needs also comes into many discussions of marital happiness. A dominant, assertive male is happier if married to a submissive female; and occasionally the very opposite works out fairly well. Two strongly assertive personalities, on the other hand, can easily run into trouble.

Divorce rates   In all Western countries the divorce rate has tended to rise in recent decades, but at present the rate is higher in the United States than in any part of Europe.[22] Although it is perfectly true that this rate is partly a reflection of our values of independence and the right to the pursuit of happiness, a high divorce rate creates many problems. The decision to break a marriage is an unhappy one for the marriage partners, often damaging to self-concept and to relationships with old friends of the married couple. In recent years a majority of divorces have occurred in families with children.[23] The shock of divorce is severe for most children, although the problem of living in a family devoid of love is often more severe. One study found that those children who expected a divorce because of the quarrelsomeness of their parents sometimes felt a sense of relief when the break finally came.[24] However, there was always shock, there were attempts to hide the event from friends, and there was a lowering of self-confidence for the children of divorce, especially in their relationships with members of the opposite sex.

Stability and social class   One factor that is positively correlated with marital stability is social class, as mentioned in Chapter 1. Proneness-to-divorce tables show that laborers are about three times as likely to divorce as professional persons, and that the higher the income the less

[21] William J. Goode, *The Family*, Prentice-Hall, Inc., Englewood Cliffs, N.J., 1964, pp. 33–35.
[22] *Ibid.*, p. 96.
[23] Murray Gendell and Hans L. Zetterberg, *A Sociological Almanac for the United States*, Bedminster Press, New York, 1964, p. 47.
[24] Jack Harrison Pollack, "Are Children of Divorce Different?", in Judson R. Landis (ed.), *Current Perspectives on Social Problems*, Wadsworth Publishing Company, Inc., Belmont, Calif., 1966, pp. 190–193.

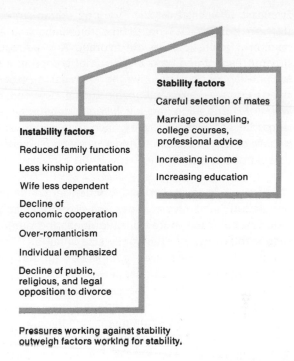

Instability factors

Reduced family functions

Less kinship orientation

Wife less dependent

Decline of
economic cooperation

Over-romanticism

Individual emphasized

Decline of public,
religious, and legal
opposition to divorce

Stability factors

Careful selection of mates

Marriage counseling,
college courses,
professional advice

Increasing income

Increasing education

Pressures working against stability
outweigh factors working for stability.

likely the couple is to seek divorce.[25] Since larger numbers of people are achieving professional and semiprofessional positions, it would seem that the divorce rate might eventually decline. However, the undermining factors already mentioned—less economic need to stay together, emphasis on the individual's rights, and more permissive attitudes in law and public opinion—seem to more than offset this possibility (see Table 10-2).

FAMILY VARIABILITY   Much of what has been said about the American family has been based largely on studies of middle-class families of white Anglo-Saxon Protestant (WASP) descent. Catholic divorce rates are lower than Protestant rates, largely because of the strong opposition of the church to divorce, but inclusion of statistics on separation without divorce tends to lessen the total Catholic-Protestant difference.

[25] See Chapter 1, p. 11 of this text.

Americans of Oriental descent   Various ethnic groups show considerable difference in family type. Chinese and Japanese Americans continue to be more familistic than the average Anglo-American. Parents receive greater respect and have more authority than in most American families, but the family does not give the impression of being ruled with an iron hand. Usually easy relationships exist between parents and children, with little generation gap, low juvenile-delinquency rates, and low divorce rates. Recent years, however, have seen a marked change in the familial pattern of San Francisco's Chinatown where juvenile rebellion is emerging as a serious problem.

The Mexican American family   A much larger segment of the American population is of Mexican descent. The Mexican American family also tends to be much more consanguineal and patriarchal than the Anglo-American family, and the family size is larger.[26] Ties to more distant kin are maintained, and even *compadres* (godfathers) remain important. The father is a rather august person whose wishes are followed, but the direct responsibility for the children is in the mother's hands. Since "father always knows best," independence training is not emphasized. Although the children might quarrel among themselves, adults are treated with respect and good manners. This makes Mexican American children quite acceptable to their teachers, in some respects, but at the same time

[26]Celia S. Heller, *Mexican-American Youth*, Random House, Inc., New York, 1966.

TABLE 10-2   Marriage and divorce rates per thousand population

Year	Marriage	Divorce
1910	10.3	0.9
1915	10.0	1.0
1920	12.0	1.6
1925	10.3	1.5
1930	9.2	1.6
1935	10.4	1.7
1940	12.1	2.0
1945	12.2	3.5
1950	11.1	2.6
1955	9.3	2.3
1960	8.5	2.2
1965	9.2	2.5
1967	9.7	2.7

Source: U.S. Dept. of Commerce, Bureau of the Census, *Statistical Abstract of the United States*, 1968, p. 47.

there is a tendency for the family to preserve old traditions that lessen achievement drive. The school is not always thought of as a friendly road to upward mobility. If the family is still close to Mexico in its customs, elder brothers insist on a protective role toward their sisters, who are expected to be pure and chaste, although the same young men may boast of their own sexual exploits; the "double standard" is still strong.

Naturally, this description does not fit all Mexican American families. The very term "Mexican American" is a little vague. Some people of Mexican ancestry have preserved their older culture with little change, and others are much closer to the Anglo-American culture. In the latter case, women are more nearly equal to their husbands in status, and brothers lose most of their superior role relative to their sisters. The family is also more apt to look upon the school as the proper road to the future.

Black American family types   The Negro family can hardly be described as one type, because the middle-class black family closely resembles the middle-class white family. There are many lower-class black families, on the other hand, that still bear resemblance to the Negro families of slavery days. The prominent Negro sociologist E. Franklin Frazier views the origin of a mother-centered family among the poor of his people as a legacy of slave days when a man was unable to remain with his family, and marital ties for field hands were discouraged. Even today there are economic factors helping to maintain a woman-centered family; often in the impoverished neighborhoods the woman is more employable than the man. The Moynihan Report[27] not only finds urban nonwhite unemployment to be twice as high as that for whites, but higher for men than for women. Nearly one-fourth of the births in the black ghetto are illegitimate. Many children of the urban ghetto are reared without fathers, a serious psychological problem for growing boys. A recent study contradicts the fairly widespread idea that many Negro boys have difficulty with masculine identity because of an absence of fathers. The conclusion is that a definite type of male-role model is always present in the persons of more-or-less steady boyfriends. A male role is observed and learned, but not the conventional middle-class one, and not one that makes for success by middle-class standards.[28] Recent black militants have been aware of the need for a more responsible type of male image. The Muslims have been especially insistent on a respectable and dominant male role.

Even in the middle-class black family there is evidence that the role of the woman, on the average, contrasts with that of the white family.

[27] Lee Rainwater and William L. Yancey, *The Moynihan Report and the Politics of Controversy*, The M.I.T. Press, Cambridge, Mass., 1967, pp. 51–58.
[28] Ulf Hannerz, "Roots of Black Manhood," *Transaction*, vol. 16, October, 1969, pp. 12–21.

In 1960, 53 percent of the nonwhites who had graduated from college were women, compared to only 39 percent of women among all college graduates.[29] A change may be coming; by 1963 men slightly outnumbered women among nonwhite college students, and by 1965 there were more men than women graduates. There is no indication of a corresponding change away from the matricentric family among the poor, however. In 1970 the Census Bureau reported that the number of poor black families headed by women had increased by one-third in the 1960s.[30]

These are only a few of the varieties that can be found in American family types. There are also distinctions between rich and poor, between rural-farm families and urban families, between foreign-born and native-born, and between the average American family and the family of such tightly structured religious communities as the Amish. The attempt here has been to describe the dominant type of American family and its problems and to give one or two examples of numerically important subcultural types. All of these family types have their special problems, and all have the common problem of adjustment to an increasingly mobile, urban-industrial society.

SUMMARY Although the family is regarded as a virtually sacred institution, there is considerable worry about its future. The modern family is often compared unfavorably with that of the past, probably partially because of a tendency to idealize the past.

Comparisons of family types show that they must fit the requirements of the societies in which they are found. A contrast between the ancient Oriental family and the modern American family points out the strengths and weaknesses of two of the world's most frequently found family types. The Oriental family has greater permanence and status security; the modern American family provides greater independence for its members. The two types of family are basically adapted to different types of societies.

An analysis of the functions of the family shows that many traditional functions have undergone change. Sex relations have never been as strictly limited to matrimony as the Puritan ethic would imply, and norms have gradually grown more permissive. More fundamental in its impact on family relations is the change in economic functions of the family. Since the family farm and other family businesses have virtually disappeared, the family is no longer an organization with the highly integrative task of cooperating for its economic subsistence. The result is that the young learn less of their adult roles from parents than in the

29 Rainwater and Yancey, *op. cit.*, p. 77.
30 "Poor Families Headed by Negro Women Rise," *Los Angeles Times*, January 10, 1970, part I, p. 14.

past, absorbing less of their information and, probably, less of their misinformation. Status is still provided by the family, but there is less general awareness of family status in urban life than in the older, rural life. Education, recreation, and care of the aged have become more specialized tasks, with less family involvement.

In interpreting the changes in family, it is not to be concluded that they are "bad" or "good," but rather that they are adaptations to a changing way of life. This point of view is stressed by Parsons and Davis. There are, of course, some authorities who argue that the new type of family develops special psychological strains. Green stresses this theme in his analysis of conflicting pressures in modern societies and families.

Other analyses of the effects of changing family type focus on the roles of family members. Historical evidence casts doubt on the common assumption that we are much more lenient with our children than were our ancestors. The role of the mother in the family relationship seems to have become more dominant, as seen by the children, because job requirements keep the father away from the children more of the time. There is some suggestion that the central position of the mother places a strain on the male ego of growing boys.

Studies of children and their socialization patterns have stressed such ideas as "fun morality" and "other-directedness," but these patterns are not entirely incompatible with many types of societal demands. A study of the bureaucratic family, for example, indicates that family-training patterns are changing to fit the requirements of people who will spend most of their lives working for corporations and who probably need other-directed personalities.

Over the last half century there has been a gradual increase in the divorce rate of Western countries, especially in the United States. The United States divorce rate reached its highest level immediately after World War II, then declined slightly, and remains fairly constant at present. Research in marital stability indicates that a similarity of interests and beliefs are closely associated with a successful marriage and that marital stability correlates positively with social-class position and education.

Although the discussion of family has tended to center on the white middle-class family, there are many variations in American families. Many Chinese and Japanese American families retain greater stability and familism than is common in most of the United States. The middle-class Negro family is similar to that of the middle-class white family, but the lower-class Negro family is strongly mother centered, often without a male head. The Mexican American family tends to be a little more male dominated than the average Anglo-Saxon American family. There are other variations in the American family pattern, but many of them are undergoing change to meet the requirements of urban-industrial society.

Comfort ye, comfort ye, O my people,
saith your God,
Speak ye comfortably unto Jerusalem. . . .
Isaiah 40: 1–2

Think not that I come to send peace on earth;
I come not to send peace but a sword.
Matthew 10:34

RELIGION IN SOCIETY

Cultures have come into existence in the company of their gods. Sometimes these gods bring comfort and serenity, and sometimes they fill the heart with terror. Sometimes they fire the imagination with dreams of worlds to conquer; sometimes they are themselves conquered, their temples broken, their statues defaced, and their people dispersed or enslaved. Usually the gods are unseen beings, but sometimes they exist in the flesh, as in the person of the ancient Egyptian pharaohs or as the frenzied leaders of more recent totalitarian states. Sometimes tensions exist between the high priests and the rulers of the state, but more frequently, the gods and their state live amicably together, coexistent and inseparable.

Perhaps this description of gods seems a mere flight of fancy in an age of secularization, when science seems to explain all, and when the types of gods described are fading from the consciousness of man. This will depend partly on how we look upon religion. In sociology we study religion mainly in terms of the functions it performs for society, for it is not within our competence (nor that of anyone) to evaluate and say whose religion is "best." We question whether the functions performed by the gods are still called for and whether they are still performed by the religions of today.

THE CONFLICTING FUNCTIONS OF RELIGION   The functions that religion accomplishes for society are often of opposing types. Seen in the short run, they seem contradictory; in the long range of history they may be complementary, the one supplying stability and the other providing for change. Religion generally supports the societal norms, reassuring the people that their ways are right and their cause is just; but at the same time the great religious prophets have all been critics of their societies. Religion tells us that man has an important place in the universe and that he is made in the image of God; it also emphasizes our insignificance in his awesome presence. Religion tells us that there is an ultimate justice in the divine will, yet it admonishes us to achieve that justice ourselves. Religion says, "Comfort ye, O my people," but for many it brings also anxiety and vexation of spirit. Research has shown that the strongly religious person rates higher in anxiety level than the less religious.[1] The religious leaders of society have generally taken a place in the social system just below that of the leaders of the state, high in prestige and position;[2] yet many religions have spoken out for the poor and humble. Finally, religion unites people into one great community of the faithful, but under some circumstances it has been one of society's most divisive forces, resorting to the pillory, the rack, and the stake in its zeal to stamp out heretics.

Religion as a unifying force   Recall that in the discussion of culture, evidence was presented to show that the primitive man tended to conceive of a divine order that bore a striking resemblance to his social order. This tendency relates closely to the function of religion as a unifying force and is what Durkheim had in mind in his statement, "Is it not, then, that God and society are the same thing?" Many religious skeptics have said that "man creates God in his own image"; Durkheim's view was that man creates God (or gods) in the image of his society. This definition of the sacred is part of the explanation of the social order—social class, laws, legitimate rule, ethnocentric attitudes toward one's own group, and the many folkways and mores. In support of Durkheim's view, it is interesting to note that historically many conquests have resulted in the destruction of the enemy gods, as when the idols of Baal were destroyed by the Israelites. Conquest of the enemy gods, apparently, meant conquest of the enemy people. At the very least, tremendously important "symbols of collective identity" were being destroyed.

What bearing does this have on religion today? Certainly modern man is much too sophisticated to create an ethnocentric God. Or is he?

[1] James A. Glynn, *An Investigation of the Relationship between Degree of Religiosity and Degree of Manifest Anxiety among Catholic College Students*, unpublished master's thesis, San Jose State College, San Jose, Calif., 1966.
[2] Kingsley Davis and Wilbert E. Moore, "Some Principles of Stratification," *American Sociological Review*, vol. 10, April, 1945, pp. 242–249.

When nation fights nation, each calls upon God for help. In wars between Christian nations each has called on precisely the same God, but have they not thought of God in ethnocentric terms, as a God more interested in their cause than in that of the enemy? The American said "In God we trust," and the German soldier had inscribed on his belt buckle "Gott mit uns" (God with us). In times of emergency there is still the tendency to call upon a deity. Even atheistic Russia had an increase in church attendance during World War II and a more tolerant attitude toward religion than had existed for many years. Some of Hitler's most fanatical followers even wanted to revive the old Nordic gods, but the general policy in Nazi days was simply to require ministers to take the "Aryan Oath." Hitler was seen as a messianic character. In countries with more conventional religious attitudes, more people prayed than before, and always with the expectation that God would listen to them and not to the enemy. In America great appeals were made to Catholics, Protestants, and Jews to attend religious services. A broadly tolerant attitude seemed to say "Regardless of which church you go to, you are worshipping a God that will aid our cause; He believes our way."

Will Herberg, in his book *Protestant, Catholic, Jew,* develops the same theme to describe recent American society. In his analysis, the religion underlying all the denominations is "the American way."[3]

A plausible argument is also sometimes made that some modern nations have created a new kind of god—a totalitarian state—defining man's place and his rules of conduct in terms of a new ideology. It would be possible to call such an ideology a religion only in a limited sense of the word, but many of the unifying functions of religion were present in the ideology of the Nazi state, and the same is true, to a great degree, of the Communist state. Drawing the analogy even further, a Communist hierarchy of secular saints can be named, especially Marx and Lenin (in China, Mao Tse-tung), and their writings have become a Communist equivalent to holy writ. Possibly the attitude analogous to religious fanaticism that has existed in Russia is now on the wane, but the fanaticism of China continues unabated. Some theorists believe that a loss of traditional ties, including traditional religion, in modern society helps to set the stage for the fiery political movements that are looking for new meanings and new gods. This is part of the explanation that Erich Fromm gives for the rise of Nazi Germany in his *Escape from Freedom.*

Religion as a divisive force   Religion becomes a divisive force in history when a society is faced with conflicting and mutually intolerant religions or conflicting and mutually intolerant interpretations of the same religion. Religion also has been divisive at other times, as when a new religion

[3] Will Herberg, *Protestant, Catholic, Jew,* Doubleday & Company, Inc., Garden City, N.Y., 1960, pp. 75–90.

began to spread in a society whose institutions and values were incompatible with its doctrines. The latter occurred when Christianity began to penetrate the Roman Empire and more recently when Christian missionaries introduced new ideas and practices into societies firmly rooted in different beliefs and values. Colin Turnbull, in *The Lonely African,* tells the story of the clash of religious beliefs and practices in a Congolese society and the disorientation of human lives in the process.

The clash between Christians and Moslems in the early days of Moslem penetration into the Circum-Mediterranean world is one of the best examples of societies being torn apart by two distinct and bitterly conflicting religions. Christendom saw the armies of Islam as armies of heathen darkness, trying to destroy all that was good in the world. Later, in the days of the Crusades, the Moslems saw the Christian armies in exactly the same light.

The results of the Protestant Reformation illustrate the divisiveness of conflicting interpretations of the same religion when the two interpretations are regarded as irreconcilable. Fear, wars, executions, and a witchcraft hysteria wracked Europe for centuries. The Thirty Years War depopulated parts of Central Europe as no other war has done, including the Napoleonic Wars or two world wars.

Religious controversy played an important part in early America. Many people migrated for religious liberty, but many were unwilling to grant such liberty to others. It was against this background that the doctrine of religious tolerance grew in the United States, with a fairly complete separation of church and state implicit in the First Amendment to the Constitution. In spite of the doctrine of separation of church and state, problems have arisen over religious rights. Court decisions have gradually eliminated many Sunday closing laws and other "blue laws," and the Supreme Court has handed down rulings that try to prevent religious indoctrination in the public schools. The Court feared that such practices would give preferential treatment to majority views and would tend to make outcasts of the children of non-Christian families. By such decisions, and by the gradual increase in religious tolerance, the problems of denominational divisiveness tend to recede. Probably the most important division remaining is the division between religious liberalism and religious conservativism, which, to some degree, cuts across denominational lines.

STABILITY AND REFORM   Religion has generally tended to act as a conservative force, preserving the social order in which it is found. Today the average American feels that a democratic way of life is implied in Christianity, but this was certainly not the view in the Middle Ages. Then the

Functions related to stability	Functions related to social change
Supporting the social order	Criticizing the social order
Institutional stability	Charismatic leadership and change
Comfort and reassurance	Anxiety and feelings of guilt
Uniting society	Dividing society
Promising divine justice	Demanding man-made justice
Reassuring the wealthy and prestigious	Providing hope for the poor and humble

highly structured social system was seen as the will of God; the doctrine of the divine right of kings emerged, generally gaining religious sanction. A good indication of this tendency to support the social order was the message of many southern ministers in the days of slavery, approving the institution, and even defending it on religious grounds. Two of the recent prime ministers of South Africa, strong supporters of *apartheid* (a doctrine of extreme racial segregation and unequal treatment), have been ministers of the Dutch Reformed Church. In addition, it should be pointed out that conservative points of view regarding morals, changes in fashion and entertainment, and new ideas from the world of science are all more closely associated with the religiously orthodox than with the less religious.

The radical criticism of religion   It is such examples of the conservative nature of religion that have led many liberals to be anticlerical and have made many radicals, most notably Marx, want to throw out the whole of religion. Marx's famous phrase "Religion is the opiate of the masses" implies that religion blinds people to their troubles and makes them ready to accept things as they are. The much less radical but strongly reformist British Prime Minister David Lloyd-George had the same feeling about some of the traditional ideas taught to him as a child, particularly the prayer:

> *God bless the squire and his relations*
> *And keep us in our proper stations.*

In America a radical labor unionist wrote in a marxian vein about religion:

There'll be pie by and by
In that sweet land beyond the sky;
Work and pray, live on hay;
You'll get pie in the sky
By and by when you die.

Religion as a reforming force   The radicals, however, are not the only people who sometimes show resentment against religion. Criticism also comes from the extremely conservative. Spencer had a strong distaste for religion because it usually preached doctrines that mitigated the philosophy of unbridled competition and struggle. In recent years the ultraconservative American writer Ayn Rand has expressed similar views about what she considers are the softening effects of religion. More frequently the conservative criticism is aimed at particular ministers whose activities are seen as "improper" rather than at religion as an institution, but it is clear that religion can draw the fire of the right wing as well as the left. A brief analysis will show why this is true.

Although the religion of a society tends to be linked to other parts of the social order, and hence to support them, the links are never perfect. Since religion upholds the idealized norms, and there is always a gap between idealized norms and actual practice, normative strains appear. The type of man to whom religion brings more anxiety than comfort is troubled by these imperfections and cries out against the evils of the system, as did the prophets of the Bible:

Woe unto them that decree unrighteous decrees . . .
to take away the right from the poor of my people,
that widows may be their prey, and that they may
rob the fatherless!
Isaiah X: 1–2

At times such voices seem to have been raised feebly or not at all. The wretchedness of the medieval peasant seems to have bothered few people of importance. Even Martin Luther, the reformist, was horrified by the peasant uprisings of his day and strongly supported the established political order. In his attempt to end corrupt practices within the church, however, he illustrates the reformist element of religion.

More recently, in spite of the fact that churches often condoned slavery, many ministers were counted in the ranks of the early abolitionists. Many became supporters of the suffragette movement or reform for conditions of labor for women and children, of prison reform, and of reform of mental institutions and orphanages. In recent years a small but dedicated minority of church leaders has been prominent in the civil rights movement; several have given their lives in the cause. Ministers working among the poverty-stricken migratory laborers and in rural and urban slums become highly critical of the unequal opportunities offered by society. Occasionally modern clergymen boldly take part in such unpopular causes as repeal of abortion laws and merciful treatment of drug offenders and homosexuals. Such activities represent only a small minority of religious leaders, but it is enough to illustrate that religion is not, in all its aspects, a conservative, self-righteous supporter of the existing order.

Religion is in a position to perform this function because it represents an important source of norms that, in the eyes of the believer, are stronger than those of the state, law, or tradition. When troubled times and normative strains occur, voices are raised for reform. These voices are by no means always those of religious leaders, and never do all religious leaders join in a reform movement; many remain placid and uninvolved. However, the issues of reform are raised often enough to make this one of the major functions of religion, complementing the function of support for the existing order. The marxian indictment is not always founded in reality; the ultraconservative often fears the inspired religious reformer as much as the radicals fear the religious establishment.

Although many laymen and nonbelievers take part in the same types of reforms, the religious man sometimes approaches the problem with greater zeal and conviction. Bertrand Russell, when he was a boy, met the British Prime Minister Gladstone, whom he described as the most frightening person he had ever met. Gladstone, said Lord Russell, was so full of religious certainty that he seemed always to be speaking with the voice of the Almighty. Many years later the same Lord Russell had the experience of meeting Nickolai Lenin. The same frightening righteousness beamed from the face of the godless radical as it had from the face of the proper and godly British liberal. The religious emotion is apparently the same whether the god is the well-known Jehovah or the pagan god called *dialectical materialism*.

CHARISMA TO INSTITUTION: THE DEVELOPMENT OF THE CHURCH   The word "charisma" denotes a characteristic of a person with strong personal magnetism who attracts devoted followers. To a limited degree the term "charismatic" can be applied to almost anyone with strong qualities of leadership, but by usage it is reserved for the dynamic, irresistible type of leader—the man who has an aura of magic about him, who can make men dream dreams of new worlds to come: the "earth shaker," the "mover of mountains." He comes as an innovator, unsupported by established institutions, but challenging the established order. The word originally referred to religious leaders, but since Max Weber's time, also includes leaders of political movements. As an "ideal type" the charismatic leader is the opposite of the bureaucrat; his power is personal, not institutional. He asks for the complete surrender of his followers to him: "Forsake all else and follow me." Zoroaster, Jesus, Mohammed, and Buddha are all early examples of charismatic leaders, but the term also applies to leaders of a very different type—Hitler, Fidel Castro, Lenin, Kemal Ataturk.

The church in adversity   Eric Hoffer describes the charismatic phase of a religious movement as one that tends to attract the wretched of the earth, the poor, the outcast, and the miserable, giving them cause for hope.[4] "Great is your reward in Heaven" is an exciting promise to those who have known only poverty and oppression. Actually, not all religious movements have started among the poverty-stricken; those of Luther, Calvin, Cromwell, and Henry VIII were among the rich. Nor have new religions in areas outside the Christian world necessarily won their first converts among the poor; but early Christianity and many recent sectarian movements have been of the type Hoffer describes.

Because the message of early Christianity was to the poor and lowly, it is small wonder that it was among such people that the faith spread rapidly throughout the Roman world, coming to be looked upon as a subversive force, not just by such insane tyrants as Nero and Caligula, but by such able emperors as Marcus Aurelius and Diocletian. During the reigns of many Roman emperors life was precarious for the Christians, and only the true believer dared stand up for his cause. Gradually the church triumphed, the pagan gods of Rome were overcome, Constantine embraced Christianity, and the time came when it was unsafe not to be a Christian. Julian "Apostate" made a last futile attempt to stem the new order and restore the "ancient virtues," but the old Roman way was gone, and the church was triumphant.

The church in triumph   The church in its triumph became a different type of social force. No longer was it concerned exclusively with the promised paradise to come. It began to change into an institution. The inspiring, charismatic leader, exciting but unpredictable, an innovator by nature, a disturber of established order, no longer was allowed to trouble the waters; a new order was established, guaranteed by a powerful and "infallible" institution whose leader was seen as God's representative on earth. How different were the problems: negotiations with the mighty of the earth, wars, diplomacy, collecting of funds, establishing new bases of power, settling theological and jurisdictional quarrels, and even humbling the Holy Roman Emperor at Canossa! How different were the leaders,

[4] Eric Hoffer, *The True Believer*, Harper & Row, Publishers, Incorporated, New York, 1966, pp. 38–48.

dressed in clerical splendor, supported by the princes of the earth! With the triumph came also corruption. The persecuted church took in only saints; the church triumphant took in also the sinners. One of the great stories in Bocaccio's *Decameron* is of the wise and kindly Jew whose Christian friend feels that he must be converted to Christianity for the sake of his soul. The Jew decides not to accept the faith until he has traveled to Rome. The Christian is aghast. How can he ever be converted after seeing such a den of iniquity! Nevertheless, the Jew returns from Rome ready to embrace the Christian faith, for, he says, only with the blessing of God could such a church flourish in all its branches when its very roots are rotten with unspeakable corruption.

The irreverent Bocaccio may have exaggerated but probably not much. His point is valid: an institution that embraces all elements of society can no longer retain its pristine purity. The conservative phase comes about. This is the situation in which the god and the state approximate the phrase "coexistent and inseparable."

So far the discussion has centered on Christianity. The process of institutionalization has never been as thorough in the Moslem faith because of less centralization of religious authority and the extreme religious democracy of Islam. Although very different from Islam, Buddhism is the opposite of the Catholic Christian model in some of the same ways, such as not having an equivalent to the Pope and oardinals. Yet it can be said of both these religions that they have gone through phases of rapid growth, missionary zeal, and then greater complacency and possibly even decline. Perhaps modern Arabic nationalism will rekindle the zeal of Islam to make it a more dynamic force again, or perhaps the Arabic world will find its new religion in more worldly ideologies.

Denomination and sect   The contrasts that have just been described in a historical framework reappear in contemporary society in the contrast between denomination and sect. A few definitions are now necessary. The *ecclesia* is the type of religious organization in the strongest position in a society—an established church claiming to represent national religion officially, such as the Catholic Church in Italy, the Lutheran Church in Sweden, and the Orthodox Church in Greece. They are no longer as exclusive as was the Medieval Church (others are tolerated), but they do hold a special position and often have considerable influence in education. The *denomination* is a large and relatively stable group, usually having been in existence for a considerable period of time, well organized, and institutionalized. The *sect* is generally smaller, with less formality, appealing more to the poor, and usually gaining members through the emotional experience of conversion rather than through the slow process of socialization, as in the denomination. The word "cult" also applies to a smaller group and especially to one emphasizing a particular phase of religion that does not appear as strongly in the major denominations — faith healing, for example.[5] For our purposes the major interest is in the distinction between denomination and sect, very well described by the German sociologist Ernst Troeltsch, but note that he uses the word "church" for our word "denomination."

> . . . The fully developed church . . . utilizes the State and the ruling classes, and weaves these elements into her own life; she then becomes an integral part of the existing social order; in so doing, however, she becomes dependent upon the upper classes, and upon their development. The sects, on the other hand, are connected with the lower classes, or at least with those elements in Society which are opposed to the State and to Society; they work upwards from below, and not downwards from above.[6]

Some denominations fit Troeltsch's description of *church* better than others, and they range in their religious orientation from very conservative to liberal, but they are generally "an integral part of the existing social order." The sects vary considerably, too, and it is hard to get a single term to fit every case. Jehovah's Witnesses fit Troeltsch's description almost perfectly in their lack of interest and participation in affairs of the state and the military service and in turning their backs on this world, which they believe is now entering its last days. The Pentecostal Holiness groups are other examples of sectarian development because they are an exclusive brotherhood of the faithful. The sects are apt to be made up of the outsiders — the poor and the disoriented, the people looking for new meanings, for emotional release through religious ecstasy, and for a sense of belonging and self-worth. The sect, more than the denomination, is inclined to see itself as a community of the righteous pitted against the outside world.

Liston Pope, in his book *Millhands and Preachers,* tells the story of a series of such sects whose sermons tend to emphasize some of the doctrines of early Christianity — "Blessed are the meek," and "The first shall be last, and the last, first." Contrast such statements of the high religious status of the lowly with the status of labor as seen by industrialist George F. Baer in the great coal strike of 1902:

[5] Terminology is not uniform as regards sects and cults. Bryan R. Wilson in *An Analysis of Sect Development,* describes and categorizes many differences. Our word "cult" is approximately equivalent to his "gnostic sect." Bryan R. Wilson, "An Analysis of Sect Development," in Seymour M. Lipset and Neil J. Smelser (eds.), *Sociology: The Progress of a Decade,* Prentice-Hall, Inc., Englewood Cliffs, N.J., 1961.
[6] Ernst Troeltsch, *The Social Teaching of the Christian Churches,* Oliver Wyon (translator), The Macmillan Company, New York, 1931, pp. 331–332.

Denomination	**Sect**
Institutionalized, formal, trained ministry	Informal, self-anointed leader
Membership through socialization	Membership through emotional conversion experience
Quiet, reserved service	Emotional service
Appeal to middle and upper classes	Appeal primarily to the poor
"Integral part of existing social order"	"Forget worldly things; the last days are at hand"

*The rights and interests of the laboring man will be
protected and cared for—not by labor agitators, but
by the **Christian men to whom God in His infinite
wisdom has given control of the property interests of
the country,** and upon the successful management
of which so much depends.[7] (Emphasis added)*

There was no doubt in the mind of Baer as to who would be first and who last! His statement was considered excessive even then, but it points out in exaggerated form the contrast between the religious views of the rich and the poor. To the rich, religion justifies the established order; to the poor it promises better things to come in the next world or possibly even in this world.

[7]Mark Sullivan, *Our Times: The United States, 1900-1925,* Charles Scribner's Sons, New York, 1927, p. 425.

The serpent handlers   A good illustration of the impact of faith upon the emotional lives of the poor and needy is contained in a recent study of the serpent-handling religions of West Virginia.[8] The serpent handlers take the following quotation from Mark as a commandment and bravely carry it out, even taking up dangerous snakes:

> And these signs shall follow them that believe; in my
> name they shall cast out devils; they shall speak with
> new tongues; They shall take up serpents; and if
> they drink any deadly thing, it shall not hurt
> them; they shall lay hands on the sick, and they
> shall recover.
>
> Mark 16: 17–18

If a member is bitten by a snake and dies, as has happened, he has proved the true depth of his faith. If the member recovers he has proved that the Lord blesses the sect. The location of the church is at Scrabble Creek, West Virginia. The Scrabble Creek people are poor, of the "stationary working class," and do not expect to get anywhere. Many other people in this depressed area are gloomy, and there is much that is depressing for the serpent handlers as well. However, they look forward to their frequent religious meetings with their fervor, emotional outpouring, ecstatic dancing, talking in tongues, feeling the touch of the Holy Ghost upon them, faith healing, and finally the greatest of all: the serpents. The rest of the service is similar to that of many other Pentecostal Holiness churches, but the serpent handling is unique.

Nathan Gerrard, the author of this study, speaks of the serpent cult as one of *religious hedonism,* the gaining of great immediate joy out of the religious experience. Although the result is not hopeful from the point of view of upward mobility in this world, its psychological results, especially for the aged, are remarkable.

> While the older members of the conventional church
> seemed to dwell morbidly on their physical
> disabilities, the aged serpent handlers seemed
> able to cheerfully ignore their ailments. . . . Three
> old serpent handlers we knew in Scrabble Creek
> were suffering from serious cardiac conditions.
> But when the Holy Spirit moved them, they danced
> ecstatically and violently. And they did this without
> any apparent harm.[9]

[8] Nathan L. Gerrard, "The Serpent Handling Religions of West Virginia," *Transaction*, vol. 5, May, 1968, pp. 22–28.
[9] *Ibid.*, p. 24.

Religion makes various promises and serves various needs for different groups. For the mighty of the earth, it supports the established system. For the poor and lowly, it gives reassurance that there is a better world, here or in the future, and promises that they will not always be the wretched of the earth. For these same people the ecstatic side of religion relieves boredom and alienation. The serpent handlers are an extreme and sensational case, but the feeling of being "possessed of the Holy Spirit" is widely known in sect and cult, as it was known by the Apostles at Pentecost.

LATENT FUNCTIONS OF RELIGION   Beside the obvious functions of religion previously discussed, there are examples of latent functions, not originally intended and sometimes unobserved. For example, missionary activity has sometimes paved the way for traders, exploiters, and even conquerors, although this was not the intent of the missionaries. Missionary activities sometimes upset old customs in such a way as to turn younger generation against older. This, again, is an unintended result, but a very common one.

Weber's theory: latent function of Protestantism   Weber's famous book *The Protestant Ethic and the Spirit of Capitalism* is the best known sociological work that deals mainly with a latent function of religion. Weber notes that modern industrial capitalism seems to have arisen first in Protestant countries, and he argues that one of the reasons was that certain teachings of the early Protestants, especially those of Calvin, created an ethic particularly useful for the development of modern capitalism. Those Protestants most strongly affected by the teachings of Calvin — Puritans, Presbyterians, and German Pietists — were rendered extremely uneasy about the future of the soul. Calvin taught that insofar as God is infinite in His wisdom and power, He must know all that has been and all that is to be. This would not be possible if everything was not already predetermined. We are born with or without the grace of God. Some will be saved, and many will be cast into hell.

Such a doctrine is an uncomfortable one to live with. How does one know whether he is of the chosen of the Lord? Increasingly, Weber says, the belief began to emerge among the Protestants that "God blesses the works of those He loves." It would seem likely, then, that the blessed would be people who work hard and accomplish much; hence, the emergence of the doctrine of hard work. Since extravagance is evil, the products of one's labor could not be squandered idly; rather, they were reinvested. What could possibly be a better ethic for the beginning of one of the most highly competitive systems the world has ever known?

The ethic adds honesty, for it is impossible for a system of free capitalism to develop unless there is a certain amount of faith in contract. However, there is another side to the honesty ethic; it is a matter of policy. The best way to succeed in the world is to be known as an honest man. Virtue and utilitarianism are combined. Of course Weber did not naively contend that all early capitalists were honest, but he did say that the system contrasts sharply with many in which the road to wealth is through gathering taxes and cheating the government (as in the latter days of Rome), oppressing the peasant, or military conquest and plunder.

The Protestant ethic was not the only ethic to have taught the importance of work, but it was peculiarly intense in its devotion to the idea. Once such a highly competitive system started, Weber reasoned, it would tend to spread and draw in other members of society to some extent, Catholics as well as Protestants, but some differences might persist.

Gerhard Lenski finds that differences still exist between Catholics and Protestants in some of the respects that Weber's theory would suggest. White, middle-class Protestants are more upwardly mobile in their orientation than are Catholics, and they place a higher amount of faith in the rewards of hard work as compared with family connections as a source of success.[10] An analysis of family life among Catholics and Protestants shows more familism for the Catholics and greater individualism for the Protestants. This relative release from family ties makes the Protestant freer to pursue his career, and he is already likely to be more success oriented.[11]

Puritanism and science   Another latent function of religion has been suggested by Robert K. Merton, the leading sociologist to develop the concept of latent function. It is his contention that the Protestant point of view had a bearing on the development of modern science because of its emphasis on the study and glorification of nature as the handiwork of God.[12] He documents this viewpoint with quotations from many leading scientists of Puritan conviction and with interesting statistics on the religious identification of scientists in the Royal Society of the seventeenth century; practically all of them were Puritans. It is ironical that by the time of Darwin science and religion were in sharp conflict. In short, a latent function of Puritanism was the promotion of science, which in turn led to the undermining of many of the beliefs of Puritanism and of fundamentalist Christianity in general. This undermining of the fundamentalist view (the seven-day creation, the Garden of Eden story, etc.) is part of the general process of secularization in modern societies, related to many factors beside the latent functions just mentioned.

[10] Gerhard Lenski, *The Religious Factor*, Doubleday & Company, Inc., Garden City, N.Y., 1963, p. 321.
[11] *Ibid.*, chap. 5.
[12] Robert K. Merton, *Social Theory and Social Structure*, The Free Press of Glencoe, Inc., New York, 1957, pp. 576–577.

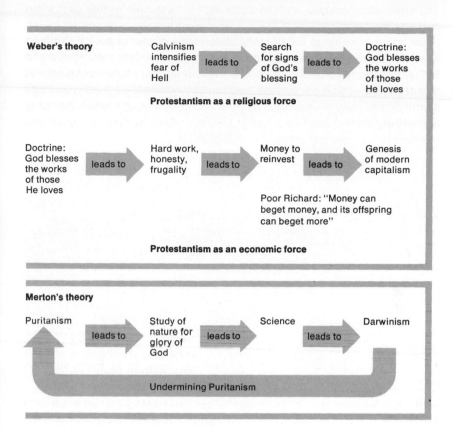

Weber's theory

Calvinism intensifies fear of Hell → leads to → Search for signs of God's blessing → leads to → Doctrine: God blesses the works of those He loves

Protestantism as a religious force

Doctrine: God blesses the works of those He loves → leads to → Hard work, honesty, frugality → leads to → Money to reinvest → leads to → Genesis of modern capitalism

Poor Richard: "Money can beget money, and its offspring can beget more"

Protestantism as an economic force

Merton's theory

Puritanism → leads to → Study of nature for glory of God → leads to → Science → leads to → Darwinism

Undermining Puritanism

THE PROBLEMS OF AN AGE OF SECULARIZATION   There are conflicting points of view about the fate of religion in modern society, but few would deny that one of the trends of the world is toward secularization and that this tends to place certain limits on religious interpretations. No longer does religion provide a picture of the workings of the universe, with a comfortable, self-assured world around which revolve the sun, the moon, and all the stars. This is part of the contrast between sacred and secular society, but the terms need further definition.

The sacred society   A *sacred society* is defined as one that sees all its customs and institutions as being of divine origin. Misfortunes are generally explained as the result of the breaking of divine law, and man holds close

215

responsibility to nature and the spirit world. Even the fertility of the soil and the abundance of nature are man's responsibility, regulated by his ritual observances and conduct. Although man often makes a distinction between the things that are sacred and those that are not, the distinction is not too great in the sacred society. Religion is a pervasive, everyday affair that regulates law, marriage, moral obligations, taking of food, planting and harvesting, curing of illness, and all the multitudinous aspects of culture.

The secular society   A *secular society*, on the other hand, can have its religious rituals and mores, but most social arrangements are thought of as simply the practical ways of meeting the material problems of life. Laws are rules made by legislatures, not by the divine will of God. Planting and harvesting are arranged on the basis of scientific knowledge, as are all aspects of the economy. Religious views still enter the picture when new social and moral issues are at stake, but in most of the everyday routine of life religion is less evident. Many members of society no longer engage in any type of religious observance, and many others think of religion as strictly a Sunday affair. Today's secular societies hold much greater funds of knowledge than the societies of the past, but sometimes a sense of loss is experienced in other respects. Whereas the sacred traditions usually look upon man as the finest handiwork of God, a modern biologist of philosophical bent can say "The human brain, monstrous tumor of the universe, in which questions and agonies proliferate without curb, like malign cells!" and "Man is far from being the creation of a lucid will; he is not even the culmination of a confused and blurred effort."[13]

Secularization does not always reach this outcry of despair, of course, for the secular society still has its faithful, and the United States actually saw a steady increase in church attendance in the 1940s and 1950s. The explanations given for a renewed interest in religion in those decades vary considerably, but probably the uncertainties of the war period and the unifying function of religion in such emergencies played a hand. There are also conflicting views on how healthy the institution of religion is in the United States today. Yinger criticizes the tendency of some writers to speak of secularization as though it means the abandonment of religion or false piety.[14] He prefers the words "religious change" to "secularization" for describing the situation in the United States today. He rejects the view of many critics that religiosity of recent times is not "really" religion: if people attend church and think of themselves as

[13]Jean Rostand, *The Substance of Man*, Doubleday & Company, Inc., Garden City, N.Y., 1962, pp. 58, 65.
[14]J. Milton Yinger, *Sociology Looks at Religion*, The Macmillan Company, New York, 1963, p. 63.

religious, then let us accept them as such, even though some of their views might be quite different from religious views of the past. Yinger believes that if humanistic and nationalistic themes become a part of religion it is still religion. The conspicuously churchlike behavior that is often an outward manifestation of middle-class values is definitely religious. The Norman Vincent Peale positive-thinking approach to religion may be philosophically shallow, but has there ever been a time when all men were philosophically profound? Lenski's conclusions are rather similar to Yinger's in some respects because they question the viewpoint that the urban society is so secularized as to make religion irrelevant.[15] Many traditions continue in urban life, including religious identification.

Others are more doubtful about some modern religious trends: " . . . a kind of creeping piety, a false piety and religiosity which has slithered its way to astounding popularity."[16] The writer Eric Goldman gives examples of dial-a-prayer, pray your weight away, and a quotation from a Hollywood actress, "I love God. And when you get to know Him, you'll find He's a livin' doll," as false religiosity. At the present time, people in the Los Angeles area can tune their television sets on a Sunday evening to "The Swingin' Gospel." Recently there has been a development of *scientology*, an amateur approach to a wedding of religion and psychiatry. Even psychedelic drugs have taken on a cultist facade as a dangerous shortcut to the ecstacies of religious mysticism. One should be cautious, however, in giving such developments as evidence of an "unhealthy" state of religion in modern society. Many strange ideas and practices have come and gone—apocalyptic prophecies, strange messiahs, bleeding icons, visions, dancing manias, and flagellation, to name but a few.

The churches and the college generation   The vast majority of the religiously committed do not follow strange cults but remain in the major churches— Catholic, Protestant, Jewish, and Orthodox. What are the trends in these churches so far as attendance is concerned? Dr. Gallup's figures on weekly church attendance show 49 percent in 1955, the high point of the century, and a decline to 44 percent in 1966, 45 percent in 1967, and 42 percent in 1969.[17] Much more disturbing for the churches than this minor decline in church attendance are the trends reported by Stark and Glock, who find a sharp distinction between older and younger generations in church attendance, a distinction that seems to be increasing.

[15]Lenski, *op. cit.*, pp. 8–12.
[16]Eric F. Goldman, "Goodbye to the Fifties, and Good Riddance!", *Harper's Magazine*, vol. 220, January, 1960, pp. 27–29.
[17]George Gallup, "Church Going in the United States Continues to Decline," *Los Angeles Times*, December 27, 1969, p. 19.

Among young adults there was a drop of 11 percent in church attendance in the years 1958 to 1966.[18] In 1957, 69 percent of the people interviewed by Dr. Gallup thought that the influence of the church was increasing; in 1966 only 23 percent thought that its influence was increasing. These figures suggest that for many young Americans the church brings neither the comfort suggested in the opening quotation of this chapter nor the sword of reform.

Declining attendance is only one of several problems that Stark and Glock see for contemporary religion. Although the vast majority of Americans believe in God in some definition or other, orthodoxy of belief is declining. This decline creates a serious problem for church support because it is the strongly orthodox believers who are most likely to attend church and provide its financial support. The dissociation of the unorthodox from the church is a likely explanation of why such a liberal denomination as Unitarianism remains small in membership. Only a few of the unorthodox are committed to the church. Yet another dilemma, according to the same findings, is a contrast between belief in religious ritual, tradition, and doctrine on the one hand, and ethics on the other. In their measurement of "Christian ethics" (defined as agreement with the importance of "loving your neighbor" and "doing good for others"), the unorthodox measured slightly higher than the more conventionally religious. It is this dilemma of the stronger supporters of Christian ethics being little committed to the church that causes Stark and Glock to say "Today the acceptance of a modernized liberal theology is being accompanied by a general corrosion of religious commitment."[19]

Comparison with Europe   Despite the suggested decline of religious commitment, the United States stands very high in stated religious belief compared with most of Western Europe. The April, 1968, issue of *Catholic Digest* reports findings indicating that 92 percent of Americans think religion is important to them. A 1960 study of several Western nations finds the following percentages of people believing in life after death:[20]

United States	74%	Great Britain	56%
Norway	71%	Switzerland	55%
Canada	68%	Sweden	40%
Netherlands	63%	West Germany	38%

Statistics on prayer were given for only two countries: 92 percent of Americans claimed to pray at least occasionally; only 54 percent of Swedes indicated that they ever pray.

[18] Rodney Stark and Charles Y. Glock, "Will Ethics be the Death of Christianity?", *Transaction*, vol. 6, June, 1968, pp. 7–14.
[19] *Ibid.*, p. 11.
[20] Richard F. Tomasson, "Religion is Irrelevant in Sweden," *Transaction*, vol. 6, December, 1968, p. 47.

Whether Stark and Glock have detected a trend that will eventually make the United States more like Western Europe in skepticism cannot be said for sure. Trends do not always continue. Another uncertainty is that of defining "religious." The above statistics of 92 percent saying religion is important to them, and the same percent claiming to pray at least occasionally, combine strangely with only 74 percent believing in life after death. It is clear that many people consider themselves religious even though their views are not the traditional ones. The reader must decide for himself whether religion includes not only commitment to God or the gods but also commitment to causes, to humanitarianism, to unfulfilled searches for meanings, to modern existentialist thought, and even to the "God is dead" philosophy of some of the religious *avant garde*.

The opening statement that "cultures have come into existence in the company of their gods" does not mean that no individuals of today live without their gods. There seems to be widespread skepticism in a secular age and in a troubled age looking for new meanings. Nevertheless, it would be rash to announce the demise of faith, even very fundamentalist faith. Recently, the Southern Baptist Convention, representing over 11 million members, adjourned after giving its overwhelming vote to the believers in the literal truth of the Bible and dedicating itself to its traditional soul saving.[21] For the foreseeable future we can expect to see large numbers of religious believers. Some will seek inner peace; some will seek emotional excitation. They will argue and debate and sometimes show animosities, but in times of societal adversity they will tend to unite. There will be the traditional churchgoers supporting the conservative norms of society; and there will be lesser numbers of the religiously committed persistently challenging society for its shortcomings. Such are the many faces of the gods of mankind.

SUMMARY   Throughout all known history societies have had their religions. Sociologists approach religion from the point of view of social function, i.e., what are its consequences for society? At first glance the functions of religion seem rather contradictory. Religion generally supports the society and proclaims its "rightness" above that of others, but at the same time the great religious prophets have been critics of their societies. Religions assign man an importance in the universe but also stress his insignificance. Religious leadership often is accompanied by high worldly status, but many religions (including Christianity) give sacred status to the poor and lowly. Religion unifies its followers and is

[21]"Southern Baptists Reaffirm Traditions," *The Bakersfield Californian*, June 21, 1969, p. 2.

sometimes the embodiment of the society itself. Under other circumstances, religion can be a divisive force, causing internal conflict, as in the Thirty Years War.

These contradictory functions of religion can also be thought of as complementary, providing for opposite needs of social systems. There are conservative implications of religion, appealing to the well-placed members of society and sharply criticized by the radicals. The reforming zeal of religion, on the other hand, has caused great criticisms from conservatives. In this sense, different aspects of religion can be thought of as supporting and challenging the status quo. Except in time of considerable turbulence, the fearless social critics constitute only a very small minority of religious leadership.

The charismatic leader, with a magnetic, emotional appeal, characterizes the beginning phase of a new religion or of a new movement within an old religion. Often the charismatic movement provides a challenge to the old order, as was the case with Christianity in its early history in the Roman Empire. Eventually a successful religion becomes established and central to the society, as happened with the Roman Catholic Church at the height of its power. Within Protestantism there has been a partial parallel to the development of the Christian church of earlier times: new sects have appeared, largely among the poor. These sects often stress the doctrines of early Christianity—the unimportance of low status in this world, promise of better things to come, and the idea that the first shall be last and the last first.

Religion also has its latent (unintended or unnoticed) functions, for example, the frequent cases of missionaries unintentionally helping to pave the way for imperialism. Weber has the most famous thesis on the latent functions of religion. He contends that calvinist doctrine accidentally contributed to the intensely competitive economic system known as capitalism. Merton shows that a latent function of Puritanism was the study of nature as the handiwork of God. The Puritan's study of nature contributed to the development of modern science, which, in turn, undermined many Puritan beliefs.

The present age is generally characterized as an age of secularization—one in which everyday life is no longer permeated by religion. Is such a society necessarily in a state of religious decline? Researchers differ to some degree in their conclusions. Yinger prefers the term "religious change" to "secularization," noting that churches are well supported in spite of a decline in religious orthodoxy. It must also be pointed out that interests in new religious philosophies, mysticism, and humanitarianism cannot be dismissed as irrelevant to religion. Stark and Glock, on the other hand, reviewing statistics on a decline of commitment to the church, speak of a decline in religion, especially on the part of college youth. Others wonder if the much greater decline in church attendance in many parts of Europe will be duplicated here. Presently, however, fundamentalism and evangelism have great popularity among many segments of the American population. Church attendance has declined from a high point in the late 1950s, but the decline is only slight. It would be an overstatement to say that religion has lost its functions in an age of secularization.

*The scholar may not be without breadth of
mind and vigorous endurance. His burden is
heavy and his course is long.*
THE ANALECTS OF CONFUCIUS, BOOK VII, NO. 7

twelve

EDUCATION

Education has the universal function of contributing to
the perpetuation of societies, transmItting their ideas from
generation to generation, and preparing the young for
active roles in the culture. Education is therefore a
reflection of the culture itself, and In complex and
changing societies it displays some of the value conflicts
and strains between real and ideal norms that are typical
of all cultures. Since social change is an inevitable part
of societies, especially modern societies, education does
more than merely transmit the accumulated wisdom of
the past. It has the function of adding to the knowledge
of the past, helping to select what is to be retained, and
making critical evaluations of tradition. For this reason,
education, like religion, has complementary and
sometimes conflicting functions — those of preservation
and innovation. Schools can be so rigid in their attempt
to instill loyalty to old traditions that they become stifling
to the needs of social change; or they may virtually ignore
tradition, making their cultures seem rootless and lacking
in sense of identity. The latter is more likely to be the fate
of ethnic minorities than of the traditions of dominant
groups.

　　Another set of educational functions is that of
preserving social status for well-placed families and
attempting to achieve upward mobility for those of lower
status.

Although education serves as a major track for upward mobility, our discussion of both high school and college will show that the lower-class family often finds major barriers in the way of realization of this goal. There are, of course, many other functions of educational systems. Among the most obvious are those of contributing to socialization, providing the manpower resources needed by the society, and training people for the duties of citizenship.

As is the case with other institutions, education has latent, unintended functions. The needs of societies for adjusting to new technologies and ideas can result in demands for higher levels of education, and often the highly educated become the intellectual critics of the very social system that produced them. Education is a vital necessity, but its consequences in periods of change can be disturbing to old ways, not just in tradition-ridden or dictatorial countries, but in all social systems.

CHANGING FUNCTIONS OF EDUCATION   For preliterate people education was not separated from the remainder of life as a specialized institution but was a day-to-day process of imitation of elders, listening to instructions in necessary techniques, and learning the myths and the folk wisdom. Until the last century or two the pattern of education in the Western world had not differed too greatly from this same tradition, except for the upper classes. The common people learned from their parents; they learned how to farm and to care for children and learned the wisdom and the old wives' tales of the culture. There was less to learn than now, but learning was immediate and practical and possessed the self-assurance of long tradition. There was no long gap in years between learning and the application of learning.

Education in early America   Although the United States was a new nation with new ideas, there were ways in which education in its early history seemed to stress the preservation function more than that of innovation. In Puritan New England, schools had started as a means of giving everyone the ability to read the Bible for the sake of his soul's salvation. Later the jeffersonian ideal of an educated electorate became a major inspiration for the building of schools in America. Along with educating a people to be competent to govern themselves, there was a great emphasis on patriotism and American heroes and the building of national tradition.[1]

A certain amount of ethnocentrism is a part of the instruction of all people, and America was no exception. Immigrants arriving in America

[1] J. Merton England, "The Democratic Faith in American Schoolbooks, 1783–1860," *American Quarterly*, vol. 15, no. 2, Summer, 1963, pp. 191–199.

learned to adopt its heroes and identify with the country, partly through
the public education system. An important part of the school systems of
midnineteenth-century America were the McGuffey Readers; they were
high in morality and sentimentality and in the idea of inevitable progress.
There was a constant emphasis on the good American virtues of morality,
sobriety, and diligence. Over long years these readers preached to
generations of school children, helping "shape that elusive thing we call
the American character."[2] They also emphasized the obvious value of
education as a way of getting ahead in the world. Thus, education in
much of American history has stressed the conservative values of building
and romanticizing a cultural tradition. It was seen as the business of the
growing public school system to equip individuals in their loyalties and
skills to fit into the society, not to become its critics.

The triumph of mass education   Our early schools were small and were
taught by poorly trained teachers, so it sometimes seemed that the blind
were leading the blind. In the early years many curious European visitors
scoffed. Others began to take real interest. The first British commission
to study the American system arrived in the 1860s.[3] Before the end of
the century many European visitors, official and unofficial, came to study
and to learn. The idea of mass education was taking root and spreading.
In America there was a gradual increase of literacy, with more and more
people completing high school. Mass education was obviously becoming
increasingly functional for a society moving into the modern age of
science, industry, and commerce. Other industrial nations began to move
along similar lines in mass education.

By 1964 young adults aged twenty-five to twenty-nine averaged
twelve and one-half years of schooling. Approximately 70 percent of
young adults were high school graduates, and 13 percent had completed
four or more years of college. It is expected that these figures will inch
upward to nearly 80 percent high school graduates and 20 percent college graduates by 1985.[4]

Mass education seemed to be an overwhelming success, and yet
criticisms were growing. Colleges were not the needling critics of society
that they are today, and educators aimed their criticisms more at education itself than at the total society; but the implications of the progressive
educator, following the philosophy of John Dewey, were to equip people
for a more cooperative society. With the passing of time the criticisms

[2] Henry Steele Commager, *The Commonwealth of Learning*, Harper & Row, Publishers, Incorporated, New York,
1952, p. 102.
[3] Ruth E. Maguire, *English Commentary on the American Common School 1860 to 1900*, unpublished doctoral
dissertation, University of California at Los Angeles, 1961, vol. 1, pp. 19–20.
[4] Francis Keppel, *The Necessary Revolution in American Education*, Harper & Row, Publishers, Incorporated,
New York, 1966, pp. 18–19.

have come to cover a much wider range, including the charge of inadequacies in such educational functions as equality of opportunity, upward mobility, training for democracy, and relevance to modern life.

New educational demands   As the United States and other technical societies adjust to the modern world that they have created, strains are placed on their educational systems. There is a demand for more schooling and more funds for the purpose. Since societies need large numbers of college graduates, they must tap the intellectual resources of a larger segment of the population, rather than drawing leadership mainly from a self-perpetuating elite. For upper-class families an extra four or five years of maturing at college has long been traditional, but to many middle- and lower-middle-class people this seems to be an incredible lengthening of the period of youth. Youth is greatly played up to in song and advertisement, but has an extremely ambiguous status—"a romantic but surplus commodity," Kvaraceus has called it. A period of ill-defined status is lengthened. The young person once looked upon his high school graduation as a "coming of age" ceremony, almost as definitive as primitive "rites of puberty," changing him from a boy to a man. Now its significance is downgraded in that more schooling lies ahead before full adult status is reached.

THE MODERN HIGH SCHOOL AS A SOCIAL SYSTEM   Although the demands for college education increase, a majority of people only finish high school and some drop out before completion. The functions of the high school, of course, are generally seen as those of occupational training, citizenship training, furthering socialization, and delaying entry into the labor market. The functions are usually innovative only in the sense of personal preparation for a society that is constantly undergoing change and for the creation of teen-age norms. How does the high school function in the accomplishment of its intended purposes, and what unintended results does it help to bring about?

In some respects the average high school shows the same bureaucratic tendencies as the rest of the society. The student enters a high school in which personal contact with the teacher is very limited. There are counselors, of course, but they are often kept so busy with the role of disciplinarian that the well-behaved student seldom sees them. From the first day the bureaucratic side of school makes a very strong impression. Individual reputations earned in grammar school are often ignored, and the student is rated on the basis of a battery of tests, processed, scheduled, assigned, and pigeonholed into the right academic level. He is now in a school that is part of a large city system, with its "better" schools, its

Then

Pinnacle of success

Small, personal

Sink or swim

Community center

Strictly book learning

The select few

Now

A minor step

High school

Bureaucratic

Principal

Administrative Assistants

Counselors | Records | "Hookey cop"

Teachers

Students

Choose your level

Level 1 Brilliant
Level 2 Good
Level 3 Average
Level 4 Nonacademic
Level 5 Potential dropout

In the shadow

University

High school

High school subcultures

Popularity kids

Athletes

Student government

Delinquents

The mass

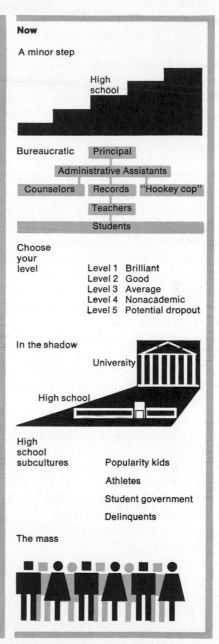

average schools, and its "Siberian exiles," correlating with the socio-economic composition of the community.

In an age when college expectations are high, the high school is less a center of community pride than it once was. Its enrollments grow rapidly, however, and so do its costs. The massive enrollments contribute to high school discipline problems until some schools take on the atmosphere of a reformatory, with rigid and absolute rules. In the opinion of one critic, the rigidity tends to "infantilize adolescence," slowing down maturation in decision making and hampering ability to be heard and taken seriously.[5]

High school subcultures   Within the high school many of the characteristics of any social system emerge, with new subcultures coming into existence, the largest one being a kind of "social popularity subculture." As in the larger society, there is competition for status, but status is defined by the high school students themselves, not the outside world. James Coleman did an extensive study of ten high schools and found none in which status is gained primarily by being a good student. Criteria of status are more apt to be skill in athletics, school politics, dating, entertaining, and going to parties. Coleman speaks of this as an *adolescent subculture* "with values and attitudes quite distinct from those of the adult world."[6] In some respects the adult world and the high school society are distinct, and they are certainly treated as distinct by the entertainment and advertisement interests, but the distinction can be overdrawn. Certainly the adult world also spends more time at parties, night clubs, athletic events, and at watching television than it does reading the world's great books.

There are ways in which the popularity subculture is functional to the school system. It prevents the total annihilation of those who are not academically gifted and relieves a long four years that many students find boring and not very fruitful. Athletic competition gives a place for some who might otherwise become high school dropouts, but this point can be overemphasized. There is a tendency for students who participate most in this type of youth subculture to be those with at least fair academic potential.

A *delinquent subculture* is also evident in most high schools. Delinquency as an occasional illegal act involves large numbers of high school students, but "delinquent subculture" as used here refers not to the occasional offenders but to perpetual offenders. These are the students who want out but are held in school by state law. They openly flaunt

[5] Edgar Z. Friedenberg, "The Modern High School: A Profile," *Commentary*, vol. 36, November, 1963, pp. 9–21.
[6] James S. Coleman, "The Academic Subculture and Academic Achievement," *American Journal of Sociology*, vol. 65, January, 1960, pp. 337–347.

their contempt for the school.[7] Inwardly they feel that the system has no place for them; they are defeated before they start. They are contemptuous of the values of the school and express their contempt in the dirty words scrawled on lavatory walls. This is part of the situation that makes many slum schools a teacher's nightmare, although delinquent subcultures are by no means confined to the wrong side of the tracks or to minority groups. Neither do such subcultures suddenly arise in high school; often the hostility typical of such groups is observable by the first few grades of school. The children fail and react to failure with aggression. Teachers, worn by the system, find it hard to give patient understanding. Often a vicious cycle develops, with hostility leading to punishment, and punishment in turn leading to greater hostility, until the student finally drops out. The school, again, reflects many of the strains of the adult world: social-class differentiation, subcultures, and contracultures.

Often in the school there are those who make up another subculture, almost hidden away from the rest of the students. These are the M/Rs (mentally retarded). They are the true pariahs (untouchables) of the system, so low in caste that even the teachers specializing in their care tend to take on a debased status. State laws say that these pupils must stay in school until age 16 (in some cases 18) or until they have graduated from high school. Occasionally, trained specialists work with such children and make their lives more productive and hopeful than they would otherwise be, but often there is no real place for them. They are an embarrassment to an ethic that says everyone can succeed if he will only try. If some of the recent studies in differing types of intelligence are correct, quite a number of students given the stigma of M/R will seem much less deficient in the world beyond the school walls than in the classroom.

Ability grouping and social-class perpetuation There are many levels of ability among the students in high schools, and something must be done to make the whole heterogeneous mass teachable. One alternative would be to have very small classes so that a teacher could give special attention to each student. Since this policy is too costly for most districts, there remain two other alternatives: throw them all into the same class to sink or swim, or "ability group" them. Ability grouping makes it possible for bright students to be in competition with and be challenged by other bright students. It just as assuredly weeds out any possibility of much intellectual challenge to those students in the lower groups, and it makes the job of teaching the lower groups appalling to all but the most dedicated teachers. Then there is another problem: children from poverty areas

[7]Edgar Z. Friedenberg, "An Ideology of School Withdrawal," in Daniel Schreiber (ed.), *The School Dropout*, National Education Association, Washington, D.C., 1964, pp. 25–39.

start school under a cloud, and the cloud grows more impenetrable with the passing of years. Lack of good reading habits at home leads such children to a slower start in the first grade, which causes them to be assigned less challenging work. By the time such children are in high school there is no way of knowing whether they ever had academic potential; possibly it once existed but was stultified by miserable self-concept fostered by the ability-segregation system. A disproportionate number of minority students follow the long trail through school on the second, third, or fourth level below the top.

Intelligence tests as normative strain   Much of the assignment of students to various academic levels is done on the basis of intelligence tests, which have recently come under heavy attack. The intelligence test scores are, on a general average, a fairly good prediction of academic work, but averages often hide many exceptional cases. Some students perform better than the tests would indicate but have their confidence shaken by unfavorable test scores. More important than a few individual cases is the tendency for the intelligence test to be unfair to students from a subcultural background that differs substantially from that of the white middle-class family. This problem was mentioned previously in relation to race and ethnic group, with the general conclusion that intelligence tests do not work except for the culture on which they are standardized.[8]

Zealous attention to intelligence quotients can run into normative dilemmas of other types besides that of unfairness to minority groups. It is easy to use intelligence scores to explain too much and to warrant giving up on some students, although the educational norms call for the highest possible development of each individual. The school system is also charged with the responsibility of producing the kinds of talents needed by today's society. If the testing system discourages capable people from developing their potentials, it adds to social wastage. Robert Faris contends that we set too many aspirational boundaries for both society and individual. By *aspiration boundaries* he means limits beyond which we dare not aspire. Once it is realized that there are no insurmountable barriers to a particular field of achievement, more people try, and many of them succeed.[9] Several studies have shown marked improvement in ability scores among children with improved opportunity and improved self-image. At the same time, one can hardly assume that there are no individual variations in human potentials.

[8] Carolyn Stern, "The Changing Concept of the Changing I.Q.," *California Teachers' Association Journal*, May, 1969, pp. 13–15.
[9] Robert E. L. Faris, "Reflections on the Ability Dimension in Human Society," *American Sociological Review*, vol. 26, December, 1961, pp. 835–843.

Bruce K. Eckland,[10] in his study "Genetics and Sociology," reviews the literature in the field and comes to two important conclusions: (1) observed intelligence differences between social classes are partly caused by assortative mating and heredity, but this is probably not true of observed differences in races; (2) despite some average differences observable on a social-class basis, many lower-class children have high intelligence and vice versa. Because his first statement sounds a little contradictory, it requires an explanation. Members of the majority race have had a reasonable opportunity to better their position, so that some upward mobility among the most able would seem likely. Since the road to upward mobility has been closed for Negroes, there is no reason for assuming that low class position on their part is necessarily connected with low ability.

If we accept Eckland's conclusions we shall perceive a society in which abilities are evenly distributed among races but which are distributed with slight inequality across social-class lines. Even granting this, there are very large numbers of children whose potential is wasted for themselves and for society. One-fourth of slum children in northern cities have IQs of 109 or above.[11] Too many of them represent a waste of human resources, partly because of lack of encouragement and partly because of lack of funds to go to school. It seems likely that we can add to this the possibility that ability-grouping systems close doors to many students before they get far enough into high school to be measured for college. The "measuring-for-college" system is another barrier.

THE UNEVEN RACE TO COLLEGE   In most European educational systems examinations are given by the age of sixteen to determine whether people have the academic potential to go on to college. The competition for college is much greater than here, and the pressure is greater. The system effectively excludes those who have not passed their examinations.

The barriers   In the United States the pressure is not so great, but the trend seems to be in the same direction. Where junior colleges are not available, one can eliminate himself from consideration by a state college or university by doing poorly in high school or on the College Entrance Examinations. Junior colleges generally admit all applicants, but they have to "wash out" a great many along the way. They do, however, serve

[10] Bruce K. Eckland, "Genetics and Sociology," *American Sociological Review*, vol. 32, April, 1967, pp. 173–194.
[11] Kenneth Eells et al., *Intelligence and Cultural Differences*, The University of Chicago Press, Chicago, 1951, p. 154.

the function of helping people who are late to mature or to become motivated.

Much of the motivation for college is a matter of family socioeducational background, which is found to be even more predictive of college entrance than is ability.[12] In a study completed in Wisconsin in 1968[13] it was found that high school graduates with high ability eventually graduated from college in 63.4 percent of the cases if their parents had high educational achievement. However, if the parents were low in educational achievement, the rate of college graduation for their offspring was only 21.1 percent, even for high-ability students. This is not just a reflection of economic ability to pay college tuition. Of the sons and daughters of well-educated parents in the study, 95.4 percent reported parental encouragement to go to college. Only 51.9 percent of those whose parents had little education reported such encouragement, even among high-ability students.

Lack of parental encouragement is not the only factor, of course, in college plans. Both money and ability are needed. Money is especially important in states that do not have tuition-free junior colleges or low-tuition state colleges. But even where the cost of tuition is held to a minimum, costs are high, and there is a great economic differential in the ability to enter. Often students have to go to work to help with family expenses; or, at best, they cannot hope for any financial aid from home but must earn their own way completely. This can be done with great effort but at a sacrifice of the time needed for reflection and for taking advantage of the cultural opportunities presented by the college.

The road to college is strewn with barriers: insufficient ability or motivation, lack of financial means, low test scores, the draft, and too few openings in the college. The effort is great enough that many do not choose to go even if the means are available. A rather small percentage of Vietnam War veterans are taking advantage of the GI Bill of Rights that enables them to go to college. Probably one important reason for this small percentage is a difference in composition of the present veterans and those of World War II. The draft system has generally exempted those most determined to get through college and has taken a disproportionate number of those who had no college ambitions in the first place. The result clearly demonstrates differences in motivation regarding college and an unfortunate waste of potential.

One final problem concerning the entering of college is that many students have not yet been able to make up their minds about vocational

[12] Burton R. Clark, *Educating the Expert Society*, Chandler Publishing Company, San Francisco, 1962, pp. 61–62.
[13] William H. Sewell and Vidal P. Shah, "Parents' Education and Children's Educational Aspirations and Achievements," *American Sociological Review*, vol. 33, April, 1968, pp. 191–209.

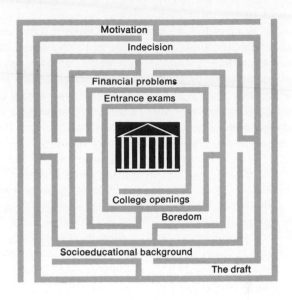

choice. There is a tendency to be most aware of jobs that are represented by family and acquaintances, and this raises a difficulty for low-income youth who have little knowledge of the types of jobs open to college graduates.

The college   Barron's *Profiles of American Colleges* lists over 1,200 regionally accredited four-year colleges and universities in the United States, ranging in size from 200 or 300 students to 17,000 at Columbia, 25,000 at UCLA or Berkeley, and 27,000 at the University of Washington. Today the large schools are more typical than are the smaller ones. The major state colleges and universities are impressive in size and academic staff, drawing large research grants from government and industry and hiring many of the world's greatest scientists and experts in all fields of learning. Their presses are busy turning out the books and research papers of their professors. Their diplomas are envied, especially those awarding higher degrees. Certain schools—Berkeley, Harvard, and Columbia, for example—are honored with many Nobel Prize winners and other great names in the academic field.

233

The trouble is that the undergraduate students are but vaguely aware of the most distinguished members of the staff. They are often taught in classrooms consisting of hundreds of students by young assistants who must publish or get out. Education departments complain that too little attention is given to the techniques of teaching.[14] The impersonal, bureaucratic atmosphere of high school is multiplied many fold in the large colleges and universities. Even school spirit and involvement are hard to develop. Many students are involved only in small primary groups of their own, and there are also "loners" who seem to need the atmosphere of the small college but cannot afford it.

Attitude change   Whether the student goes to a small college or a large university, it is generally assumed that his education will broaden his perspectives, removing some of his prejudices and provincialism. Whether as a result of instruction or maturation and being away from home, certain attitude changes usually do take place. Not all surveys agree, but a majority show a slightly greater tolerance of conflicting political opinions on the part of college seniors than of entering freshmen. There is a decline in racial prejudice, an increase in religious tolerance, and less religious fundamentalism. To a slight degree this is the result of a selective function of the college, weeding out some of the more narrow minded, but to a great degree it also shows a change of attitude with increasing education.[15]

Charles Stember did a study on education and attitude change that is not quite as encouraging as most.[16] The simplest stereotypes, he admits, are seldom found among the educated—such stereotypes as "all Germans are brutal," or "all Orientals are sneaky." Anti-Jewish prejudice declines with every step of the educational ladder, but a decline in anti-Negro prejudice occurs mainly at college, with earlier schools showing little change. The remaining difficulty, as Stember sees it, is that sometimes prejudices are simply a little more sophisticated in their justifications. Higher-class people usually preserve enough of a pattern of discrimination to maintain considerable social distance from minority groups. Education tends to remove prejudice, but the higher-class position that goes with it does not. The conditions that reinforce the favorable effect of education on racial attitudes are urbanization and personal contact with Negroes of equal status. Education widens the gap between the prejudiced and nonprejudiced more in the South than in the North and more among people with foreign-born parents than among those with American-born parents.

[14]James B. Conant, *The Education of American Teachers*, McGraw-Hill Book Company, New York, 1964, pp. 1–14.
[15]Clark, *op. cit.*, pp. 30–37.
[16]Charles H. Stember, "Education and Attitude Change," in James L. Price (ed.), *Social Facts*, The Macmillan Co. of Canada, Limited, Toronto, 1969, pp. 287–298.

In political matters, the effects of education seem to foster liberal attitudes. Research at the end of the conservative decade of the 1950s found that a majority of the very vocal conservatives on college campuses came from conservative homes. Although the liberals were less vocal then than later, there were considerably more students rating themselves as "more liberal" than their parents than "more conservative."[17] In a more recent study by Free and Cantril,[18] it was found that 45 percent of those offspring who classified their fathers as "very conservative" classified themselves as "very liberal." Only 1 percent of "very liberal" parents had offspring who classified themselves as "very conservative," although a majority (80 percent) moved slightly to the right—"moderately liberal" or "middle of the road." When political activism shows a strong revolt against the parents, it is likely to be a revolt against strong conservativism. Gallup's figures for 1969 showed a liberal trend on the part of college students. In his survey, 21 percent of the students called themselves "conservatives," 24 percent "middle of the road," and 53 percent "liberal."[19] Only time will tell whether the liberal convictions will change with the passing of years and greater vested interest in the status quo.

Vocational selection   College education generally shows results in the most practical of respects—occupation and income. The income of the college graduate has long remained about three times that of the grammar school graduate and about twice that of the high school graduate. Professional and technical workers were largely college graduates by 1940, but at that time only 23 percent of managers, officials, and proprietors were college graduates; by 1960 the corresponding figure was 35 percent.[20] Clerical, sales, and kindred workers, and farmers and farm managers had attended college in smaller numbers, but their percentage of graduates was also increasing.

By 1970, it began to appear that there would be employment difficulties for some categories of college graduates.[21] Sometimes the problem was created in the engineering and technical fields by changes in aircraft production and in construction. A more serious problem was that, for the first time in many years, there seemed to be an oversupply of Doctor of Philosophy degrees in some fields. Graduates were seeking

[17] Russell Middleton and Snell Putney, "Student Rebellion against Parental Political Beliefs," *Social Forces*, vol. 41, May, 1963, pp. 377–383.
[18] Lloyd A. Free and Hadley Cantril, *The Political Beliefs of Americans*, Rutgers University Press, New Brunswick, N.J., 1967, p. 139.
[19] "Gallup Poll: Strong Swing to the Left Noted on Campuses," *Los Angeles Times*, May 27, 1969, part I, pp. 10–11.
[20] John K. Folger and Charles B. Nam, "Trends in Education in Relation to the Occupational Structure," *Sociology of Education*, vol. 38, Fall, 1964, pp. 19–33.
[21] "The Doctoral Glutt," *Newsweek*, March 16, 1970, p. 114.

jobs rather than choosing among offers. Although the diploma becomes more important for more jobs than ever before, and the years in school continue to lengthen out for more people, there is no absolute certainty at the end of the academic road.

The diploma mills continue to grind out the needed degrees, with a few surpluses, and with critical shortages in medicine and some scientific areas. The student enrollment increases steadily, and the population rises in its average level of formal education. To some educators it seems that the golden age has arrived. For others there is the disturbing thought that thousands of people hardly fitted by temperament or interest for college are being ground through the machine, while many able people of depressed social background have been excluded by the hard facts of economics. There is also the worry that a college education is not accomplishing what the academically minded would like to see— graduates with awakened, inquiring minds, interested in the world of ideas, science, and society. The attention to graduation and to vocational preparation in a specialized age can be too narrowly instrumental. The national rivalry attitude toward education, observable especially in the years immediately after the Russians launched their first Sputnik in 1957, can lead in the same technically specialized direction. Most colleges are aware of this problem and try to avoid the training that Burton Clark characterizes as *technical barbarism* (more fully defined later), but the more narrowly technical training is a trend in much of the world.[22] A glance at the student subcultures within the universities will show many divergencies of opinion and interest but not too strong a concentration on the world of the intellect.

THE COLLEGE SUBCULTURES   The college student bodies of today are quite different from those of the past, especially if we take the large colleges and universities as models. Clark, using some of Martin Trow's terminology, describes four distinctive college subcultures, showing the gradual change in dominant student type.[23]

The first, the *collegiate subculture*, consisting of the "Joe College, rah-rah type," has long been on the decline, although it never completely disappears. "Joe College" was a loyal supporter of old alma mater, a faithful follower of the team, and a man who would eventually join the alumni association. Although he would never be an intellectual, he would identify with the school. His subculture was not serious enough for the academic professors, but it was functional to the school system in that it found outlets for youthful exuberance that supported the school rather than protesting its policies.

22 Clark, *op. cit.*, p. 288.
23 *Ibid.*, pp. 202–203.

The *academic subculture* has never made up a majority because not that many people are truly scholarly. There are probably as many members of the academic subculture today as ever, but they are lost in the growing mass of less academic students. The academics are the people devoted to learning and loyal to the school as a place of enlightenment. They are the types of scholars referred to in our opening quotation from Confucius with "breadth of mind" and "vigorous endurance."

A decline in the relative importance of the academic subculture could be dysfunctional to democratic societies. It has long been the viewpoint of liberty-loving nations that their freedom of expression, although sometimes disturbing, provides them with the very self-criticism that is needed. Social criticism is most likely to be given consideration if it comes from men of scholarly training. Autocratic regimes often find it expedient to promote expensive systems of technical and scientific education, but they take precautions against the development of cliques of intellectual critics. A system that supports science and technology, at the same time discouraging the critical capacities of the intellectual, is characterized by Clark as *technical barbarism*.

The majority college subculture is the *vocational subculture* that consists of people attending college to prepare for jobs. This subculture is a serious one but not necessarily in the sense of a love of knowledge for the sake of knowledge. Often the students are married, with home responsibilities, and sometimes making their way through school by slow degrees in night-school classes. Even the unmarried often do not have enough financial support from home. The result is that their hours of work interfere with much of the collegiate-subculture type of activity. The vocational subculture is a reflection of the change that has brought larger numbers of aspiring people from lower-middle class and working class into college.

The last of the subcultures described by Clark is the *nonconformist subculture*—a small one once but on many campuses a rapidly growing one. Furthermore, the nature of this subculture has changed as it blends increasingly with student activism. As originally described, the nonconformists were interested in art and music, dressed distinctively to the point of being shocking to the "squares," and generally did not relate to the college in loyalties. Their basic disregard for what they considered false middle-class standards made them ready recruits, or even leaders, for the student activism of today.

STUDENT ACTIVISM   Colleges and universities have been political storm centers in many countries of the world. During periods of national crisis student groups have been political activists in various countries of Europe, Asia, and Latin America. Even in the United States many college campuses were characterized by active political factions during the Great Depression, but they lacked the ability to mount the massive demonstrations of the 1960s and 1970. Student activism falls clearly into the category of latent functions of education, never intended by college governing boards or political administrations. Student-activist leaders see themselves as performing the critical, reformist, and innovative functions of education.

Normative strain is always present in a politically aware college generation that has been reared in a system that emphasizes the ideal norms of society. As students mature, they become aware — sometimes acutely so — of the gaps between ideal and reality. Nevertheless college campuses are usually quiet, as they were in the decade of the 1950s. There must be other ingredients besides normative strain to create an explosive situation: a generalized belief in the evils and incompetence of the "establishment," precipitating incidents, organization and leadership, and failures in social control — all traits included in Smelser's analysis of hostile outbursts (Chapter 7).

As is to be expected, there are widely differing evaluations of the student movements among members of the community. Some see them as the vanguard of a great new age of social justice. Some disapprove in relatively mild terms, pleased to see student political interest, but worried over excesses. Others see such movements as cases of the misplaced idealism of youth expecting to suddenly bring about an age of utopia. Some of the critics fear that student movements will only result in conservative reactions. Others, not at all unhappy about conservative reactions, think of student activists as the pawns of "reds" with completely unexplainable convictions.

A long and frustrating war has perpetuated student activism in the United States and brought it to unusual heights, but other complaints against society have also played a major part in student uprisings. The first student movements of the 1960s started over issues other than the Vietnam War, but at an earlier time an unpopular war in Korea had not caused similar student reactions.

During the 1950s, the college campus was disturbingly quiet — a tomb of learning. A favorite theme of many professors was expressed in T. S. Eliot's *The Hollow Men*. The poem, written in 1925, depicts Western civilization as a receptacle for mundane ideologies and populated by individuals fed on predigested opinions. The world will end with a whimper.

Reviewing the "silent fifties," Daniel Bell wrote that no new philosophies were emerging in Western thought and that, perhaps, we had reached the "end of ideology."[24] He asserted that radicalism was becoming extinct in a mass society. The radical, the discontent, the disenchanted, and the disenfranchised could only attack "the culture" as a whole and,

[24]Daniel Bell, *The End of Ideology*, Collier Books, The Macmillan Company, New York, 1962.

in so doing, found it hard to discover who or what was the enemy.[25]

On the campus the students seemed to retreat from an encounter with the mass society. Most students manifested the "withdrawal syndrome" by trying to achieve technological excellence. Science and mathematics classrooms were overflowing; classes in the humanities, literature, and the arts were generally avoided. Those who could not accept or cope with the boom of scientism sought refuge in the coffee houses that popularized the poetry and music of the "beat generation." The poetry was nihilistic, the music was jazz. Bensman and Rosenberg observed that the "Beats represent nothing but a passive rejection of middle-class values, with no enterprise to give that rejection meaning. . . ."[26]

Eventually an enterprise was found that gave meaning to the rejection of middle-class values: the attainment of civil rights for all citizens. The nucleus of this cause centered around the desegregation movement of the midfifties, which was largely outside the academic sphere. In the sixties the movement was carried into the college and university systems. In accordance with the sentiments of the students, the humanities experienced a renaissance as classrooms filled with individuals seeking a retort to the challenge offered by President Kennedy: ". . . ask what you can do for your country." Thousands of students went off to foreign soil by joining the Peace Corps, and thousands more poured into the urban ghettos looking for solutions to the plight of minority groups. It seemed that much of the public welcomed this type of activity and viewed it as constructive activism.

Student activism did not erupt as a serious disturbance until 1964 when the free speech movement began at the Berkeley campus of the University of California. Mario Savio, the spokesman and organizer of the disturbance, spoke about man's subjection to mass society, and students carried signs proclaiming "I am a student at Berkeley. Do not fold, spindle, or mutilate." Joan Baez led 1,000 students to a sit-in at Sproul Hall. It is interesting to note at this point that the right wing and left wing had at least one common foe—an impersonalized mass society undermining the individual. While the left wing on the campus objected to being numbered by a computer at a loss of individuality, the right wing in the community expressed fear that the new postal zip-code system was a Communist plot to categorize everyone in anticipation of a United Nations take-over of the United States.

A right- and left-wing coalition, of course, could not form. The two groups became oppositional. As the rightists directed their attention at the government and the Supreme Court, the leftists turned their attention

[25] *Ibid.*, p. 312.
[26] Joseph Bensman and Bernard Rosenberg, *Mass, Class, and Bureaucracy*, Prentice-Hall, Inc., Englewood Cliffs, N.J., 1963, p. 530.

toward the educational institution. In describing the activists of the 1964 demonstrations on campus, Charles T. Powers, staff writer for the *Los Angeles Times*, stated that "A one-sentence listing of their revolutionary heroes will likely include the names of Che Guevara, Mao Tse-tung, Leon Trotsky, and Jesus Christ."[27] Although the student movement drew its first converts from the left wing, its "cause" actually reflected a confusion of ideals, including political democracy and the extreme individuation characterized by the later expression, "Do your own thing."

According to Savio, students demanded an active role in the university, less impersonal regimentation, freedom from "mass education," nondiscriminatory hiring practices, and civil rights with equal opportunity for all Americans.[28] Within the "factory system" of the multiversity the student came to view himself as a second-class citizen seeking full participation in an academic society which alienated the young people whom it was intended to serve. The situation became more complicated as the war in Vietnam continued to escalate. The archetypal demonstrations for civil rights and student power were easily transformed into antiwar demonstrations. The student activists began to view themselves not only as second-class citizens or numbers to be fed into a computer but as "cannon fodder" for a war in which they did not believe. At this point, public opinion no longer considered the student movement a mere nuisance. Suddenly student activism became dangerous and alarming according to much of the populace outside the university system.

The apathy of the "silent fifties" was but a dim memory by the mid-sixties. The change was hailed by some as a great stride forward for politically aware students. Others looked at the direction of the movement and saw it leading toward total anarchy and the ultimate demise of the university system. The student activists saw it as another source of frustration. The sentiment of the students involved in the movement seems to be well reflected in a Simon and Garfunkel song in which all words end in the "well of silence."

However, the frustrations of the students did not slow the movement. The Berkeley rebellion was followed by massive protests at Columbia University and San Francisco State College. And, although the spotlight centered on these institutions, virtually every college and university was affected by the wave of student activism, especially after the entry of United States forces into Cambodia.

There is no evidence to suggest a reversal of trend in the near future. An analysis of the present college generation by Gallup lists six dif-

[27] Charles T. Powers, "Protesters of '64: Berkeley Leaders Face New World," *Los Angeles Times*, July 6, 1969, sect. B, p. 1.
[28] Mario Savio, "Certain Things That Happened at Berkeley," in Patrick Gleeson (ed.), *American Changing. . . .*, Charles E. Merrill Books, Inc., Columbus, Ohio, 1968, pp. 272–277. Reprinted from Hal Draper (ed.), *Berkeley: The New Student Revolt*, Grove Press, Inc., New York, 1965.

ferences between it and previous generations.[29] The first three, regarding use of drugs, sexual attitudes, and nonconformist appearance are of only minor importance to an analysis of the ideals behind student activism. The next three "new traits" of college youth (discussed below) show an ideational change quite consistent with the activism of today.

Interest in social work. A majority of all students report that they have done some social work. Sixty-five percent of campus demonstrators have engaged in this type of activity; only forty-five percent of nondemonstrators have. Working among the poor and underprivileged is now considered to be part of one's college experience.

Future occupation and goals in life. Earning a great amount of money and making one's mark in the world are no longer the chief goals of college students. Most students seem to prefer occupations directed toward helping others.

Attitude toward society. Generally, students behold the world with an extremely critical eye. The "credibility gap," which was expanded during the Johnson administration, has not closed in the years since.

These three interests and points of view may be interpreted as the results of growing awareness of the social-class inequalities in an "equalitarian" society. They also show a confidence on the part of the young that they are capable of initiating important improvements. To a large degree the role of social critic is being taken over by college students, not by the seasoned scholar whose "burden is heavy and whose course is long." Such a change is obviously disturbing to those who expect criticism to be fairly polite and to emanate from within the system and not from impetuous youth. To the student activist, the only real critic must be the person still uncontaminated by the system and not aware of a vested interest in it.

Whatever the eventual outcome, it seems that at present the critical function of education has become more dominant than ever before. The criticism reflects a society in a state of restlessness and uncertainty, not because of a general decline in societal welfare, but because of a widening gap between social custom and what is perceived as desirable. Mass education has a great potential for widening this gap, especially in times of unpopular wars and other crises.

SUMMARY   In all societies, education has the function of transmitting the accumulated culture of the past to future generations. In modern societies especially it has the additional function of developing new ideas in order to remain abreast of present developments and prepare for

[29] George Gallup, "The Gallup Poll: Today's Student New Breed in Six Respects," *Los Angeles Times*, May 26, 1969, part 1, pp. 6–7.

the future. Other major functions of education are training needed personnel, promoting citizenship, and maintaining status for some, and encouraging social mobility for others. Educational systems also display such latent functions as the development of adolescent subcultures and various kinds of student activism.

In modern societies a gap develops between the time of learning and the time of application of knowledge, making education long and difficult.

Early American education stressed the cultural-transmission function of education and the development of national feelings. As education became increasingly universal, it began to be seen largely as a vehicle for upward mobility, but for many people there were barriers in the way.

Since educational systems are a reflection of their societies and influence the growing generation, an examination of high school and college reveals many of the distinguishing traits of the society. In the United States, a fun and popularity subculture in high school, although criticized by adults, is a fair reflection of a fun-loving adult world. Ability grouping in schools reflects the strain between the ideal of equality and the realities of differing starts in life and differing academic possibilities.

The path to and through college can be viewed in some respects as a long, uneven race, with high hurdles to be surmounted by those of working-class or depressed ethnic-group background — the problems of initial motivation, "knowing the ropes," and raising the money.

Whatever the criticisms of college, it accomplishes the task of training the needed personnel for the job market, with a few exceptions, especially in the field of medicine. The college probably also has the function of liberalizing attitudes toward racial and ethnic groups and increasing tolerance of opinion differences. In spite of these changes, the higher-class position achieved by many college graduates tends to separate them from minority racial groups.

The college subcultures that have been analyzed are the collegiate, academic, vocational, and nonconformist. Clark suggests that a decline in the academic subculture and rise in the practical, vocational subculture may lead to a technically expert society, but a society without enough reflection on purpose, direction, and philosophy.

The last of the college subcultures, nonconformist, has merged with student activism, and student-activist movements attract many other students as well. Student activism can be analyzed as a development made possible by a somewhat separated college world developing an antagonism toward what it sees as "the establishment." Other developments are necessary before such attitudes erupt into demonstrations, but these developments have been frequent in recent years. Although antiwar sentiment is a major factor, student activism of recent times started with other causes, such as free speech and civil rights.

Critical and innovative functions of education have become more prominent now than in the past. They developed in a society torn by normative strains, acutely aware of its ghettos, racial inequalities, depressed areas, and unsure of its cause in war. The critical function, usually thought of as the job of trained intellectuals, has been taken over by the young. The older generation sees the young as too visionary for the world of reality and lacking in maturity of judgment. The young activists, in turn, see the older generation as too thoroughly engrossed in the system to be capable of meaningful criticism and strong action toward reform.

thirteen

THE ECONOMIC SYSTEM

Economic systems are the institutionalized arrangements
worked out by societies for the production and distribution
of goods. These systems differ widely and usually develop
through long custom and necessity rather than through
consciously stated economic philosophies. Nevertheless,
there is a close relationship between economic systems
and other aspects of a culture. Often in hunting and
gathering societies, for example, land, hunting and fishing
areas, and food-bearing plants are thought of as communal
property that are not parcelled out to individuals.[1]
Close cooperation and food sharing are so necessary for
survival that they become part of the moral order. In
later agricultural societies, productivity becomes great
enough to support upper classes who often rationalize
the uneven division of rewards on the basis of their own
superiority or even of God's will. The very need for
rationalization, however, indicates that societies have
seen something of a moral issue in their systems of
production and reward.

[1] E. Adamson Hoebel, *Anthropology: The Study of Man*, McGraw-Hill Book Company, New York, 1968, pp.
415–416.

In modern societies the concept of "just rewards" is constantly referred to in every labor dispute. The regulation of industry, tendencies toward monopoly, conflicts of interest in economic and political power, and threats to free enterprise are all viewed as issues of right and wrong.

We shall study the historical rise of our modern economic system and then we shall return to the issue posed by our opening quotation from Durkheim—whether the system can "satisfy the need for justice." We shall look also into the problems and prospects of an economy that meets at least some of the requirements of free enterprise but becomes increasingly regulated because the struggle between free enterprise and social regulation is also seen as a normative issue.

CAPITALISM IN HISTORICAL PERSPECTIVE   The medieval economic systems were very different from those of today. There were a few wandering merchants and a few trade centers, but for the most part the economy was of a subsistence type, with peasants producing their own goods. Most economic arrangements were based on obligation to the feudal lord whose lands had to be worked by the serf. Lands belonged in feudal estates and were not for sale. To suggest the sale of manorial estates would be as much out of order as to suggest that the United States sell Texas to Mexico.

Emergence of the competitive economy   In contrast, a highly competitive exchange economy emerged with the passing of the Middle Ages. The new economy was still somewhat encumbered by fees and obligations and the granting of special monopolies to favorites of the Crown, but it was moving in the direction of control by supply and demand. Adam Smith, the great champion of the new system, wrote in the late eighteenth century that an "invisible hand" would guide a free economy to make sure that the goods needed by society were produced in the quantities called for by a competitive market. Distribution would be fair and just, with the businessman earning his share in repayment for his enterprise, skill, and risk; the laborer would receive a lesser share for his work, which required less planning and risk. Since labor was plentiful, the laborer would be in a poor bargaining position but at the very worst would have to be paid enough to stay alive and to reproduce his kind.[2]

Smith's idea had great appeal to the rising business classes who wanted greater freedom of the economy, a policy called *laissez faire*, meaning literally "to let alone." The government was not to interfere with business. The encumbrances of the mercantile system were broken,

---

[2] Robert Heilbroner, *The Worldly Philosophers*, Simon & Schuster, Inc., New York, 1958, chap. III.

especially in the newly independent United States, and the new laissez-faire economy seemed to be off to a good start. Malthus and his friend David Ricardo saw the possibility of an economy that would produce too many laborers. Ricardo especially thought that if the laborer earned too much money he might cease to work, or even more likely he might produce and successfully rear enormous numbers of ragged children. This would mean that in the next generation there would not be enough jobs, and the result would be unemployement and starvation. (Ricardo incorrectly assumed that deep poverty would cause people to practice restraint in their breeding habits.) Therefore the safe policy would be to pay labor only the barest minimum of survival wages, an idea known as "the iron law of wages." Small wonder that Carlisle spoke of economics as "the dismal science."[3]

Conditions of labor   Descriptions of the conditions of labor in the late eighteenth and early nineteenth centuries indicate that Ricardo was taken seriously in the emergent industrial nations. The English Factory Acts of 1833, in the name of reform, forbade children under nine to work in textile factories and ruled that children less than thirteen could not work more than forty-eight hours/week in factories or mines. Nine years later it was decided that it was improper for women to pull coal carts through the mines, and women and girls and boys under ten were forbidden to work in the mines.[4] Reform was running wild!

As was to be expected, labor agitation was on the rise, and many thoughtful critics questioned whether the "invisible hand" was working in behalf of the people. Heinrich Heine expressed the bitter mood in his "Song of the Weavers": "Old Germany, listen, e'er we disperse; we are weaving your doom with a triple curse!" In England, Elizabeth Barrett Browning pleaded against the conditions of child labor. She wrote in 1843 "Have you heard the children weeping, O my brothers (while) All day long the iron wheels go onward, grinding life down from its mark, (and) A child's sob in the silence curses deeper than a strong man in his wrath." While reformers pleaded, angry revolutionists called for an end of the system: "Let the ruling classes tremble . . . the proletarians have nothing to lose but their chains. They have the world to win," declared the *Communist Manifesto* in 1848.

Rising productivity and reform   Actually, revolutions of the type Marx called for were thwarted, and even today such revolutions are much more the

[3] *Ibid.*, chap. IV.
[4] J. Salwyn Shapiro, *Modern and Contemporary European History*, Houghton Mifflin Company, Boston, 1951, pp. 133–134.

phenomena of peasant and "underdeveloped" countries than of the industrial societies in which Marx had expected revolution. Although the capitalistic system did not deserve the rapturous praise given it by Smith, its very productivity began to frustrate its most bitter enemies and to undermine the "iron law of wages" policy. The "quantum theory"—the idea that there is only so much to go around, and so it would be disastrous to raise wages—became less convincing. The economic system was showing enough growth so that wages could rise slowly without destroying profits. The dogged resistance to labor unionism broke down slowly in several Western capitalistic countries, and in Germany the powerful Chancellor Bismarck attracted worldwide attention by granting sickness insurance, accident insurance, and old-age pensions. This, said Bismarck, makes working men "far more contented and easier to manage. . . . A great price is not too much to pay if the disinherited can be made contented with their lot."[5] What happened in Germany in the 1880s has finally become common practice in all the major capitalistic nations.

THE DIVISION OF LABOR AND THE MORAL ORDER   One of Durkheim's most important works is *The Division of Labor in Society*, in which he speaks of a new moral order resulting from the increasingly complex division of labor in industrial societies. Before industrialization, people were held together by the traditional norms that they followed rather blindly because they were all socialized into the same pattern. They were as alike as though they had been "turned out of the same machine," and it was this culturally induced likeness of belief and habit that gave society its cohesion and its moral order. In the modern society, with its intricate division of labor, each man is an exchangist, Durkheim goes on to say, contributing the product of his labor and depending on the product of the labor of others. In this type of society a new moral order must be worked out based upon the increasing feeling of interdependence. Hence new rules and regulations arise. Each man can be different; there can be a growing amount of individuality, but the society will be cohesive because new norms based on interdependence will determine what is just.

New norms of industrialism   Following Durkheim's line of thought, we could speak of the new pension and insurance laws as a first step toward the new moral order, alleviating the poor conditions of labor and, hopefully, winning the loyalty of labor to the economic system. Later, the recognition of labor unions, negotiating terms and conditions of labor,

5 *Ibid.*, p. 396.

shortening hours of work, and in some cases, even adopting profit-sharing schemes all came as further steps in this new normative adjustment.

Other regulations illustrate the same trend toward a new type of equity: pure food and drug acts, fairness-in-advertising legislation, and laws to curb monopoly in order to keep competition alive. All of these are ameliorative traits of the free-enterprise system and have helped to make it a more attractive system than the Marxists foresaw. At the same time, such policies have curbed the purely laissez-faire features of capitalism.

Growing interdependence   The interdependence produced by the division of labor in society has had its counterpart in world trade. Not only was each man an "exchangist," but so was each nation, and the dynamic industrial systems of the West began to have a sweeping influence on other parts of the world. Marx, the arch enemy of the system, saw clearly what was happening. As usual he placed the blame at the feet of the "bourgeois" class—the leaders of industry, trade, and finance. Note that the words "industrial society" could easily be substituted for his word "bourgeoisie" without changing the aptness of his description.

> The bourgeoisie, by the rapid improvement of all
> instruments of production, by the immensely
> facilitated means of communication, draws all, even
> the most barbarian nations, into civilization. The
> cheap prices of its commodities are the artillery
> with which it batters down all the Chinese walls,
> with which it forces the barbarians' intensely
> obstinate hatred of foreigners to capitulate. It
> compels all nations, on pain of extinction, to adopt
> the bourgeois mode of production; it compels them
> to introduce what it calls civilization into their
> midst, i.e. to become bourgeois themselves. In a
> sense, it creates a world after its own image.
>
>   The bourgeoisie has subjected the country to
> the rule of the towns. It has created enormous
> cities, has greatly increased the urban population
> as compared with the rural, and has thus rescued a
> considerable part of the population from the idiocy
> of rural life. . . ."[6]

Whatever else could be said of the economic system, it had achieved a devastating level of productivity, drawing the whole world into its vortex, as Marx predicted. It had also accomplished a higher standard of living than its earlier critics had thought remotely possible, had added

[6] Karl Marx, *Manifesto of the Communist Party,* Charles H. Kerr, Chicago, 1888, p. 20.

many of the rules of Durkheim's "new moral order," had swept agriculture into its system, had found its needed markets and resources, and had displayed great vitality and inventiveness. It also had necessitated international cooperation in trade and science and would eventually bring about similar cooperation in monetary policy and even in "common-market" agreements.

Persistent problems Was the "new moral order" complete? A long list of problems arose. The industrial system, in its rapid development of resources, had often been wasteful. Forests were devastated, marginal lands were eroded, mines scarred the earth, mountainous slag heaps rose skyward, and in petroleum areas sump holes spread their miasmatic stench over the countryside. Not enough attention was paid to waste; rivers and lakes often became cesspools, fish and wildlife died, and supplies of drinking water were contaminated. Living species were being exterminated by insecticides and other chemicals used for the increase of production. Worries grew about the contamination of the atmosphere with automotive and industrial smog. In the summer of 1969 all the fish in the lower Rhine River (an estimated 40 million) were accidentally killed by pesticides. In some respects it seemed that modern industrialism, whether developed by free enterprise or by other systems, was running too fast to think of consequences.

A problem that harassed the capitalistic systems was the business cycle. Depressions followed prosperity, and some of these depressions were devastating, plunging people into hopeless despair for long periods of time and resulting in loud attacks on the capitalist system itself. At other times inflation became a danger to the system, tending to wipe out the savings of the thrifty and to be particularly hard on the elderly and other persons living on fixed incomes.

The system even had a tendency to limit the very competitive motif on which it was based by the growth of monopoly or, more commonly, *oligopoly*—a condition in which a few producers control practically all of a particular area of production, as in the automobile industry.

There also remained a number of problems concerning the distribution of wealth. No economic system distributes its wealth with complete evenness, nor is this expected. In the 1960s an increasing number of studies began to document the fact that some elements of the population did not share in the productive prosperity in any way; they remained in a well of poverty, isolated outside the system. This was especially true of aged people and many inhabitants of bypassed rural areas and city slums, as pointed out by Michael Harrington in his book *The Other America* and by Myrdal in *Challenge to Affluence*. The problem became particularly

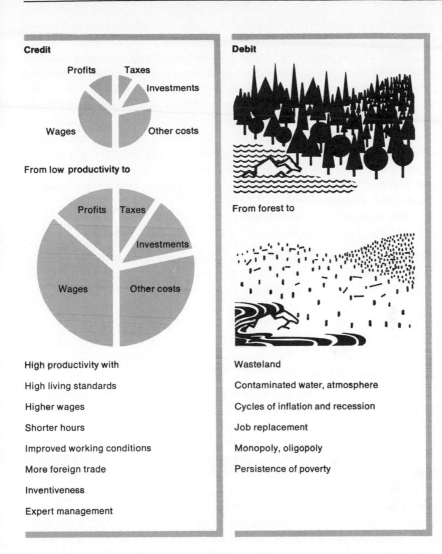

Credit

Profits Taxes
Investments
Wages Other costs

From low productivity to

Profits Taxes
Investments
Wages Other costs

High productivity with

High living standards

Higher wages

Shorter hours

Improved working conditions

More foreign trade

Inventiveness

Expert management

Debit

From forest to

Wasteland

Contaminated water, atmosphere

Cycles of inflation and recession

Job replacement

Monopoly, oligopoly

Persistence of poverty

bitter in an age of racial tensions because the largest concentrations of poverty were to be found in the Negro ghettos, the Mexican American *barrios*, and the Indian reservations. Congressional committees that investigated the problem of poverty in 1969 were shocked to find malnutrition common in some regions. In some cases the protein shortage was sufficient to show up in cases of *kwashiokor*—an African name for severe protein deficiency characterized by a distended stomach and skinny arms and legs.

One of the problems of the modern economic system is controversial and ill defined but nevertheless should be mentioned. Was the prosperous economy of the United States getting so involved in war, preparation for war, and the supplying of military equipment that it could rightly be called a *military-industrial complex*, with the implication that pressures would be exerted to keep up military spending because of vested interest in such spending? Left-wing critics consider the answer undoubtedly "yes." More conservative people hate to accept this view, and yet this is the very possibility that President Eisenhower warned against in his farewell address to the nation.

Obviously, Durkheim's "new moral order" is a long time being born.

TRENDS IN THE MODERN ECONOMY   For many years numerous writers have noted the decline in the directive role of the individual entrepreneur, the type of man represented by the picturesque giants of the past: Rockefeller, Carnegie, and Henry Ford. These were people who were both owners and managers. All decisions were their decisions. They had the advantage of quick decisions and innovation and the disadvantages of lack of consultation with technical experts.

The technostructure   One of the first books to document a new trend in the management of large enterprises was *The Managerial Revolution* by James Burnham. More recently, Bell has described much the same phenomenon in "The Break-up of Family Capitalism," [7] noting that the control of great corporations is today less likely than in earlier times to pass from father to son and that control comes from college-trained managers who arise from outside the ownership family. In *The New Industrial State*, John Kenneth Galbraith speaks of much the same phenomenon under the concept of *technostructure*. [8] The technostructure is always a committee of experts, acting jointly to reach decisions. An interfering owner cannot overrule the technostructure for fear of creating tensions that would disrupt the system. If a group is hired to do a study, make itself expert, and reach conclusions, and its conclusions are then overturned, a likely result is demoralization and possibly resignation. Consequently, the staff is depended upon completely. It becomes a cohesive group, planning together and drawing in the best advice from each area of expertise. It almost resembles a plot for gaining government contracts, increasing its share of the market, outdistancing competitors, and creating greater consumer demand through advertising. Although small busi-

[7] Daniel Bell, *The End of Ideology*, Collier Books, The Macmillan Company, New York, 1962, pp. 39–45.
[8] John Kenneth Galbraith, *The New Industrial State*, Houghton Mifflin Company, Boston, 1967, pp. 60–71.

nesses continue to exist, the large corporation of this type has many advantages, gradually making the concentration of industrial power more and more unchallengable.

The technostructure depends upon a stable economy and therefore is concerned with the fiscal and monetary policies of the government. Social security and other devices that tend to keep buying on an even keel are generally seen as beneficial to such organizations because they help to give the stability needed for long-range planning. In other respects the industrial order becomes more enmeshed with and dependent upon the state, and the situation is mutual. The industrial system serves the purposes of the state, doing the research work necessary for weapons development, space programs, and other new advances in science. "The state, through military and other technical procurement, underwrites the corporation's largest capital commitments in its areas of most advanced technology."[9] State and industry merge in ends and methods.

The corporation that supplies equipment for the Navy begins to identify with the Navy. It takes the Navy point of view, and customer and industry pull together for larger appropriations. The interrelationship of corporation and state is not apt to be based on old-fashioned bribery for special favors (as when railroads virtually owned state legislatures) but is based on commonality of interest. In a broader sphere, both are dependent upon a stable economy, a well-supported educational system, expansion and growth, scientific advancement—in short, national goals.[10] The military-industrial complex is at hand especially where military, industry, and government develop a mutual involvement and vested interests in weapons development. The real question is whether this is a complex that rightfully prepares the defenses of the United States against possible foreign aggression or whether it is a complex with a dynamic of its own, leading to more and more arms expenditure regardless of need and constituting a threat to peace.[11]

The concentration of wealth   The late C. Wright Mills wrote a book titled *The Power Elite* in which he contended that power tends to concentrate in the hands of the few, and he noted the same interrelationship between government, military, and industry that was just cited from a more recent work by Galbraith. In the same book, Mills also presents evidence to prove that there is a "hardening of the arteries" insofar as the ready mobility of Americans from low to extremely high status is concerned. In part of his work he uses the example of only the very wealthiest families in the United States, those with holdings of an absolute minimum of

[9] *Ibid.*, p. 308.
[10] *Ibid.*, p. 309.
[11] Marc Pilisuk and Thomas Hayden have an excellent discussion of this problem in "Is There a Military-Industrial Complex Which Prevents Peace?", *The Journal of Social Issues*, vol. XXI, July, 1965, pp. 67–117.

30 million dollars. Among these families he finds a tendency toward greater and greater stability in position. Of the holders of the greatest fortunes of the nineteenth century, 39 percent were born poor; of the last group in his study, the 1950 generation, only 9 percent were born poor.[12] The Mills analysis contrasts with many studies finding as much mobility as ever in American society, so his analysis must be considered open to controversy. A partial explanation of these differences in findings is that Mills was speaking of only the very wealthiest, and most mobility studies have been done in middle ranges.

The offhand impression of many people is that income and inheritance taxes have had a powerful leveling effect so that change could be noted in the years since Mills wrote *The Power Elite*. In "The Future of Capitalism" Robert Heilbroner looks into this possibility.[13] In his opinion the maldistribution of income is not sufficient to constitute a threat to capitalism, but he thinks it is greater than desirable and is not becoming less. Although a generation has passed since high inheritance and gift taxes were initiated, concentration of stock ownership has "shown no tendency to decline since 1922," and wealth held has declined only slightly (from 33 percent to 29 percent). "The statistics of income distribution show a slow but regular drift toward the upper end of the spectrum."[14]

Recently much comment and discontent has arisen over the matter of income-tax evasion. If regulations are tightened, they may have more of a leveling effect on wealth and income.

The position of labor and the impact of automation   *Automation*, originally defined as the "automatic handling of parts between progressive production processes,"[15] has come to mean any type of automatic process that replaces or improves human control of production. Sometimes the word "cybernation" is used, meaning full use of computers along with other types of automation. In some respects it is a continuation of the increasing industrial efficiency that started with the first days of the Industrial Revolution and the later growth of assembly-line production. One effect of the long process of change in production techniques has been to make work monotonous, and a corollary effect has been to do away with pride in craftsmanship and identification with the product. The resistance of labor to new techniques and the drive for efficiency is an old story, at least as old as Hargreaves and his spinning jenny that was attacked and destroyed by an angry mob. Will automation also reduce worker satisfaction and increase worker anger, or will it alleviate some of the problems of the industrial system?

[12]C. Wright Mills, *The Power Elite*, Oxford University Press, New York, 1958.
[13]Robert L. Heilbroner, "The Future of Capitalism," *Commentary*, vol. 41, April, 1966, pp. 23–35.
[14]*Ibid.*, pp. 23–35.
[15]Paul A. Samuelson, *Economics: An Introductory Analysis*, McGraw-Hill Book Company, New York, 1964, p. 333.

Bell shows how management attitude toward labor has gradually changed from speed-up to worker satisfaction. The cult of the efficiency expert reached its heyday around the turn of the century with Frederick W. Taylor and his stopwatch and with Frank Gilbreth (Father in the well-known story *Cheaper by the Dozen*). Gilbreth reduced all mechanical operations to their smallest component parts, called "therbligs" (his name spelled backward), in an attempt to speed up each movement.[16] The compulsive nature of the assembly line was heightened as never before, and the resentment toward management and its efficiency experts was correspondingly heightened. The modern policies of coffee breaks and improved conditions of all kinds, along with more of a labor union's definition of what constitutes a fair day, have changed the situation considerably; still it is difficult to make people happy with most kinds of menial jobs, even by such devices as calling garbage men "sanitary engineers." In a 1955 study only small percentages of workers in the following categories said they would choose the same kind of work again: service workers, 33 percent; semiskilled operatives, 32 percent; unskilled, 16 percent. Professional, managerial, and sales personnel indicated much greater satisfaction with their jobs.[17]

The general discontent with jobs requiring lower skills and greater satisfaction with jobs requiring more education leads some to see automation as a great boon to labor. Bernard Asbell writes:

> We are engaged . . . in one of history's most grand
> and pure acts of humanity. We are making it
> unfeasable for masses of men to live like animals.
> To those millions still entrapped in the animal pens
> of our old ways, we are showing the way—even
> compelling them down the way—to dignity, physical
> freedom and the joys of intellectual discovery.[18]

Although not many researchers in the field are quite as ecstatic in their praise of automation as Asbell, many others point out its ultimate advantages: fewer monotonous jobs paced by the machine and more jobs in which man is in control of the machines. There will be no more need for Markham's "Man with the Hoe" — "distorted and soul-quenched . . . stolid and stunned, a brother to the ox."

Automation and job replacement   One can hardly mention automation without entering into a discussion of job replacement. There are some areas in which the loss of jobs in recent years has been a cause for

---

[16] Bell, *op. cit.*, pp. 227–272.

[17] Nancy C. Morse and Robert S. Weiss, "The Function and Meaning of Work and the Job," *American Sociological Review*, vol. 20, April, 1955, pp. 197–198.

[18] Bernard Asbell, *The New Improved American*, Dell Publishing Co., Inc., New York, 1965, p. 23.

alarm. There has been a loss of 435,000 railroad jobs, 265,000 jobs in textile mills, 310,000 jobs in coal mining, and 3,600,000 jobs in agriculture.[19] Many of these job losses have resulted from new automated techniques, although some have been caused by the decline in demand in some industries — coal, for example. An argument arises over whether new jobs are being created by the new machines or whether much of labor is simply becoming obsolete.

If the number of man-hours of labor required to produce and maintain the machine were the equivalent of the number of man-hours of labor the machine would replace, it obviously would not pay for production. There are two somewhat more sophisticated ways of analyzing the possibilities. (1) It is possible that automated processes will be able to reduce the price of goods sufficiently so that more goods will be consumed and that, therefore, almost as many people as ever can be employed regardless of machine displacement of some of the workers. (2) The other possibility is that a high enough level of prosperity will keep employment high regardless of machine efficiency. This seems to have been true in recent years, in spite of rapid growth of the labor force, partly augmented by more women at work. The professional, trade, and service areas have expanded employment while jobs in other areas have declined, but there are differences of opinion regarding the net result. It is small satisfaction for a replaced coal miner to be assured that somewhere else in the economy somebody is getting some new type of job. There is also less than full agreement about whether the new jobs are always better than the old. Harrington complains that often well-paying jobs, protected by powerful labor unions, have been surrendered for service jobs that are far below union standards. The process of retraining such workers for other types of industrial jobs also has its problems. As one union official states, "The trouble with retraining is that nobody knows what the hell to retrain them for. We may teach them a new skill that itself may be automated in six months. . . ."[20] Even the service trades are not immune to automation, as noted by Donald Michael's examples: self-help markets, department stores, and service stations, automated food dispensers, automatic elevators and escalators. The R. H. Macy Company even has an automatic sales girl: a machine that can dispense thirty or forty items in different sizes and styles. It is intelligent enough to make change and to recognize and reject counterfeit money.[21]

Another example of this kind of concern about jobs is implicit in the following advertisement:

[19] *Ibid.*, pp. 173–174.
[20] Harold H. Martin, "Has Success Spoiled Big Labor?", *Saturday Evening Post*, December 8, 1962.
[21] Donald Michael, "Cybernation, the Silent Conquest," *A Report to the Center for the Study of Democratic Institutions*, The Fund for the Republic, Inc., 1962, pp. 14–24.

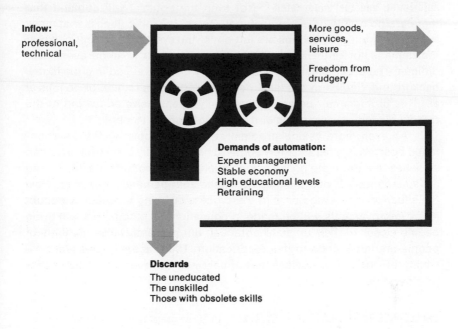

Inflow:
professional,
technical

More goods,
services,
leisure

Freedom from
drudgery

Demands of automation:
Expert management
Stable economy
High educational levels
Retraining

Discards
The uneducated
The unskilled
Those with obsolete skills

*TransfeRobot 200 will pick up, turn over, insert,
transfer, shuttle, rotate, or position parts accurately,
and will control secondary operations such as
drilling, stamping, heat sealing, welding, embossing,
forging.*[22]

Such machines are always frightening to the worker and perhaps even to the disinterested layman.

To return to the more optimistic analysis, Asbell contends that the loss of jobs in rails is matched by gains in the aircraft industry; losses of jobs in textiles are more than matched by gains in merchandise-store employment; losses in coal jobs are more than matched by gains in petroleum and chemicals; and the huge two-decade decline of 3,600,000 in agricultural jobs is evenly matched by the tremendous gain in employment in teaching. The largest percentage gains are in professional, semiprofessional, and white-collar jobs that are generally preferred to those being replaced, in spite of exceptions noted by Harrington.

[22]Asbell, *op. cit.*, p. 30.

Automation and the uneducated   Not even the optimist will contend that there are no problems of employment. One of the difficulties is that many members of minority groups are left out of the system at present and that the demand for more advanced skills makes their position even more difficult. The urban black, generally already disadvantaged in educational background, finds only the least desirable jobs open to him, or no jobs at all. This problem can be ameliorated only by intensive education of the disadvantaged — a strong demand of minority-group leaders.

An even more vexing problem arises for people whose disadvantaged position is a result of low ability. It has generally been true in human societies that there are only a few positions calling for unusual talent and an abundance of jobs making no intellectual demands whatever. Now the situation is reversed or is in the process of being reversed. No doubt many improvements will be made in educational methods that will bring people closer to their ultimate potential, but presently large numbers of people are impervious to much education. There is the unpleasant possibility of creating a society that simply has no need for a significant portion of its population.

CHALLENGES TO THE ECONOMIC SYSTEM   In this chapter we have been concerned with a series of challenges that interrelate the economy with sociological problems and perspectives. A new value system has evolved in which many of our national leaders have come to look upon the solutions to problems of welfare, poverty, inflation, growth rates, and unemployment as the essence of the art of government. Attempts to solve such problems, however, lead to other problems — high taxes and increased governmental functions — leading us ever further from the laissez-faire economy that was the dream of Smith. This leads to special types of challenges, fundamental and interrelated, that must be examined.

Free enterprise   One of the major questions of the future is whether the economy can maintain a healthy degree of freedom. In an economic system that most people characterize as *free enterprise,* it is surprising to realize the extent of government involvement. That regulations should be imposed on interstate commerce, including railroads, trucks, airlines, and the like, has long been accepted. Controls of other kinds are becoming increasingly necessary for the protection of health and welfare: food and drug laws, supervision of insecticides and pollutants, safety regulations, and regulations concerning conditions of labor. Other groups of controls include meeting government standards in building and the avoidance of racial discrimination in hiring. Altogether, the regulations, increasing taxes, and the monetary and fiscal manipulations already mentioned are sufficient to cause our economists to speak of ours as a *mixed economic system* rather than a system of pure private enterprise. It should be noted, however, that at present the private sector of the economy remains strong and flourishing. We trade at privately owned markets and department stores, buy our houses from private builders, pay privately owned corporations for our gas, electricity, and telephone services, deposit our money at privately owned banks, buy our automobiles from giant, but privately owned, corporations. This is a long way from a socialistic economy.

The Communist challenge   In reviewing the history of the capitalistic system it was mentioned that the stronger industrial-capitalist nations have not been subject to Communist takeover, although this has long been the nightmare of many people, especially members of the far right. It was also mentioned that the greatest danger seems to be to countries characterized as underdeveloped, just beginning the industrial revolution. Benjamin and Kautsky have recently done a study documenting the idea that the danger of large Communist parties is greatest in countries with considerable industrial development, but with much lower average annual incomes than the major capitalist nations. The preindustrial societies have almost no Communist Party members. Those In the earliest stages of industrial development have a small Oommunist group consisting mainly of intellectuals educated abroad. Those with considerable industrialism, but less production than the major industrial powers (France, Greece, and Italy), and with a GNP of only $600 to $1,200 per capita have the largest Communist parties. Those with the highest level of industrial development show a great drop in Communist sentiment (Australia, Canada, Sweden, Japan, Great Britain, and the United States).[23]

There remains, of course, the challenge of the Communist world in another sense: will free economies be able to maintain their lead over those of the Communist bloc? The industrial output of the Soviet Union increased at an average annual rate of 5.9 percent in the years 1950 to 1966,[24] but it has been slowing slightly since. During the same period the United States output increased at a rate of 3.9 percent. Part of the reason for the difference is that the later entrants into the industrial system can benefit from the accumulated technological knowledge of the world, and this advantage lessens with the passing of time. It should also be realized that percentage increases per year are sometimes easier to achieve if the original production is small than if it is already adequate or nearly adequate to the needs of the nation. In spite of the percentage gains of the

[23] Robert W. Benjamin and John H. Kautsky, "Communism and Economic Development," *American Political Science Review*, vol. 62, March, 1968, pp. 110–123.
[24] George Leland Bach, *Economics*, Prentice-Hall, Inc., Englewood Cliffs, N.J., 1968, p. 199.

Soviet Union the standard of living remains far below that of the United States. Per capita output in 1966 was estimated at $3,770 for the United States and $1,450 for the U.S.S.R.[25]

Dynamism and drive   A point of view variously called "the decline of the Protestant ethic," the rise of the "organization man" (William H. Whyte), or the emergence of the "other-directed personality" (Riesman) has its implications for a dynamic, competitive economic system. A strong supporter of the capitalistic economic system, the economist Joseph Schumpeter, answered the question "Do you think capitalism can survive?" with "No, I don't think it can."[26] His gloomy prognostication was based on his conviction that capitalism requires a dynamic personality type, individualistic in methods and approach as well as in economic philosophy. The modern trend toward large-scale bureaucratic organization, with its emphasis on predictable outcomes, is simply contrary to the adventurous spirit of capitalism. Although he gave no name to the system to replace capitalism, Schumpeter seems to have had in mind a semi-private economy, but one so controlled as to no longer be thought of as free enterprise.

Heilbroner, in "The Future of Capitalism," analyzes the changes that are and are not possible within capitalism.[27] Capitalism is a system that can be modified in the direction of government control, welfare measures, close interrelationship with the military complex, and even a limited amount of leveling through the tax system. However, the economic system is not only a system of production and distribution but a system of privilege based on wealth, and there will be strong resistance to the surrender of such privilege. For this reason Heilbroner does not see an indefinite movement in the direction of socialism. For many years he predicts the continuation of the present system, probably further modified, but still recognizable as capitalism. In the long run, however, the requirements of technical and scientific expertise may result in a system in which such experts are in control rather than owners and managers.[28] Whatever the future, the mixed economic system, which has shown great adjustability in the past, will probably have to show even greater adjustability in the future.

STABILIZING THE ECONOMIC SYSTEM   One requirement for keeping a relatively free-enterprise system is the avoidance of depression and run-away

25 *Ibid.*, p. 3.
26 Heilbroner, *The Worldly Philosophers, op. cit.*, p. 278.
27 Heilbroner, "The Future of Capitalism," *op. cit.*, p. 33.
28 Heilbroner, *The Worldly Philosophers, op. cit.*, p. 235.

inflation. A stable economy can prevent the kind of massive unemployment and business failure (so typical of the Great Depression period) that cause many to despair of the system. Stability is also needed for the high levels of productivity necessary for increased education, urban renewal, and antipoverty programs demanded by a large segment of the population.

Monetary and fiscal policy   The age of Woodrow Wilson brought a new concept into the management of the national economy—*monetary policy,* which is the attempt to control inflation and deflation through control of the money supply. The Federal Reserve System can lower or raise rediscount rates, which in turn increases or lowers interest rates to the borrower. The principle is if money is cheap (interest rates are low) more people will borrow, and if money is costly (interest rates are high), fewer people will borrow. The record indicates that monetary policy has had only a very limited effect. It certainly was not sufficient to control the Great Depression or inflations that have taken place since. More governmental policies were to be tried.

The new policies were started during the Roosevelt administration, without a clear theory or mathematical analysis of just what the result to the economy would be. The vague term "pump priming" was used to describe the intended effect; but soon a new economic analysis of the government role in a depression was provided by John Maynard Keynes of England, and the science of economics has never been the same. Keynes started by discovering an economic dilemma that had been overlooked before his time: individual savings can have the effect of slowing down an economy if there is no outlet for their investment.[29] This slowing down has a snowballing effect that can eventually end in a new equilibrium of permanent depression. Vast new discoveries or other sources of new investment could reverse the cycle, as could the wasteful expenditures of war. The first alternative does not always appear, and the second is too horrible to be a purposeful solution, but there remains a third alternative. Let the government spend large amounts of money, in deficit spending if necessary, to make up for the shrinkage of private investment. The management of the money supply started in Wilson's time is called *monetary policy;* the pumping of money into the economy by direct government action is part of what is called *fiscal policy.*[30]

Distribution of gross national product   Neither policy is enthusiastically endorsed by all economists, but they have become so important in governmental policies as to be essential to economic institutions. Even the public

[29] Samuelson, *op. cit.,* p. 242.
[30] *Ibid.,* chap. XII.

is forming the habit of thinking in terms of modern fiscal policy and other words associated with modern *macroeconomics,* that is, large-scale analysis of economic issues. "Gross national product" has become a part of the common vocabulary, although "net national product" is a little more meaningful for the following equation. *Gross national product* is the sum total of all goods and services produced in a single year. *Net national product* equals gross national product minus depreciation and will be referred to as NNP.

$$NNP = C + I + G$$
where C = consumer expenditure
I = private investment
G = government expenditures

To keep the equation balanced it would be necessary to increase G if there is a decline in C and/or I. If C, I, and G all increase rapidly, as in war-time, there are strong inflationary pressures which can be headed off by higher taxes, price and wage controls, or possibly by forced savings of part of income (to reduce C in the formula). Manipulation of the economy is not always successful, but it is hoped that this brief glance at theory will at least help to clarify the methods that are attempted.

There are other reasons why the layman should understand something about the ideas of monetary and fiscal policy. (1) Monetary and fiscal policies, plus the economic characteristics that have already been discussed under technostructure, show the degree to which ours is a managed economy, not depending entirely on Smith's "invisible hand" of supply and demand. (2) Since enormous new pressures and demands are constantly being placed on the economy, this type of analysis is necessary to make a guess at how much government spending is necessary to maintain a healthy rate of growth and to determine at what point it can get out of hand and contribute to inflation, as in both the Korean and Vietnam Wars. (3) It should demonstrate that government spending is not exactly the same as private spending. The individual reduces spending if times are hard; the government, by keynesian logic, should increase spending.

How much the public sector of economic spending can increase without inflationary pressures is not agreed upon by all economists. Leon Keyserling thinks that there is little danger of large infusions of money into the economy, provided that there is a balance between consumption and investment. President Kennedy thought of a 6 percent growth rate (over a long period we have averaged just over 3 percent) as very possible, aided by deficit spending, and eventually paying off in tax revenues to the government through a much higher GNP on which to collect taxes. His opponents believed that this might be too inflationary.

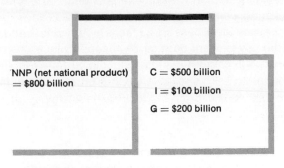

NNP (net national product) = $800 billion

C = $500 billion

I = $100 billion

G = $200 billion

Economy in balance NNP = C + I + G

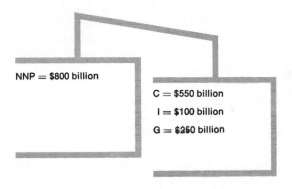

NNP = $800 billion

C = $550 billion

I = $100 billion

G = $250 billion

Economy out of balance NNP < C + I + G

Inflationary pressures at work. Policies to prevent inflation could involve high interest rates to discourage I (investment), or higher taxes to reduce C (consumer spending), or government economies to reduce G (government expenditures).

Regardless of which opinion is correct, it can be seen that if we wish to keep up the large investment needed to educate the disadvantaged, renew our cities, and keep employment levels high enough to make real inroads on poverty, the economy must be kept in high gear. One problem at present is that military spending accounts for more than half of C in our equation NNP = C + I + G. In one respect government spending has something in common with private spending: money can be spent for almost anything within our income range, but we cannot buy everything at once. If the individual does so, he faces indebtedness and, possibly, bankruptcy. If the government does so, the economy faces inflation. Therefore we are faced with choices about what must be done with the products of industry and labor. In this respect, as in so many others, the economy is closely involved in the normative values of society.

SUMMARY   Economic systems are the institutionalized means for production and distribution of goods. Particularly where distribution is concerned, the problem of "just rewards" is viewed by members of society in moral terms; various attempts are made to rationalize uneven reward systems or to change them.

The system that we call modern capitalism emerged slowly out of systems based on the privileges of feudalism but changed with the advance of the Industrial Revolution. Adam Smith, the best-known early champion of a free-enterprise system, expected capitalism to be a nearly perfect system, distributing goods fairly on a basis of supply and demand. His ideas were widely accepted by rising business interests, but bad conditions in factories and mines caused protests and revolutionary threats. However, capitalism developed such high productivity that it was possible for wages to increase without cutting out profits, and labor reforms gradually came about. Bismarck was the first powerful statesman to grant pensions and other modern benefits to labor, hoping therewith to buy their loyalty for Germany.

As Durkheim pointed out, the intricate division of labor in modern society calls for new norms based on interdependence and rewards rather than punishments. Greater rewards for labor were a part of the new moral order made possible by high productivity. Even Karl Marx was aware of the great productivity of the capitalistic system and its power to supersede other economic systems, but he expected it to deepen the poverty of the poor. The system did not lead to the ever-deepening poverty Marx foresaw, but it lacked much of what might have been implied in Durkheim's new moral order.

Despite slowly rising standards of living, new problems arose—waste of natural resources and contamination, business cycles and depressions, monopolistic trends in many industries. In spite of a generally improved standard of material well-being, poverty persisted. Another problem was the increasing involvement of the economic system in military production; a decline in military spending could injure the economy.

Major trends in the modern economy include greater control by expert management in systems that Galbraith has characterized as techno-structures. Although there are conflicts in interpretation, many agree with the late C. Wright Mills that there is an increasing concentration of wealth and power—a "power elite" of business, government, and military.

A worry to labor has been the increase in automation in modern industry. There is no question that many people are replaced in their jobs and that many jobs protected by union pay scales and benefits have declined sharply. On the other hand, many of the new types of jobs required by automation bring greater worker satisfaction than those being replaced.

An assessment of the record of the modern mixed economic system shows that it has great adjustability and is not on the verge of being surpassed in productivity by the Communist states. Some wonder if the real challenge to the American economic system is not a more subtle one—the tendency for it to lose some of its drive as independent business concerns are replaced by industrial giants under increasing managerial and governmental control.

Economic analysis makes it clear that although the government has vast financial powers, it cannot afford to accomplish all of its aims at once. Choices must be made as to how much should be spent on military and space programs as opposed to antipoverty, urban-renewal, and educational programs. Just as the division of rewards between industry and labor can be seen as part of the new moral order, so can the decisions of how to use the financial resources of the government.

*Inherent in all democratic systems is the
constant threat that the group conflicts
which are democracy's lifeblood may
solidify to the point where they threaten
to disintegrate the society.*[1]

SEYMOUR MARTIN LIPSET
Political Man

fourteen

POLITICAL INSTITUTIONS

Political or *governmental institutions* are societal
arrangements for making and enforcing laws, protecting
the public health and welfare, distributing public funds
and tax burdens, conducting foreign affairs, and
deciding the issues of war and peace. Political
institutions are the ultimate source of legitimate power
in a social system, whether the system is based on rule
by the many or rule by the few. The state seeks to achieve
a monopoly of power and a primary claim on the devotion
of its people. In return it offers its people a sense of
common identity and social cohesion. The word "state"
is used here to designate the nation and its government,
rather than subordinate governments such as Florida,
California, White Russia, or the Ukraine. The word
"state" is used in this way in most parts of the world,
referring to a government with full independence or
sovereignty.

An understanding of political institutions calls
for an analysis of the characteristics of the nation-state,
the types of leadership that emerge, the interplay of
political conflict and national consensus, the patterns of
social-class participation, and the possible threats to
political systems. Is the force of nationalism too powerful
to be subordinated to regional or worldwide interests?

[1] Seymour Martin Lipset, *Political Man*, Anchor Books, Doubleday & Company, Inc., Garden City, N.Y., 1963, p. 70.

Against a background of conflicting interests, can democratic states achieve sufficient agreement to maintain cohesion, give all classes and ethnic groups a sense of belonging and participation, and avoid being torn apart by extremist movements of right and left? Are comparable problems faced by urban-industrial nations whether their governmental systems are democratic or not?

THE NATION-STATE   There is a sense in which the nation-state of today is an obsolete institution, for markets and resources cross boundary lines, as do problems of the world economy and money market. Economic turbulence in one country has its repercussions throughout the world. All nations have a vested interest in trade and commerce, although occasionally national ambitions or animosities become so great as to blind people and their leaders to this fact. Despite the economic arguments for a world united, the world is very much disunited, and nation-states remain virtually sovereign; that is, within the limits of their military might, they are able to control all of their affairs without the intervention of a higher authority.

Historical forces have welded the nations of today into their present patterns, sometimes suddenly, as for example the independence of the United States or the unification of Italy and Germany. More frequently, nation-states have grown through slow accretion, adding territories, enduring common trials and ordeals, and finding common sentiments and heroes until the bonds of unity are secure. This potential unity does not always materialize and result in nationhood; whether it will do so in such new states as Nigeria and Zambia remains to be seen. If the nation-state is successful, it helps to fill man's need for identity, common cause, and the grouping of ethnocentric attitudes around a center of devotion.

National fanaticism   There are recent cases of devotion to the nation-state rising to fanatical heights. Mussolini spoke of the state as not just an association of people but as a spiritual entity. "Fascism conceives of the State as an absolute," he said, "guiding the play and development, both material and spiritual, of a collective body. The Fascist State is itself conscious and has a will and personality. . . ."[2] Communism, on the other hand, is supposed to be an internationalist movement, one in which the state will eventually "wither away." Nevertheless, the appeal of devotion to Mother Russia seemed to do more for rousing a fighting spirit in World War II than the appeal to ideology. At present the Communist states, especially Russia and Red China, cannot maintain monolithic unity as

[2] Benito Mussolini, "The State as Life," *International Conciliation*, Carnegie Endowment for International Peace, October, 1926.

differences in national interest arise. Hitler's Nazi movement was intensely nationalistic, just as was Mussolini's fascism, but it added another ingredient that is a nightmare to the modern world — racism. If race should become the intensely emotional unifying force for human groups, the world could be torn apart in new ways even more devastating than those we have known in the recent past. Whatever the dangers of nationalism may be, it has at least generally united people within their particular territories. Racism has a potential for tearing them apart.

Whether the time will come when man can be united, taking pride in the accomplishments of common humanity, remains to be seen. Fiction writers have foreseen this possibility only in the event of having to unite against a common enemy from outer space. George Orwell saw no possibility for unity, but imagined a future world divided into supernations, all keeping up a flagrant nationalism in order to control their people under the rule of "Big Brother." A constant state of near-war was necessary, but all the rulers realized that actual all-out war had become an impossibility. Of course, we have no guarantee that states will display even the minimal wisdom Orwell suggests. Certainly we see no sign that the state is about to "wither away."

There are, however, certain centrifugal forces at work within many nation-states, tending to pull them apart. Some of these forces are social-class and regional divisions. Some states, such as the Soviet Union and the United States, contain many racial and ethnic differences. Nearly all modern urban societies face mobile populations with constantly growing economic demands. The complexities of urban-industrial systems call for greater organization to appease all conflicting demands and coordinate efforts. One result of new organizational demands is a changing type of leadership.

POLITICAL LEADERSHIP: THE BUREAUCRATIC TREND   Political leadership can be of many kinds, with absolute monarchy or dictatorship at one extreme and a pure town-meeting type of democracy at the other. The distinction between the extremes of democracy and dictatorship seems clear and unequivocal when such democratic countries as England, Canada, or the United States are contrasted with Hitler's Germany, Communist Russia, or Red China. However, the distinction is not quite complete. Dictators can go only so far in defying the traditions of their countries, and elected leaders do not go all the way in responding to the will of their people. They sometimes fail to sense the public will or find themselves unable to accomplish the programs which they think the public demands. More important, the public cannot possibly feel close to decision making in the Pentagon, or to such regulatory agencies as the Interstate Commerce Commission or the Federal Reserve System. Both democratic and authoritarian leaders are dependent upon large administrative bureaucracies necessary for keeping the machinery of government going, but responding only slowly to demands for change. Bureaucratic growth probably mitigates the fanaticism of the totalitarian state to some extent, but in democratic countries it often seems merely to interpose an unresponsive officialdom between the people and their elected leaders.

Weber's analysis of bureaucracy   Weber was the classical sociological writer on the subject of bureaucracy, describing its characteristics thoroughly and noting the bureaucratic trend of government and industry. In many respects he was strong in his praise of bureaucracy for its "purely technical superiority over any other form of organization,"[3] although he was pessimistic about the effect of bureaucracy on individualism and liberty. *Bureaucracies*, in his description, are large, hierarchically arranged organizations with precise assignments of duties and powers, well-defined qualifications for positions, and precise rules and directions tending to make them foolproof; they are impersonal in the sense that their services and positions are open to all people irrespective of race, family, or status. Bureaucracy is frequently charged with inefficiency, but Weber attempted to show that it is the most efficient organizational form ever devised. Perhaps the apparent contradiction comes about because earlier forms of administration were much more lacking in efficiency than are modern bureaucracies. A view of the contrasting possibilities for leadership and administration will help to clarify this point.

There are, says Weber, three ways of legitimizing authority: (1) it can be made legitimate on traditional grounds, resting on a belief in the sanctity of custom and inheritance; (2) it can be based on charismatic principles, resting on devotion to the heroic leader; or (3) it can be based on rational grounds, resting on belief in the authority of those who have risen to power through tested competence.[4]

The traditional leaders are best illustrated by systems of monarchy and nobility in which rights to rule are recognized by inheritance. Important administrators and courtiers, and even army and navy officer corps, are recruited from the upper classes, more on the basis of kinship or family tradition than on qualification or efficiency. If the system must adjust to the modern business world, then pressure is exerted for de-

[3] Max Weber, *Essays in Sociology*, H. H. Gerth and C. Wright Mills (eds.), Oxford University Press, New York, 1946, p. 240.
[4] Max Weber, *The Theory of Social and Economic Organization*, A. M. Henderson and Talcott Parsons (translators), Talcott Parsons (ed.), The Free Press, Glencoe, Ill., 1947.

veloping an efficient civil-service system based on competitive tests—
an administrative bureaucracy.[5]

Charismatic leadership, as we saw in the study of religion, is based
on intense personal loyalty to a magnetic leader. In government this is
often the revolutionary leader who brings about great changes in the
social order. Eventually the charismatic leader dies or is replaced. A
successor might try to hold control of the movement entirely in his own
hands, but eventually the changes have to be institutionalized and
administered through a bureaucracy. Sometimes bureaucratization is a
long, slow process, as it was in the United States, where the famous
"spoils system" for recruiting public servants was very evident until
the era of civil-service reform after the Civil War. It also should be noted
that charismatic qualities are not the monopoly of revolutionists. Many
constitutionally elected presidents have had charismatic qualities,
exciting strong loyalties and bringing about major changes—Jackson,
Lincoln, the two Roosevelts, and Kennedy, for example. The person who
sees his role simply as carrying out legislation and avoiding drastic
change might be characterized as the *bureaucratic type*. All those presidents whose names no one can remember might be called bureaucratic
types, although Weber considered the definitive type of bureaucrat to
be an appointive official.

The third means of legitimizing authority, on rational grounds, is
characteristic of the trend of the industrial world. Powers and duties are
carefully assigned to leaders and assistants in the hierarchical manner
typical of bureaucracy. Bureaucracy provides the expertness that traditional arrangements often lack and the continuity that charismatic leadership often fails to provide. It is the most rational means of organization
and administration.

Criticisms of bureaucracy   The foregoing discussion, consistent with
Weber's views, shows the positive side of bureaucracy and, to some extent, the ideal of a bureaucracy rather than the reality. In actual practice
some of the rules of impersonality and impartiality are violated. Even in
bureaucracies it often helps to know the right people. Even more important
than the failure of bureaucracy to live up to its own rules are problems that
many critics see as *latent functions* of bureaucracy—unforeseen and unintended results inevitable in the system. One latent function is confusion
of ends and means. Bureaucrats can become so absorbed in the rules that
they forget the actual purposes for which the rules were made.[6] In schools,

[5] Seymour Martin Lipset, "Bureaucracy and Social Reform," *Research Studies*, Washington State University,
vol. 17, 1947, pp. 11–17.
[6] Robert K. Merton, *Social Theory and Social Structure*, The Free Press of Glencoe, Inc., New York, 1957, pp.
19–84.

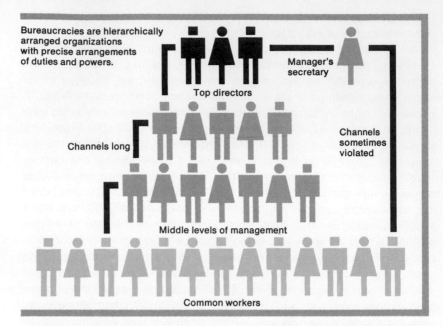

Bureaucracies are hierarchically arranged organizations with precise arrangements of duties and powers.

Manager's secretary

Top directors

Channels long

Channels sometimes violated

Middle levels of management

Common workers

Sometimes bureaucracies proliferate officials, having more chiefs than indians.

Top directors

Middle levels of management

Common workers

for example, the desired end is education; attendance and grades are only means to this end. Yet for some administrators attendance records and grades are the overriding concerns of the institution. Another problem is that bureaucracy consists of so many levels of officialdom that it is hard to reach the person holding ultimate authority. "Going through channels" becomes a tedious process, and often it is necessary to find "unofficial channels" to cut through too much bureaucratic red tape. Thus the person who happens to know the secretary to the top official can save much bother, but this undermines the impersonality that is supposed to be part of the bureaucratic ethic. Sometimes a bureaucracy seems to proliferate officials, resulting in "more chiefs than Indians." This is the type of situation lampooned by C. Northcote Parkinson in *Parkinson's Law*.[7] Parkinson makes it appear to be a "scientific law" that much of the work of bureaucracies consists of men making work for each other and that the number of bureaucrats increases whether the bureau has anything to do or not. He exaggerates, of course, but voices the feelings of many people about bureaucracy. A writer on the same subject, Laurence J. Peter, has come up with the term "level of incompetence." His idea, which he calls the "Peter Principle," is that in a bureaucracy people are promoted if they do their jobs well. They finally get promoted into jobs that they are unable to perform well, and the promotions stop at that point. They have "reached their level of incompetence," and there they remain, inefficient and exasperating.[8]

Lipset shows how the routinization of government bureaucracies makes them conservative and unable to adjust to new ideas.[9] Alfred Weber raises a more disturbing thought about bureaucratization—it is inconsistent with liberty. He decries the growth of great business and military bureaucracies that promote an increase in standardization and a decline in individual initiative.[10] Bureaucrats tend to become entrenched for long periods of time. One need only consider the history of J. Edgar Hoover, head of the FBI since 1924, or of General Hershey, head of the Selective Service System from World War II until 1970, to realize the truth of this assertion.

Bureaucratic growth   Business bureaucracies become as gigantic as those of government. General Motors employs 600,000 people, exceeding the combined payrolls of the state governments of California, New York, Illinois, Pennsylvania, Texas, and Ohio.[11] The fifty largest companies in the

[7] C. Northcote Parkinson, *Parkinson's Law and other Studies in Administration*, Houghton Mifflin Company, Boston, 1957, pp. 2–13.
[8] Laurence J. Peter and Raymond Hull, *The Peter Principle*, William Morrow & Company, Inc., New York, 1969.
[9] Lipset, "Bureaucracy and Social Reform," *op. cit.*, pp. 11–17.
[10] Alfred Weber, "Bureaucracy and Freedom," *Modern Review*, vol. 3, March-April, 1948, pp. 176–186.
[11] Andrew Hacker, "A Country Called Corporate America," *New York Times*, July 3, 1966, pp. 8–9.

United States have almost three times as many employees as the fifty states. In spite of these impressive figures, it is government employment that is growing most rapidly, showing a 25 percent increase between 1957 and 1965, whereas corporation employment increased 15 percent during the same period.[12] Government grows not only in employment but in costs, responsibilities, and powers.

THE GROWTH OF GOVERNMENT   It was pointed out in the discussion of the economic system that the government has become the regulator of the economy and is held responsible for seeing that the economy flourishes, unemployment does not become excessive, and funds are available for large numbers of programs including urban renewal, retraining workers, and assistance to depressed areas, as well as the astronomical amounts needed for the military establishment. A glance at the federal and state budgets of the United States will show the size of government and give a good indication of the enterprises to which it is committed.

The budget for the 1971 fiscal year called for expenditures of $201 billion dollars. Of these expenditures, $73 billion dollars was for national defense—by far the largest item. Other large items (in billions) were: health, labor, and welfare (including social-security payments), $62 billion; interest on the national debt, $17 billion; veterans, $8 billion; education and manpower, $8 billion; agriculture, $4.5 billion; national resources, $2.5 billion; housing and community development, $2.5 billion; foreign aid, $2 billion.[13] State- and local-government costs have also mounted, totaling $95 billion dollars in 1968. One-third of this amount goes to education, and equal amounts (approximately 13 percent each) go to highways and welfare.[14]

Rising governmental costs is a widespread phenomenon in countries where concern for social programs has become an important political issue. Tax revenues have risen to 28.8 percent of the GNP in the United States. In Germany and France, the figure is higher, 34.9 percent and 38.6 percent respectively, and in Sweden the tax revenues are 41.1 percent of the GNP.[15] Governments perform larger numbers of services, and costs increase even in countries without vast military commitments.

There are always complaints about the cost of government, high taxes, and the welfare state. At the same time there is the general feeling

[12] *Ibid.*, p. 9.
[13] *The Budget in Brief*, Executive Office of the President, Bureau of the Budget, Fiscal Year 1971, p. 29.
[14] *Ibid.*, p. 404.
[15] Alfred G. Buehler, "The Cost of Democracy," *The Annals of the American Academy of Political and Social Science*, vol. 379, September, 1968, pp. 1–12.

Where It comes from...

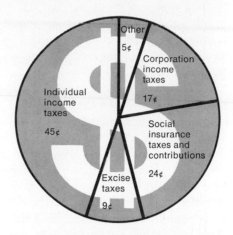

Where it goes...

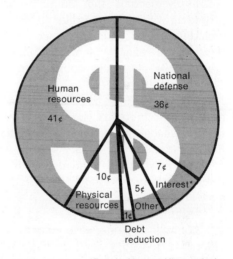

(Source: *The Budget in Brief,* Executive Office of the President, Bureau of the Budget, Fiscal Year 1971, p. 1)

*Excludes interest paid to trust funds

that much welfare-type legislation is here to stay. Public-opinion polls in the 1930s found the public to be generally in favor of the New Deal reforms, and similar polls in the 1960s showed support just as strong for similar types of legislation, including antipoverty programs. A 1967 public-opinion poll showed half the people in favor of the extension of medicare to all members of the family, not just the aged.[16] Even a questionnaire on whether the federal government wields too much power showed similar results. Only 26 percent of the public said "Yes, federal powers are excessive." However, 52 percent thought we were spending too much money on the military.[17]

The Presidency   Although the powers of the Presidency are enumerated in the Constitution, the office has grown beyond its explicit constitutional limits. Besides his extensive constitutional powers as Chief Executive, his appointment powers, and his powers as Commander in Chief, the President wields great power as leader of his political party. His ceremonial powers as Chief of State help make him the center of national attention as no other governmental official can be. Modern television and other communications media have furthered the constant exposure of the President to the public limelight. His messages to Congress have increasingly become the launching platform for extensive legislative programs. Clinton J. Rossiter lists ten roles of the presidential office, including all the traditional ones, and adding "Chief Legislator," "Protector of the Peace," "Manager of Prosperity," and "Leader of the World's Free People"—all roles going far beyond the explicit statement of the Constitution.[18]

Such events as the Vietnam War have caused many Americans to have second thoughts about whether the President should assume the role of "Leader of the World's Free People." Commager notes that in the past the President's military powers were used only in case of national peril, but now they are used more routinely, on a global scale, and in cases where opinion is divided about whether the national interest is immediately involved.[19]

Although a number of strong and able men, visualizing their office as a commanding one, have helped to make the Presidency the powerful office it is, sociology views the aggrandizement of the office in an institutional rather than a personal perspective. For example, Democratic Presidents in recent decades have been accused of trying to turn more and more functions over to the federal government, and the Republican party, in its public pronouncements, has made an issue of local and state responsibility instead. In spite of this, the greatest federal highway-

[16]Lloyd A. Free and Hadley Cantril, *The Political Beliefs of Americans*, Rutgers University Press, New Brunswick, N.J., 1967, pp. 10–11.
[17]Gallup Poll, *Los Angeles Times*, August 14, 1969, p. 1.
[18]Clinton J. Rossiter, *The American Presidency*, Mentor Books, New American Library, Inc., New York, 1956, chap. 1.
[19]Henry Steele Commager, "Can We Limit Presidential Power?", *New Republic*, vol. 158, April 6, 1968, pp. 15–18.

building program in history was launched during the relatively conservative Eisenhower administration and, surprisingly, sweeping, federalizing, and expensive reforms in welfare have been advocated by President Nixon. One party may add to governmental growth more slowly than the other, but neither reverses the trend.

More important than political party or personality in the growth of the Presidency has been the growth of involvement in foreign affairs. "We may take it as an axiom of political science that the more deeply a nation becomes involved in the affairs of other nations, the more powerful becomes its executive branch." [20] No other branch of government has the access to secret information and the ability to move with sufficient speed in foreign-policy crises. Other types of crises, such as depression or natural disasters, have increasingly called for Presidential action. The Presidency also seems to symbolize American democracy more than any other branch of government. No other election combines all the talents of showmanship and political manipulation in such blatant ways nor creates such a circus. But no other contest excites public interest to the same degree. Whatever the backstage manipulations, the public has the feeling that its voice is heard most strongly every four years in the Presidential elections, as is apparent in voting patterns, even though it was originally supposed that the House of Representatives would be the governmental body closest to the people. Originally, only the House of Representatives was elected by direct vote of the people.

Other areas of governmental growth   Other areas of government have grown too, for an executive cannot grow constitutionally without the explicit or implicit approval of Congress and the courts. Government has grown not only because of foreign involvement, war, and crisis, but because of the demands of the economy and of various interest groups. Agriculture and labor call for special aid and regulation, as do railroads, airlines, ships, trucks, and all other means of transportation. States demand more aid in welfare programs, road building, water projects, and educational programs. Large, congested cities have brought forth a Department of Housing and Urban Development in the federal government. Since minority groups demand laws for equal treatment, and federal government is the only agency likely to make or enforce such laws in many of the states, the area of race relations has become a concern of federal government. When funds are distributed to aid in welfare, education, disaster relief, or urban planning, the government administrative

[20] Rossiter, *op. cit.*, p. 64.

bureaucracy must grow in order to provide supervision of such expenditures. For these and other reasons, the federal government has become an agency spending close to 200 billion dollars/year and employing an administrative bureaucracy of nearly 3 million people.

PARTIES, CONSENSUS, AND CLASS VOTING HABITS   Conflicting interests inevitably arise in government. Secure monarchs of the past were able to ignore the problems of the people to a greater degree than now, but even they could not be deaf to all voices. Their ministers and courtiers were attuned to the more powerful conflicting interests within the kingdom. Modern dictatorships often give little official recognition to conflicting pressures, but behind the scenes there are struggles for influence, and there are often factional struggles for succession when a dictator dies.

Democratic systems require effective political parties — parties that give the voter a choice but that are not so far apart ideologically as to result in strong polarization into ideological extremes. There must be enough clash of interest to challenge leadership, but the differences still must be within a general area of agreement or *consensus* on democratic principles and the functions of the state. When a party turnover takes place, there must not be a vengeful undoing of all the previous legislation, as happened in the short-lived Spanish Republic and has sometimes happened in France.

Political parties   Political parties, as everyone learns in government classes, serve the function of presenting candidates and issues to the people, publicizing elections and programs, getting voter turnout, and, in principle at least, trying to guarantee that their banner carriers will perform well in office. A more subtle function that is sometimes overlooked was stated cleverly by Bernard Shaw.[21] In an imaginary conversation between William III and his crafty advisor, the Earl of Sunderland, Shaw pictures the King as being at his wit's end as to how to settle his problems with Parliament and his English subjects. Sunderland advises him to choose all his ministers from the majority party; then, when things go wrong, it will not be in any way the fault of the King, but simply of that inept political party. From that day on, Shaw continues, failures have resulted in change of parties but have not reflected on the monarchy or the country. In the United States we do not have the device of monarchy, but the failure of the party in office does not, in the public mind, reflect too strongly against the country. We simply "throw the rascals out" and try again.

[21] Bernard Shaw, *Everybody's Political What's What*, Constable & Co., Ltd., London, 1944, pp. 25–28.

Although Shaw's suggestion might sound somewhat facetious, a party system undoubtedly helps to maintain national morale as well as to serve the generally recognized function of making shifts in policy possible. Russia, in contrast, had to go through a ritual "destalinization" after the death of Joseph Stalin to convince her people that the new leadership would not be as ruthless as the old. No change of parties was possible, however, and the only political party in Russia could not avoid coming out tarnished. American and British parties also are sometimes tarnished in reputation, but the public can turn to the opposite party for a number of years while shifts in party leadership come about and the old party re-emerges, none the worse for wear, after catching up with the times.

Consensus and class difference   Not all voters shift their party alignment, regardless of declining popularity of the party in office. To a great degree the political identifications of people are based on factors other than the particular party leader or his platform. There are regional and ethnic differences in party preference, and there is also a notable difference on a social-class scale. Since 1932, poorer people have tended to identify with the Democratic party more than with the Republican, thinking of it as the more "liberal" of the two.

The word "liberal" has a variety of meanings. It once referred to the laissez-faire philosophy of as little government as possible. In popular usage the word "liberal" now refers to almost the opposite philosophy, and it is this type of definition that will be used here, following the analysis of Free and Cantril,[22] who speak .of two types of liberal philosophy — *operational* and *ideological*. *Operational liberal* refers to the person who approves minimum wages, social security, medical care, and antipoverty programs — in general, a large governmental commitment to the handling of social problems. Free and Cantril find an actual majority of the American voters favorable to most such programs, so there seems to exist a liberal consensus on the operational level. There are inconsistencies in this respect, however, with a resentment of the high taxes and governmental bureaucracies resulting from such programs. *Ideological liberals* are those who state views favorable to increasing the size of government, more regulation of property rights, more of the welfare state, and they tend not to be worried about a drift toward socialism. The majority rejects this type of liberalism. Whereas 65 percent are operational liberals, only 16 percent are ideological liberals in this sense of the word.[23]

In spite of a possible overall consensus, class differences are marked. Of those who call themselves members of the propertied class,

[22] Free and Cantril, *op. cit.*, pp. 23–40.
[23] *Ibid.*, pp. 31–32.

40 percent are operational liberals; of those claiming middle-class identification, 57 percent are operational liberals; and of the working class,
74 percent are operational liberals.[24]

On a political-party basis, the same differences in viewpoint are to
be inferred. Eleven percent of Republicans identify themselves as of the
propertied class, and only 2 percent of Democrats do so; 35 percent of
Republicans are of the working class, whereas 65 percent of Democrats
are of that class.[25] A 1969 Harris Poll presents somewhat different information from that found by Free and Cantril, especially in its emphasis on
public outrage against taxes and inflation. Even in the Harris Poll, though,
the major problem seems to be "the public loss of faith in the government's judgment and priorities" rather than a rejection of domestic
programs. Those interviewed were 69 percent in favor of cutting expenditures in foreign aid (oddly enough, at an all-time low), 64 percent in
favor of cutting Vietnamese expenditures, and 51 percent in favor of cuts
in the space program, in spite of spectacular successes. On the other
hand, only 37 percent said to cut federal welfare spending first, and 60
percent said the last thing to cut should be aid to education. Sixty-seven
percent resented "the way my tax money is being spent," and there was a
strong feeling that taxes were being rigged for the rich.[26]

All the above data reflect expressions of attitude. To what extent
these attitudes are translated into action depends partly on the voting
habits of the people. It will be seen that actual voter turnout may be more
favorable to the conservatives than the above statistics would imply.

Who votes   Our political parties are not successful in getting a unanimous turnout for elections. In 1896, 80 percent of those eligible to vote
went to the polls in a presidential election; in 1920 the figure dropped to a
low of 49 percent of those eligible to vote. The 1920 case was unusual in
that women had just been enfranchised by the Nineteenth Amendment, but
many of them were not yet prepared to participate in the vote. In recent
years voting has fluctuated greatly, always being higher than in 1920, but
lower than in 1896. The vote is always higher in presidential-election
years than in "off-year" elections, indicating that people see the presidency as more important than the legislative branch of government.[27]
For example, in 1960, 64 percent of the electorate voted for President, and
59.6 percent voted for representatives, but two years later, without a
presidential election to stimulate interest, only 46.7 percent of the people

[24] *Ibid.*, p. 18.
[25] *Ibid.*, p. 142.
[26] Joe McGinnis, "The Dollar Squeeze," *Life Magazine*, vol. 67, no. 7, August 15, 1969, pp. 18–23.
[27] Seymour Martin Lipset, *Political Man*, Anchor Books, Doubleday & Company, Garden City, N.Y., 1963, p. 85

More likely to vote	Less likely to vote
Men	Women
Middle-aged	Young and very old
Northerners	Southerners
The educated	The uneducated
Whites	Blacks
The rich	The poor

What keeps people from the polls?
Health problems
Jobs out of town
Transportation problems
Less perception of importance
Less access to information
Less group pressure to vote
Racial disabilities
More cross pressures

voted for representatives. Voter turnout is irregular, but it was over 60 percent in all the presidential elections of the 1960s.[28]

In the number of people voting there are some well-marked categorical differences. Men vote more than women; middle-aged people vote more than the young or very old, and whites vote more than blacks. More Northerners than Southerners vote, and voting goes up with both education and income. The well-to-do are better represented at the polls in proportion to their numbers than are the poor.[29]

Several circumstances surrounding nonvoting show a certain amount of hardship on the poor. Health problems, lack of transportation, or having to be at work are frequent reasons for nonvoting among the poor. Military personnel have difficulty voting and help to account for a relatively low percentage of voters among the young. Racial disabilities, in the disguised form of literacy tests or in the overt form of intimidation, have been very prominent in keeping down the size of the Afro-American

[28] Richard M. Scammon, "Electoral Participation," *Annals of the American Academy of Political and Social Science*, vol. 371, May, 1967, pp. 59–77.
[29] *Ibid.*, pp. 59–77.

vote. Although these disabilities have declined in recent years, the black vote remains lower than the white, probably reflecting larger numbers in lower-class position. Other reasons for nonvoting are often summed up as "apathy," but this may be merely an emotionally charged term by which the voter condemns the nonvoter. Sociology is interested in a further analysis of nonvoting. Lipset has some important conclusions about voting and nonvoting based on data from many countries.[30]

People are more apt to vote, according to Lipset, if they perceive the importance of government policies to them. This importance is seen most clearly by the educated upper class and in the special case of government employees, who have the highest voting record of any occupational group. Access to information is another variable that aids the educated upper and middle classes and helps the workers only when intensive political work is done by parties or unions. Group pressures to vote also have their impact, and these pressures are greatest in the middle class where voting is considered a norm of good citizenship. Finally, cross-pressures are very important. Lipset cites cases where left-wing unions almost monopolize the time and interests of workers, as in parts of France, and produce a high turnout of working-class voters, sometimes even higher than that of other classes. On the other hand, a voter may have only a vague working-class identification, along with the conflicting feeling that he is moving toward middle class. His church or neighborhood may be traditionally conservative, exerting counterpressures on him, or such pressures may come from the newspapers or magazines he reads. In cases of strong crosspressures he may decide not to vote at all, feeling uncertain and confused about his own interests. Lipset shows that these confusions are greater for working-class than for upper-class citizens and are one of the reasons for lower voter turnout and a resultant under-representation of the poor in elections. Whether differences in social-class attitudes and participation in the election process are a threat to democracy is one of the questions now to be examined.

THREATS TO THE POLITICAL SYSTEM   In addition to general worries over taxes and inflation, unequal voter turnout, and the growth of bureaucracy and executive power, there are other worries about democracy. Can true democracy survive in a mass society? What effect do economic crises and frequent wars have upon democratic societies? Are there antidemocratic groups and attitudes that menace our way of life?

[30]Lipset, op. cit., 183–229.

Alienation in the mass society   The idea of alienation in mass society is prominent in modern literature as well as in psychology and sociology. The concept of alienation is found among writers of various political persuasions, from socialists and social democrats to ultraconservatives. Basically, the mass society of today alienates people from each other and from meaningful groups in various ways, making the people prone to look for new meanings. Eric Fromm[31] and Hannah Arendt[32] attribute much of the psychosocial background for the rise of Hitlerism to the alienation of men from their old traditions, communities, and sources of identity as Germany changed into a modern mass society. In their search for a new identity the Germans chose rampant nationalism and *der führer,* losing themselves and their problems in a great new cause.

Bell gives an analysis of several writers who take the mass-society approach (Ortega y Gasset, Karl Mannheim, Karl Jaspers, and others), and tries to sum up their concepts.[33] He finds certain inconsistencies: men are linked more closely by the mass media and interdependence, yet the theory holds that they are more alienated from one another. Americans are described as lonely and isolated, and yet we are also characterized as a "nation of joiners." Specialization makes modern men develop along different lines, and yet they are characterized as a faceless, homogeneous mass. The concept of mass society, Bell goes on to say, may have its merits, but It misses much of the variety of American life with its regional, ethnic, and occupational groups, and its clash of interests and ideas. It also overlooks the remarkable persistence of primary groups in the mass society. It becomes questionable whether the mass-society concept is sufficient to explain such a phenomenon as Hitlerism or extremist groups in American society.

Extremist groups in a pluralistic society   Joseph R. Gusfield views American society in a manner similar to Bell's.[34] He does not try to demolish the picture of mass society, but he does contend that the traditional analytical tools of political science—the view of a democratic government as a system for reconciling pluralistic pressures and interests—is still valid. Extremist politics can be expected but not because of mass society. After all, there have been extremist groups in much more traditional societies. If we define *extremism* as an unwillingness to abide by democratic rules

[31] Eric Fromm, *Escape from Freedom,* Farrar & Rinehart, Inc., New York, 1941.
[32] Hannah Arendt, *The Origin of Totalitarianism,* Meridian Books, Inc., New York, 1958.
[33] Daniel Bell, *The End of Ideology,* The Free Press, Glencoe, Ill., 1950, pp. 21–38.
[34] Joseph R. Gusfield, "Mass Society and Extremist Politics," *American Sociological Review,* vol. 27, February, 1962, pp. 19–30.

of the game, then we might define the Whiskey Rebellion of Washington's administration as our first national experience with extremist politics. Certainly the decision of the South not to accept the Presidency of Lincoln was a case of extremist politics in this sense of the word, but not at a time when the United States was thought of as a mass society. Extremist politics emerge from social situations in pluralistic societies, Gusfield argues, because of disenfranchised classes (black America, for example), competing interests that see no hope (labor unions at times), doomed classes (the small farmer), or periodic crises where compromise breaks down (the Civil War). Our present concern most likely is to be with doomed classes and with groups previously excluded from the political process.

Harold Lasswell, writing during the days of the rise of Hitler, commented on the winning over to Nazism of certain groups who saw themselves as doomed classes, largely in lower-middle-class positions — small farmers, small shopkeepers, clerks, and craftsmen. These people saw themselves overshadowed by the upper bourgeoisie and by unionized labor.[35] A case can be made for calling them "alienated in mass society," but an equally good case could be made for viewing them as pressure groups with complaints to be mediated by a pluralistic society. A more recent study concludes that these people did not vote for Hitler in a majority of cases until late in the period of his rise,[36] apparently after hope for aid from the Weimar Republic had been abandoned.

The last important revival of the Ku Klux Klan in the late 1950s can be thought of as an attempt to save not a doomed class but a doomed way of life — a way of full-scale and unchallenged white supremacy. An analysis of members (not too large a group was available because of the secrecy of the organization) revealed that most of them belonged to a marginal lower middle-class group undergoing rapid change and status disorientation because of community change and differences in job requirements.[37] Perhaps both a doomed way of life and a doomed class applied to the group.

So far as the disturbance on the part of those people previously excluded from the system — the black Americans — is concerned, the subject has been discussed in Chapter 7. Frustrated and not knowing how to achieve legitimate political influence, some of their numbers have turned to violence, as did labor groups before they achieved recognition.

An interesting note on the behavior of groups with a legitimate complaint, but one ignored by holders of political power, was reported by

[35] Harold Lasswell, "The Psychology of Hitlerism," The Political Quarterly, vol. 4, 1933, pp. 373–384.
[36] Karl O'Lessker, "Who Voted for Hitler," American Journal of Sociology, vol. 74, July, 1968, pp. 63–69.
[37] James W. Vander Zanden, "The Klan Revival," American Journal of Sociology, vol. 65, March, 1960, pp. 456–462.

Harvey Molotch.[38] An oil slick, caused by leakage from offshore wells, for a time virtually ruined the beaches of Santa Barbara, a city with many wealthy residents. Unable to obtain their aim of closing the wells and bitter over their inability to influence the government, they turned to direct action: "sit-downs blocking oil trucks, yacht sail-ins circling offshore wells, 'nonnegotiable demands,'" and even murmurs about blowing up oil rigs. It seems that even a wealthy group excluded from the system can turn to nonconventional forms of collective behavior. The lower classes, however, are more likely to feel excluded more frequently. Are they a potential source of danger?

Working-class authoritarianism   Some conservatives worry about the possibility of movements on the extreme left. If threatened middle classes under some circumstances join movements of the right, will working-class members join movements of the left? Working-class people have just been characterized as "more liberal" than middle or propertied classes, but it must be recalled that "liberal" has a variety of meanings. Working-class people, according to the data from Free and Cantril, are liberal in economic issues, especially wage and welfare measures. In the political sense, "liberal" can be a synonym for tolerance of a wide range of views and of the gradualist processes of democracy. It is in this respect that the working class is characterized as less liberal than the middle and upper classes. A combination of political liberalism and the *authoritarian* desire for strong leadership and the suppression of the opposition would predispose people to radical extremism.

In a discussion of lower-class authoritarianism, Lipset notes that in many countries the Communist Party has had greater appeal to the workers than has the Socialist Party. Both are oriented to the working class, but the Communist Party is rigid and authoritarian, and the Socialist Party is not.[39] The implication is that the rigid, simplistic doctrines appeal more to the less educated segment of the population, a segment that is also more isolated from groups and associations and has had less experience with the give and take of organization life. As indicated in Chapter 12, education is positively associated with tolerance, and since the lower class is less educated it is not surprising to find it less tolerant of dissension. A lack of knowledge of the roles of other people is also closely associated with authoritarianism[40] and is more likely to be a problem of the less educated lower class than of the well educated.

[38]Harvey T. Molotch, "Oil in Santa Barbara and Power in America," a paper read at the American Sociological Association Convention, San Francisco, September 2, 1969. (Also reported in *The San Francisco Chronicle*, Sep. 3, 1969, pp. 1, 26, under the title "Rich Become Radicals.")

[39]Lipset, *Political Man*, pp. 89–90.

[40]Don Stewart and Thomas Hoult, "A Social Psychological Theory of the Authoritarian Personality," *American Journal of Sociology*, vol. 65, November, 1959, pp. 274–279.

However, the working class of the United States has not followed the Communist Party line as in France and Italy. One reason is the traditional feeling that upward mobility is possible; thus the more hopeful members of the working class take on a feeling of middle-class identity. Probably another reason is that the United States has had a particularly strong cultural orientation to democratic processes. It is also likely that the greater amount of sectarian- and revivalist-type religion in America, which, like political extremism, tends to be simplistic and anti-intellectual, may "drain off the discontent and frustration which would otherwise flow into channels of political extremism." [41]

It is also possible that the very factors that make for working-class authoritarianism are gradually declining and that such authoritarianism might be less evident in the future. The isolation of rural counties is less marked than in the past, and fewer people live in such counties. The years of schooling, even for children of the poor, are increasing. Dissemination of information (admittedly along with much nonsense) through television and other mass media certainly reduces isolation and increases social awareness.

Upper-class authoritarianism   If the working class is narrowly authoritarian in its attitudes, we might expect it to look upon society in conspiratorial terms and to agree that a small inside group of big businessmen really run the country. Actually a study by Form and Rytina found the poor taking a very different point of view, generally agreeing that the country is pluralistically run by various business, labor, religious, and political groups.[42] In comparing the rich with the poor, the researchers found certain respects in which the rich seemed more narrow-minded. They were unable to see that some strata of the population need special governmental help; 72 percent felt that the government had already done too much for the poor. The rich also were likely to choose "business and the rich" as the most powerful elements in society and to feel that this was the way it should be. They showed strong class consciousness and out-group antipathy, conclude Form and Rytina. "A good case can be made for upper-class authoritarianism." [43]

Perhaps the reference to upper-class authoritarianism seems to be a nagging case of charge and countercharge, but the point is that people are most likely to be closed-minded in matters that affect their welfare, whether they are rich or poor. Lower-class authoritarianism has appeared historically in attempts to keep out foreigners who compete on the labor market and in "white backlash" against blacks in recent elections. It

[41] Lipset, *Political Man*, p. 200.
[42] William H. Form and Joan Rytina, "Ideological Beliefs in the Distribution of Power in the United States," *American Sociological Review*, vol. 34, February, 1969, pp. 19–30.
[43] *Ibid.*, p. 30.

undoubtedly was one of the factors showing up in the Wallace vote of 1968, but that vote was not too impressive except in a few states of the South. If the wage earner voted for Wallace in the hope of keeping his neighborhood white, he was admittedly showing narrow-mindedness, but is it a type of narrow-mindedness unknown to the middle or upper classes?

Any type of change that may lead to unemployment is naturally feared by the workingman, and unemployment is associated with strong class consciousness and militancy.[44] Radical sentiments, much greater militancy of labor unions, and a tendency to join visionary movements were characteristic of the unemployed during the depression period. However, government action eventually relieved unemployment, ameliorated poverty for those out of work, and began to reduce the intensity of radical feelings. The two-party system, beginning to respond to the socioeconomic problems of the people, undoubtedly helped to prevent the rise of a radical party at that time. The Socialist and Communist parties failed to capture the working-class loyalty. There was some fear of the social movement of Father Caughlin and of the demogoguery of Senator Huey Long, but their influence eventually waned. With a government more readily geared to coping with the socioeconomic problems of the poor than in those days, there is reason for hope that radicalism would fare no better in a future depression than in the past.

There is ample evidence for narrow-minded and authoritarian attitudes in various parts of society. It is, however, the lower class that is submitted to the greatest number of frustrating pressures making for anger and extremism. If we are to avoid the possibility of frustration and anger showing up in a form threatening to democracy, we must try to avoid the types of crises that might bring forth such emotions. The crafty Machiavelli observed centuries ago that a republic must beware of war, for if the war is lost, the leaders might be overthrown by a dictator, and if the war is won, the leader will be so heroized as to be made into a dictator. In spite of our propensity for electing military heroes to the Presidency, we have never had the disaster that Machiavelli foresaw, but the passions of war have brought other problems for democracy. Free speech and freedom of the press have been drastically abridged. In World War I, we attacked and vilified German Americans and socialists. In World War II, we incarcerated thousands of Japanese Americans without trial. All segments of a population become more authoritarian in times of war, more fearful of the outsider and of the nonconformist. Although wars are bitter experiences for all nations, politically they are especially dangerous for democratic systems.[45]

---

[44]John C. Legget, "Economic Insecurity and Working Class Consciousness," *American Sociological Review*, vol. 29, April, 1964, pp. 226–234.
[45]Robert M. McIver, *The Ramparts We Guard*, The Macmillan Company, New York, 1950, pp. 84–92.

SUMMARY   Political institutions are the ultimate source of legitimate power in societies. Regardless of the system of government, the state seeks to achieve a monopoly on power and a primary claim on the devotion of its people. In return it offers a sense of common identity and social cohesion — sentiments that can sometimes rise to the level of national fanaticism.

Although nationalism continues to be a powerful force in most of the world, many nation-states are faced with certain divisive forces from within. Many countries face ethnic, racial, and regional divisions. In modern societies urban, mobile populations develop increasing economic demands, and there are always conflicts of interest between social classes.

The complexities of urban-industrial systems call for greater organizational effort that is met by increasing bureaucratization in both government and industry. Government grows in both size and expense because it must regulate the economy and provide for the welfare of its people. The growing regulatory functions of government, and in many cases mobilization for war, lead to greater concentration of executive power, as exemplified by the American Presidency.

Conflicting interests inevitably arise in government. Firmly established monarchical states of the past were relatively immune to pressures from the common people, but even they had to take notice of the varied interests of the powerful. In dictatorships there are usually factions competing for influence at governmental centers. In operating democracies, political parties attempt to win the allegiance of various interest groups by promising to serve their cause.

Democratic systems seem to function best in cases where there is a fair degree of consensus. A general acceptance of some types of welfare measures illustrates a degree of consensus in the United States, but there remain strong social-class differences in opinion as to how far welfare-state measures should go. Although working-class people have a stake in elections, they are less likely to vote than are middle- and upper-class people, for a variety of reasons.

In periods of rapid change, political systems can be placed under serious threat. In the opinion of some observers, alienation in mass society is a major source of political danger, leading to the politics of extremism and impatience with democratic processes. Lipset presents evidence that authoritarian attitudes are most prevalent among lower-class people, both in Europe and the United States. Other researchers find strongly authoritarian attitudes among the well-to-do, characterized by a very blurred perception of the problems of other classes. Authoritarian attitudes are not just matters of social-class position, however. Times of threat and crisis tend to limit tolerance and increase the fear of dissension in all economic levels of the population.

No single thing abides, but all things flow
Fragment to fragment clings;
The things thus grow
Until we know and name them. By degrees
They melt, and are no more the thing we know.

LUCRETIUS

fifteen

THE PRESSURES OF CHANGE

Throughout the major portion of human history the
process of change has been extremely slow, often
deliberately retarded by such cultural devices as the
subordination of the young to the old, reverence for
departed ancestors and their ways, and avoidance of the
ways of the stranger. At times the catastrophes of war and
famine have doubtlessly forced migrations and adjustment
to new ways, but the new adjustments have been
disturbing, breaking up the small measure of tranquility
that man has been able to attain through fixed status,
beliefs, values, and folkways.

Then came the development of agriculture and
settlement into permanent villages and towns. These
developments were the hallmark of the so-called
neolithic revolution—one of the two great ages of
invention, the other being the modern phase of history.[1]
Animals were domesticated, the wheel was invented,
writing began, and the use of metals was discovered.
The debris of the past reveals a story of the rise and fall
of civilizations, of invasion and counterinvasion, of
pillage and looting, captivity and slaughter. There is
another side to the story, however. Behind all the conflict
and destruction, invention of new culture traits was
progressing, and new ideas were diffusing from centers in
the Near East, India, and China. The social and technical
inventions of man were increasing, opening many
possibilities that the Old Stone Age had never known.

[1] Claude Lévi-Strauss, *The Savage Mind*, The University of Chicago Press, Chicago, 1966, p. 15.

CONFLICTING THEORIES OF SOCIAL CHANGE   Many of the writers of theories of social change have looked upon one or the other of these two aspects of human history: the rise and fall of civilizations and the gradual accumulation of new inventions, ideas, and possibilities. One can hardly take an interest in history without speculating about the destiny of his own little segment of mankind, wondering whether he can defy the common fate of nations or whether he, too, will be "as one with Nineveh and Tyre."

Cyclical and struggle theories   Those writers most impressed with the growth and destruction of civilizations have tended to look on social change in terms of futile cycles or even as a decline from some kind of a mythical golden age to the miseries of today. One of the well-known works on cycles of development is Oswald Spengler's *Decline of the West*.[2] Spengler thought of civilizations as similar to living organisms, with their youth, maturity, and inevitable old age and death. Each had its original inspiration and ideal, which was destined eventually to fade in the pursuit of more materialistic interests, presaging the demise of the civilization.

Many optimistic Western historians, on the other hand, have tended to give an upward-and-onward view of history and to consider history merely the history of the Western world. The cyclical theorists have avoided this easy optimism and Western ethnocentrism but have not been able to explain the mechanisms of rise and fall to the satisfaction of modern sociologists.

Another alternative view of history is that of various "struggle theorists." Hegel, for example, saw all social change as the result of struggle between opposing forces, eventually producing a "new synthesis" which would itself find new opposing forces to renew the struggle. Marx, in his theory of class struggle, was strongly influenced by the view of Hegel.

Climatic and biological theories   There have been many other interesting theories, often advanced by people with special interests in one area of investigation. For example, Ellsworth Huntington, a prominent geographer, looked upon geography, and especially climate, as all-important in the vigor of a civilization. Although sociologists regard such a view as too limited, one theme of his book, *The Mainsprings of Civilization*[3] is rather intriguing. Briefly, he contends that favorable weather cycles

---

[2] Oswald Spengler, *Decline of the West*, Alfred A. Knopf, Inc., New York, 1928.
[3] Ellsworth Huntington, *The Mainsprings of Civilization*, New American Library, Inc., New York, 1959, pp. 469–479.

permitted population growth in parts of Central Asia, and later unfavorable changes forced nomadic tribesmen out to conquer the lands of neighbors, as was the case with Ghengis Khan.

Hans Zinsser,[4] a biologist, wrote an equally interesting book titled *Rats, Lice and History*. It contended that the lowly germ has had a far greater effect on the course of history than is generally realized. Very possibly typhus destroyed the forces of Sennacherib, foiling his attempts to conquer the Israelites, and it may have wiped out thousands of the troops of Xerxes before the Persians ever reached Greece. The effects of endemic malaria are seen by Zinsser as a contributing factor in the decline of ancient Rome.

Such writers as Huntington and Zinsser do well to show us that social change can often be influenced by unobserved forces, but their conclusions are based on particular examples more than on the total record of human societies. They also tend to oversimplify, explaining too much on the basis of one factor.

Toynbee: challenge and response   Probably the best-known contemporary philosopher of history is Arnold Toynbee, whose monumental work *A Study of History*[5] seeks the general causes of rise and decline of civilizations. The idea of challenge and response as causative forces runs strongly through his work, and he makes interesting comparisons between the Greco-Roman world of antiquity and Western civilization of today. His work amounts to a vast summary of historical cultural systems but has been criticized for proving points by a careful selection of examples. It also ends in a kind of historical mysticism, expecting a new age of religion to save man from his impending doom, but not explaining how this new age of faith is to come about.

Sociologists and anthropologists, as well as philosophers and historians, have attempted to make sense and order out of the human record. In the nineteenth century they often looked at social change from the perspective of *cultural evolution* — the idea that cultures evolve in a way comparable to the evolution of species in the biological world. Evolution was central to the thinking of the sociologist Spencer and the anthropologist Lewis Henry Morgan. Morgan's theory, stated briefly, was that all cultures evolve along similar lines and with an inevitability resulting from the "psychic unity of man." His point of view was consistent with modern ideas of the potentialities of all peoples to build advanced cultures, but it failed to explain different rates of growth and the enormous range of cultural differences.

[4]Hans Zinsser, *Rats, Lice, and History*, Blue Ribbon Books, Doubleday & Company, Inc., Garden City, N.Y., 1937.
[5]Arnold Toynbee, *A Study of History*, abridgment of vols. I–X by D. C. Somervell, Oxford University Press, New York, 1947–1957.

Futile cycles (Spengler)

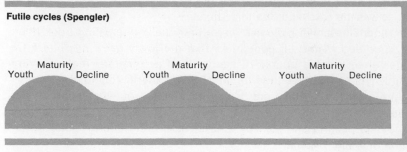

A common Western view

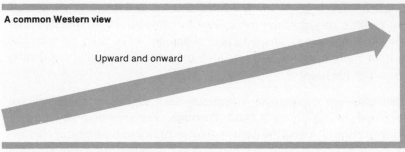

A struggle theory (Hegel)

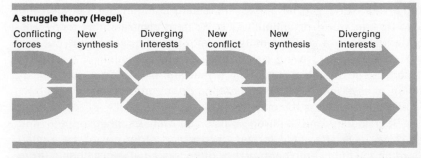

Parallel developments at different rates (Lewis Henry Morgan)

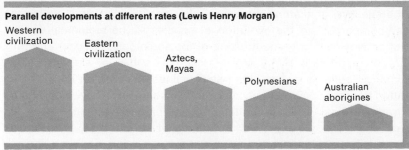

Multilineal theories   More recently, other anthropologists have attempted to give such problems consideration. Julian Stewart speaks of *multilineal evolution*—the idea that cultures can evolve along several lines but show similarities in certain areas. Karl Wittfogel, among others, gives an illustration of how geographical factors can help explain the growth of certain cultures along similar lines.[6] In his "Theory of Oriental Society" Wittfogel notes that those regions characterized by irrigation from rivers whose floods had to be controlled tended to develop a flowering of civilization at an early date and in similar ways. Control of rivers and irrigation called for massive effort and strong cooperation, forced by powerful monarchs and great social-class differentiation, but always with a free peasantry supplying the agricultural basis of support. The valleys of the Nile, Tigris-Euphrates, Indus, and Hwang-ho all supplied similar conditions and produced similar results. Even the remarkably centralized empire of the Incas was based upon intense cooperative effort to terrace hillsides and build the aqueducts needed for irrigation, although there was no single dominant river valley.

Wittfogel's analysis is only one example of the possibilities supplied by environmental factors, but such factors are never "necessary and sufficient" cause for the rise of civilizations. Not all similar river valleys have produced similar cultures. Fertile plains have not always resulted in agriculture, and even arid regions have not always prevented agriculture. The Pueblo Indians of the American Southwest developed agriculture in spite of very poor natural endowment. Such considerations prevent sociologists from believing that geographical environment alone will determine the course of a culture.

There was a tendency to reject cultural evolution in the early twentieth century, partly because cultural evolutionists had not been able to solve the problems of different rates of change without heavy reliance on geographical determinism. Another reason for this rejection of cultural evolution was that the evolutionists were, unwittingly, ethnocentric, looking for the gradual development of cultural institutions from the simple to the complex. Highly developed cultures were always those that most closely resembled the cultures of American and European sociologists and anthropologists.[7]

Functionalism   *Functionalism* became a more prominent concept for analyzing cultural change in the early twentieth century. Functionalism

[6] Karl Wittfogel, "The Theory of Oriental Society," in Morton H. Fried (ed.), *Readings in Anthropology*, vol. II, Thomas Y. Crowell Company, New York, 1968, pp. 179–198. From "Die Theorie der orientalischen Gesellschaft," *Zeitschrift fur Sozialforschung*, VII, 1938, pp. 90–122. (Translated by Far Eastern and Russian Institute, University of Washington.)
[7] Kenneth E. Bock, "Evolution, Function, and Change," *American Sociological Review*, vol. 28, April, 1963, pp. 230–231.

tries to understand cultures in terms of how their various parts contribute to the maintenance of the total system. To cite a previous example, absolutist governments served an important function in early civilizations, harnessing the energies of the people to control rivers and develop irrigation systems. It would be easy to use functionalism to explain various practices repellent to the modern world. For example, female infanticide (killing girl babies) functions to keep down the population, slavery functions to increase the power of the slave-holding class, and warfare functions to eliminate inefficient social systems. Naturally, functionalists would not go this far in a "whatever is is right" philosophy, but functional analyses do run into this problem.

Functionalism, however, makes some important advances in the understanding of social change. It helps to explain why customs persist unless new customs can serve the same functions. For example, polygyny will persist if it functions as a prestige system for important men, regardless of missionary teachings. It could possibly change, though, if a new and equally desirable status symbol could be found. Functionalism also raises the question of why change occurs at all.[8] Change can occur in two ways: as a result of strains within the system or as a result of outside forces. There are always strains within a social system resulting from individual variations. The younger generation is never a perfect duplicate of the old. Rulers attempt to solve problems in different ways. Sometimes population increase puts a strain on resources. Sometimes something new is invented. The outside forces can be the infusion of new ideas from surrounding people, competition with other groups for control of land and resources, or the crisis of war. The question remains, though, whether there is a patterning of these changes into a type of increasing complexity and specialization that can be called cultural evolution.

CONTEMPORARY THEORISTS: PARSONS AND WHITE   Several modern theorists are reexamining cultural evolution. The theories of today are improved upon by many years of research and by new theoretical perspectives. Different models of analysis are used, sometimes viewing a society in terms of *structural functionalism*, as a *moving equilibrium* (Parsons), or, as suggested by Moore, a *tension-management mechanism.*[9] The terms "moving equilibrium" and "tension-management mechanism" suggest that cultural and social systems can undergo considerable change and that readjustments of various institutions are needed and made, but behind all the changes is a certain persistence—a very different perspective from that of "decline and fall" or "old age and death."

[8] *Ibid.*, p. 232.
[9] Wilbert E. Moore, *Social Change*, Prentice-Hall, Inc., Englewood Cliffs, N.J., 1963, p. 10.

White's energy theory   Two modern theorists of society who are interested in revised forms of cultural evolution are the anthropologist Leslie White and the sociologist Talcott Parsons. Both would agree that the earlier cultural evolutionists had made a marked contribution to our understanding of human cultures, but these modern theorists depart from the simple unilineal evolutionary theory of Lewis Henry Morgan. Both recognize that the course of cultural evolution is complex and that not all societies evolve in exactly the same direction; but insofar as there has been a trend from the simple to the complex in human societies, the word "evolution" is appropriate. Parsons speaks of the advanced societies as those that "display greater generalized adaptive capacity."[10] Of the two theorists, White lays the greater stress on invention and technology. Since cultural diffusion of inventions occurs, the place of origin of a new idea is irrelevant to him. His view of cultural evolution is of the entire human race, not of any particular society. A major point of his analysis is the *energy theory of evolution*, the idea being that as man has tapped greater sources of energy he has developed greater potential for cultural advancement. Until the time that animal power was harnessed for doing the work of humans, nearly all available energy and time had to be expended in earning a living, and all people were directly engaged in food production, whether in hunting or gardening. With greater energy available, much more differentiation of labor became possible as many former gardeners were released to do some of the other work needed for cultural development—organization of effort, the building of forts and temples, advances in the arts, military protection, and so forth. Thus it was the period of man's history when he first attached the ox to the plow that can be called the first great breakthrough, and the second great breakthrough came with the Industrial Revolution. Naturally, White sees other sources of variation in cultural possibilities, including the level of organization, the tools invented, and the environment. He uses the formula

$$E \times T \times V = P$$

where E = energy
   T = tools
   V = environment
   P = potential[11]

Culture does more than provide a means for economic support; it gives people a set of values, customs, beliefs, and a system of organization. White does not omit any of these ideas. He elaborates especially on the state-church phase of cultural evolution, in which societies are often

[10] Talcott Parsons, *Societies: Evolutionary and Comparative Perspectives*, Prentice-Hall, Inc., Englewood Cliffs, N.J., 1966, p. 110.
[11] Leslie A. White, *The Evolution of Culture*, McGraw-Hill Book Company, New York, 1959, p. 49.

organized under the control of a godlike king.[12] Such a structure, accompanied by a belief system, functions to make the social system expand far beyond that of a tribal group and gives cohesion to the system. Strong kings, upper classes, and laws attributed to the gods all help to serve the function of controlling a heterogeneous population, but much of the old freedom of earlier times disappears.

White insists that societies could not have grown without an expansion of the amount of energy available for human use, increasing production and making possible a division of labor and social-class differentiation. As the modern phase of civilization is entered, the energy available increases manyfold, not only making tremendously more production possible but making it possible without slavery or divine rulers, although man is still organized and regimented far more than in his early primitive state. Technological factors, then, especially available energy, are seen as the underlying elements in social change.

Parsons: adaptive capacity   Parsons is more inclined to stress social structure and ideology first, for the advancement of adaptive capacity depends upon ever-widening bases for social structure, that is, advance from the mere band or tribal organization to that of city-state, nation, or empire. Writing is a first step in this direction, taking societies out of the primitive state. Belief systems that legitimatize authority and law in the larger societies are also basic to such organizational advance.[13] Thus the divine pharaohs of ancient Egypt represented a great advance over primitive tribal organizations because they were able to hold together large populations under one system (as White recognizes in the state-church phase). Since the divinity of the pharaohs was closely tied in with continuity, changelessness, and the Nile, the system could not easily expand to societies outside of Egypt. It also lacked the degree of separation of the supernatural sphere from the natural that Parsons contends is necessary for innovation and cultural change.[14]

Rome later supplied a legal and citizenship system that extended over a vast empire, but it fell short in some ways in the legitimatization of its authority, and it always had some people who were not assimilated into the system: slaves and the downtrodden. With regard to religion, Rome was in some ways archaic. Too sophisticated to truly adhere to the god-king idea, it nevertheless fell short of developing a religious system with universal appeal. Hence Rome witnessed a bewildering profusion of Eastern cults of various kinds. Christianity was finally accepted

[12]*Ibid.*, pp. 303–328.
[13]Parsons, *op. cit.*, p. 11.
[14]*Ibid.*, pp. 51–61.

White's energy theory: E × T × V = Potential

(Adapted from Leslie A. White, *The Evolution of Culture:
The Development of Civilization to the Fall of Rome,*
McGraw-Hill Book Company, New York, 1959, pp. 33-57.)

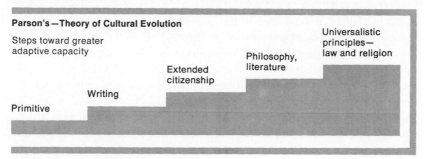

(Adapted from Talcott Parsons, *Societies:
Evolutionary and Comparative Perspectives,*
Prentice-Hall, Inc., Englewood Cliffs, N.J., 1966, p. 110.)

throughout the empire but only after Rome was already in the twilight of its development.[15]

A universalistic type of religion had been brought into the Eastern world by Buddha, but since the eventual technological breakthrough into modernity occurred in the West, Parsons gives this less importance than the religious development of ancient Palestine. The Hebrew nation was never impressive in size, and its period of glory was very short, but the Hebrews developed a religious and legal concept with a universality that made it adaptable to later Christian and Moslem people: the concept included a legal system that flowed out of the will of a universal God, as their prophets saw it, and was therefore superior to any particular society or ruler.[16] Future generations could fight over just what the will of God was, but the principle had great possibilities for generalization into many cultures, both as a religious and a legal principle.

Another people whose period of political glory was short, the Greeks, also made one of the universalistic contributions that would be necessary before larger systems of organization could develop. Ancient Greece developed a cultural system of philosophy and literature that extended far

[15] *Ibid.,* pp. 86–94.
[16] *Ibid.,* pp. 96–102.

beyond the boundaries of her city-states, influenced the Roman Empire, and later influenced all Europe with the revival of Greek learning in the period of the Renaissance. Greece also made an important contribution to the concept of citizenship. Although citizenship was limited to old families, all adult male citizens were considered virtual equals.

In the theories of both White and Parsons there is the obvious implication that cultural evolution differs from physical evolution in that cultural diffusion is possible. Some societies have made considerable advance along one specialized line or another but have left no apparent heirs. Others have come forth with the inventions—in the cases cited by Parsons, nonmaterial inventions—that have made higher levels of organization possible and that have increased cultural capacity to adapt. When these organizational capacities are combined with scientific technology the modern phase of man's development is reached. White suggests that the next phase may be one in which computers make not only greater organization but better thinking processes possible.[17]

THE INTERRELATIONSHIPS OF SOCIAL CHANGE   As functional analysis emphasizes, one of the complexities of the study of social change is the fact that the elements of a culture are interrelated in such a way that a change in one element of the society leads to corresponding changes in others. This is most easily seen in the impact of mechanical inventions, to which we will return; but for the sake of a summary of the field we have covered in this text, it will be interesting to review some of the interrelationships already mentioned or implied in the preceding pages.

Alternative reference points in change   Chapter 2 discussed human groups and the drift from gemeinschaft to gesellschaft society. The whole trend of the modern world could be analyzed fairly well in terms of these changes in group relationships, and as a matter of fact many of the people most worried about modern mass society actually do analyze our problems in this way. Changes could also be analyzed in terms of the socialization problems discussed in Chapter 4. There is an often-noted tendency for older generations to feel that the younger generation is not being socialized properly and that this is the reason for disturbing changes. Another analysis of social change starts with the differentiation of human societies by division of labor and status and class. Some of our most obvious recent changes have been in the area of greater specialization. The change in relationships between majority and minority racial and ethnic groups is another focal point in the study of social change. We also could

[17]R. P. Cuzzort, *Humanity and Modern Sociological Thought*, Holt, Rinehart and Winston, Inc., New York, 1969, pp. 232–233.

use the growth of population as a starting point in the study of social change, for the increasing population of today means that there is no possibility of a return to simple agricultural existence. Instead, there is a compulsion toward further increasing industrial production in order to take care of the people. Population pressures, along with urbanization, also create a society that calls for more controls over the lives of people — they must abide by zoning laws and building codes, pay increasing property taxes, and be careful not to disturb the peace.

Interrelationships of changing institutions   The family gradually changes to fit the conditions of society, as was noted in the contrast between consanguineal family and restricted conjugal family. However, even the family is sometimes taken as a starting point for change. The family system that frees the individual for the competitive struggle, and hence emphasizes individualism, is more congenial to modern capitalism than a more restrictive family, and there are probably even cases where family change has preceded economic change. Religious attitudes also change, perhaps in response to changing conditions, but recall that Weber saw the religious orientation of Calvinism as at least one cause of the rapid development of capitalism. In other words, religious change motivated economic change. Education also becomes a powerful force for change, and yet it is complementary with the rest of society. It is the society whose values and economy require education that develops a modern educational system. Some underdeveloped countries train a small, educated elite that can hardly be used, and it becomes a restive element, often radical and revolutionary. Recall Benjamin and Kautsky's study showing that in the countries not yet entering industrialization the few Communist members are likely to be part of the educated elite.

As Chapters 13 and 14 demonstrated, economic and political institutions are closely interwoven, especially with the mixed economic system of today. Economic changes are basic and underlying as seen from one perspective, but at the same time it is possible for poor governmental systems to greatly retard economic growth. Values and beliefs are also basic to economic change, retarding such changes if the society believes too strongly in the sacredness of the old ways. Political changes in the direction of a stronger state are of overwhelming importance today, as are changes in the equalization of political power. Whichever way we turn, we see this entangling relationship between one institution and another. It is also demonstrable that certain important inventions have their impact on practically all customs and institutions and an understanding of the interrelationships of the various aspects of society will aid to analyze the impact of one such invention.

In analyzing the impact of a particular invention, we are using the ideas of the late William Fielding Ogburn[18] but exemplifying those ideas in our own ways. In starting with a particular invention, it is first necessary to deny complete *technological determinism*—the idea that technology is always the first cause in social change. There must be favorable attitudes in a society before it will accept an invention, and even our own technically oriented society has allowed some important inventions to go without takers—the first modern submarines, for one example.

It was Ogburn's point of view that an important new invention would act on a society very much as ripples spreading across a pond until every part of the society was somehow affected. If we start with the automobile, we can demonstrate the point, although other starting points would do just as well—the railroad at one time, or the airplane more recently.

Derivative effects of the automobile   The invention of the automobile and its increasing production called for new products from the area of international trade. It was one of the industries that concentrated labor in large plants and helped to give rise to the labor movement. New supportive industries had to grow, especially petroleum and rubber, and old industries died out; buggies, horses, and hitching posts were seen no more. The government also had to become involved, making new laws for the regulation of traffic and building the roads that the new means of transportation required. Higher levels of government had to take over more of the duties imposed by the new transportation system. Local governments could not bear the cost, nor could they coordinate a national transportation system.

There are many other ramifications of the invention of the automobile. Urban growth was no longer confined to suburbs strung out along railroad lines or water courses; now the city could explode in all directions. Motels began to replace the city hotels and drive-in restaurants, drive-in movies, and even drive-in banks and drive-in churches appeared. Dating patterns and the time of coming-of-age were affected. The age at which the state law permits a driver's license is a crucial age for the young man, allowing him to join the dating whirl. Probably too much has been made of automobiles and the morals of the young, for there is no doubt that the good old horse and buggy were quite agreeable to young couples, too, but maybe the horse had an annoying habit of going home when the hour got too late!

Family mobility increased, although moving around the country was already a part of the American pattern of living. The little red schoolhouse disappeared as bus transportation made possible consolidated

[18]William Fielding Ogburn, *Social Change*, The Viking Press, Inc., New York, 1950.

The impact of an invention
spreads like ripples across a pond.

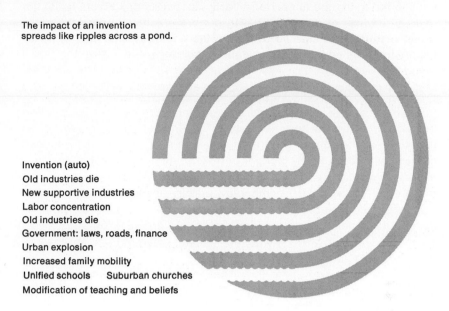

Invention (auto)
Old industries die
New supportive industries
Labor concentration
Old industries die
Government: laws, roads, finance
Urban explosion
Increased family mobility
Unified schools   Suburban churches
Modification of teaching and beliefs

schools. The "little brown church in the wildwood" was replaced by the urban or suburban church. In both institutions the growth in size had further implications. Better-trained teachers and better-trained ministers began to do away with some of the distinction between rural and urban, although some rather backward rural areas still remain. Religion became less fundamentalist; educational standards became more uniform.

Not all inventions have been as thorough in their effects as the automobile, but many have been. The invention of gunpowder eventually brought the whole age of medieval castles to an end. An earlier chapter has discussed the tremendous impact of automation on employment and education. No one knows what the ultimate effects of the discovery of atomic energy may be, but it will probably dwarf the importance of all previous inventions.

As noted, social change can be described in terms of long-range theories of history and cultural evolution. It can be described in interrelational terms and as the result of the acceptance of particular inventions. These perspectives, however, fall short of explaining all the factors involved in social change. Undoubtedly there are many that escape the attention of analysts, such as Hans Zinsser's germs, or mutation, radiation, DDT, and a host of others. However, a more practical understanding of social change can be gained by discussing a few of the commonly noted factors in social change and resistance to change.

A FACTOR ANALYSIS OF CHANGE AND RESISTANCE   *Invention* is one of the most important factors in social change, but it needs little elaboration because it has already been discussed. The kinds of inventions described (automobile, gunpowder, and atomic reactors) are *material inventions* and are the types usually thought of first. There are also important *non-material inventions:* writing, money, credit, banking, social security, monarchy, "divine right," democracy, slavery, insurance, corporations, consumers' cooperatives, and credit cards, to name but a few. The non-material inventions creating better systems of organization and universalistic principles of law, it will be recalled, are a part of Parsons' analysis of cultural evolution.

Diffusion is even more important than invention. Diffusion is the process of borrowing cultural elements from another culture. All societies have borrowed more than they have invented because many inventions are ancient and have spread throughout most of the world: the bow and arrow, wheel, plow, beasts of burden, weaving, use of metals, most types of clothing and food, languages and writing, paper and ink, glass, silverware, chinaware—the vast majority of the objects of everyday use, even including the stories we tell and the religions we follow.

Crises as change agents   *War* increases the demand for the inventions of weapons of death, very obviously, and it also increases the demand for materials from all parts of the world. Armies spread new ideas—and bad habits—from one part of the world to another. The French armies of Napoleon's time have been credited with spreading the ideas of the French Revolution wherever they went. Earlier, the Crusaders had learned much from the Saracens, and this learning helped to usher in the Rennaissance in Europe.

The *crises* of flood, drought, and other natural disasters have led to new societal adjustments. In earlier times they led to migration to new territories; now they result in greater efforts to control nature. *Depressions* are types of business crises that have resulted in many social inventions in Western societies, especially in the United States—social security and insurance of bank deposits being some of the most prominent.

Deliberate promotion of change   In the historic past it is likely that many inventions have been the result of accident rather than deliberate seeking of new ways of doing things. Accidental inventions occur even today, but most of our present-day inventions are a result of *deliberate efforts at change*. Giant corporations hire thousands of researchers to find new products, and governments do the same.

Laws are used to institute change. We are used to the idea of smog-control devices on cars and may have to get used to a substitute for the internal-combustion engine. Laws insist on education of the young. Laws promote racial equality in more and more aspects of life. Laws insist that people save toward their old age through the social-security system. Laws tell young men they must join the service, although most youths rarely express any desire to do so.

Resistance to change   There are also many kinds of *resistance* to social change. One resistance is simply the force of *habit* and another has to do with *uncertainty* about the new invention. Some people took many years to get used to television sets, having been fairly well satisfied with radios. Sometimes peculiar stories arise about the possible ill effects of a new invention. "Good old-fashioned methods" are preferred. In earlier times many people saw inventions as somewhat sacrilegious—"If God had intended us to fly, He would have given us wings."

Costs are important as a resistance to change. Spectacular achievements in space are purchased at such a high price that some taxpayers would like to slow down the pace. Ingrained habits and costs often combine as resistance factors. Nothing could facilitate some types of learning more than to simplify the spelling of the English language and also to change to a metric system instead of the cumbersome measuring system used by the United States. Yet there is almost no progress in this direction. Much new printing would have to be done, and there would have to be the unlearning of old ways and the learning of new ones. Resistance to the improvement of notational systems can be a serious detriment to a civilization. China has been "stuck" with a writing system that is extremely cumbersome compared with our Western alphabetical system.

Vested interest is very important in resistance to social change. Petroleum interests would not be happy to see a change to electrical cars. Workers are not happy about inventions that make their jobs unnecessary. The railroad interests were successful for decades in resisting the St. Lawrence Seaway because of the competition it would bring. All of these are examples of vested interest, a financial stake in the old order.

Sacred values and beliefs often cause resistance to change. The Amish still think of automobiles as worldly wickedness and refuse to use them. Printing, invented in China, spread to the Arabic lands but was rejected on the grounds that it would be sacrilegious to print the holy

Koran rather than write it by hand.[19] Insecticides were resisted in Iran because "if we kill the pests Allah sends against us, who knows what He'll send next!"[20]

Sometimes *attitudes* of a society will be resistant to a new element even though the attitudes are not what could be called sacred beliefs. Most people will not adopt such delicacies as snails, fried grasshoppers, pickled octopus, or goats' eyeballs, for example. We have borrowed various cultural traits from Mexico—a few words, styles of architecture, art, dress, decoration, and food—but bullfights, no! Our sensitivities would not permit us to watch the killing of a bull. We like to watch prize fighters beat each other into insensibility and to watch people get broken and maimed in auto races, but we wouldn't kill a bull, except in the slaughterhouse.

Resistance to change sometimes seems to be solid and immovable, and then it collapses rather suddenly, as was the case with resistance to medicare for the aged. Wilbert Moore uses the word "thresholds" to describe this situation of a poorly perceived threshold of change.[21] His example is of the sudden breakdown of resistance to birth control in some countries that have been adamantly opposed to it. The process of change here seems to be the gradual absorption of new ideas, a slow rationalization of old attitudes, and a final willingness to take action in a new direction.

Cultural lags   *Cultural lags* are periods of maladjustment created by the failure of some social traits to change fast enough to keep up with change in other parts of the social system. Technology often leads, and customs and ideas have to catch up. The idea of cultural lags was first used by Ogburn, and one of his examples was the failure to develop conservation methods in American forestry.[22] His forestry example emphasizes the persistence of an old belief that was no longer true, "there will always be plenty of trees." The cultural-lag concept has many applications. The United States was slower than most countries to adopt social-security laws because of a persistent belief in the duty of the individual to take care of all of his own economic needs. This belief had become a cultural lag in an age of unemployment caused by technology or by a downturn in the business cycle. Until recently, public interest has lagged behind the rapid pace of river, lake, and air contamination, the attitude having been that "there will always be clean water and air."

[19] Paul Frederick Cressey, "Chinese Traits in European Civilization: A Study in Diffusion," *American Sociological Review*, vol. 10, October, 1945, pp. 595–604.
[20] Margaret Mead, *Cultural Patterns and Technical Change*, New American Library, Inc., New York, 1962, p. 233.
[21] Wilbert E. Moore, "Predicting Discontinuities in Social Change," *American Sociological Review*, vol. 29, June, 1964, pp. 331–338.
[22] Ogburn, *op. cit.*, pp. 200–213.

Sometimes major aspects of a culture can be cultural lags, as with governmental systems that cannot keep pace with technical, scientific, and economic change. Certain governmental systems have collapsed in the twentieth century, partly for this reason—the Ottoman Empire, the Austrian Empire, the Manchu Empire, and the Czarist regime in Russia. In the case of old systems overthrown by revolution, various undermining forces are at work, and it is necessary to go beyond the concept of cultural lag to explain them.

SOCIAL CHANGE AND REVOLUTION   The word "revolution" has several meanings. *Revolution* can mean a fairly complete change brought about by different methods of production or by the acceptance of new ideas such as the Industrial Revolution. Another example is "revolution of rising expectations," a phrase frequently used to describe attitudes in the underdeveloped areas of the world as they begin to hope for the same material comforts that have been attained by Europe and the United States. A second type of revolution is a simple overthrow of government, with one group of rulers replacing another. A synonym for such a revolution is *coup d'etat* (literally "stroke of state"). From the point of view of the majority of common people, little has changed as a result of such an overturn of leadership. The social order remains basically the same.

Revolution as basic social change   The word "revolution" also describes basic change in a social system, usually, but not always, brought about by such uprisings against the existing government as the American Revolution of 1776, the French Revolution of 1789, and the Russian Revolution of 1917. All of these revolutions resulted in more than a simple change in the ruling faction. The French and American Revolutions replaced monarchy with republican forms of government, although the first French Republic did not last long. The Russian Revolution not only replaced the political system but made a drastic change to a Communist system of economic production. In the United States some of the causes of revolution were the tax issue, the controls of the mercantile system, and the general feeling of being crippled and frustrated by English rule. In each of the other cases the list of grievances was lengthy, but they were grievances that had long been in existence without having brought their nations to the breaking point in the past. What were the conditions that precipitated revolution at the particular point in history when it occurred?

Theories of revolution: Brinton   Crane Brinton, James E. Davies, and Talcott Parsons have all presented interesting analyses of revolutions.

Brinton,[23] drawing on information from the American, French, and Russian Revolutions, and the English Revolution of the seventeenth century, finds that in none of the cases were conditions growing steadily worse. Our American ancestors were making economic progress at the time of the Revolutionary War. It is true that France was undergoing crop shortages at the time of her revolution, but she had experienced a century of rather rapid progress in total output before then. Russia was embroiled in World War I and had suffered defeat at the hands of the Japanese in 1905, but the peasants had received their freedom in 1861, and their overall conditions seem to have been improving. Russia also was making progress in steel and oil production. The earlier English Revolution seems to have been led by a rising class of Puritans who were making considerable advances in business. In all cases, however, there was crisis at the governmental level. A need for new taxes, combined with governmental ineptitude, at a time when there was a rising class of able and determined people demanding more rights, played a part in each of the revolutions. With each revolution there were middle-class leadership and an abandonment of the old order by the leading intellectuals, but only in Russia was there outright appeal to class interest.

Theories of revolution: Davies   Davies,[24] using a slightly different group of revolutions for illustrative purposes, adds an important factor. Although there is usually a general increase in the well-being and hopes of the revolutionary elements involved, something occurs that seems to shatter their hopes. There is a downturn in prosperity or employment or a serious threat of such a downturn. In neither the Brinton nor the Davies analysis is there the implication that misery alone will lead to revolution. Many societies have existed in a state of misery too long to make this seem to be the single ingredient of revolution.

What seems obvious in much of today's world, especially in the underdeveloped areas, is a situation in which knowledge of better possibilities is at hand, especially among the educated groups. At the same time, social change in the form of new technologies, new products, foreign trade, and a movement from farms to cities strongly dislocates old ways of life. Old norms and rules of behavior are no longer applicable. A situation of anomie exists. It is easy to see the explosive potential of the modern world, but it would be rash to predict revolutions in particular cases.

[23] Crane Brinton, *The Anatomy of Revolution*, W. W. Norton & Company, Inc., New York, 1938.
[24] James C. Davies, "Towards a Theory of Revolution," *American Sociological Review*, vol. 27, February, 1962, pp. 5–19.

Theories of revolution: Parsons   In Parsons' analysis of the revolutionary movement[25] it is pointed out that a revolutionary movement demands a complex set of circumstances. The rise of a revolutionary movement demands large "widely distributed alienative elements" who are able to pull together, united by a vision of the future. This vision might be of a religious nature, in which case it will result in a religious rather than a revolutionary movement. Under the right circumstances, however, these elements can be united behind a charismatic leader with an exciting ideology of change. Even at this point there must be a weakness in the power structure or a revolution is impossible. This governmental weakness, it will be recalled, was an important point in the analyses of both Brinton and Davies.

Parsons carries his analysis of revolution a step further, showing that there is an *adaptive transformation* so that the new order retains some elements of the old. It is not surprising that Communist Russia should have retained a secret police force such as had existed in the days of the Czars, nor that in foreign policy she should again cast hungry glances at Eastern Europe and the Dardanelles, nor that a military elite would again be very prominent in the system. This is not to deny that revolutions make great and sweeping changes, but it does remind us that there is a certain persistence to a social system and a culture.

Summarizing briefly these various points of view, a rapidly changing world helps to create the tensions, dislocations, and feelings of alienation that can be mobilized by a successful revolutionary leader. It also should be added that there are ready-made philosophies of revolution exported from Russia, Red China, and elsewhere. At the same time, even moderately effective governments are not easily overthrown. No revolution has occurred in France or Italy in spite of strong Communist parties, even though their governments have suffered a number of leadership crises. Sweeping revolutions in various Latin American countries have long been predicted, but only a few have come about. Even the incredibly corrupt regime in Haiti still is, at this moment, being maintained by a system of terrorism. The study of social revolutions has clearly not brought us to a state of easy predictability. More analyses of the forces of resistance seem to be needed.

Change: despair and hope   Whether one lives in the most progressive modern society or in one of the world's underdeveloped areas, he feels the pressures of change. New products, new technologies, new ways of

[25] Talcott Parsons, *The Social System*, The Free Press, Glencoe, Ill., 1952, pp. 520–535.

organizing social institutions, new values and new aspirations are every-where in evidence. Old ways are gradually abandoned. Cut adrift as he is from the moorings of tradition, modern man can easily feel a con-fused sense of hopelessness, for the very currents of change that he has set in motion seem now to have a power of their own, sweeping him along almost against his will. The literature of our times is full of nostalgia for a simpler past. Leslie White says, for example, in comparing man's plight today with that of the primitive world:

> However crude and ineffectual primitive cultures
> were in their control of the forces of nature, they had
> worked out a system of human relationships that has
> never been equaled since the Agricultural Revolution.
> The warm, substantial bonds of kinship united man
> with man. There were no lords or vassals, serfs or
> slaves, in tribal society. . . . No one kept another
> in bondage and lived upon the fruits of his labor.
> There were no mortgages, rents, debtors, or usurers
> in primitive society, and no one was ever sent to
> prison for stealing food to feed his children. Food
> was not adulterated with harmful substances in
> order to make money out of human misery. There
> were no time clocks, no bosses or overseers, in
> primitive society, and a two-week vacation was not
> one's quota of freedom for a year.[26]

There is, fortunately, another side to the story. A modern man living in the world described by White would find it a world of unendurable boredom. Day would follow day with little happening and nothing but petty gossip to talk about, together with old superstitions and myths, and an argument about who bewitched whom. Whatever the forces of change have brought there is no way back. We live in an age when the moon and planets beckon us, and our first steps on extraterrestrial bodies have been taken. The task before us is to so organize our societies on earth that we will be free to turn our attention to the exploration of the unknown, ever increasing the freedom of the mind of man, without the fear that our planet will explode behind us in the primordial hatreds and fears that we have been unable to conquer.

SUMMARY   Change was once extremely slow in human societies, but the pace of change increases as technology grows and one development leads to another. Theorists have long attempted to explain social change

[26]White, *op. cit.*, p. 277.

in various ways, often looking for the cause that underlies all other causes. Spengler saw the cause of change as a kind of vitalistic principle, similar to growth, maturity, and decay of the individual life. Hegel and Marx both emphasized struggle as the motivating force in history, with Marx seeing the struggle as basically economic. Other theorists have tried to relate social change and the rise of civilizations to challenge and response, or climatic change, or to such biological factors as disease.

Functionalism and cultural-evolutionary perspectives have received more attention from sociologists and anthropologists than most other explanations of change. Functionalism is more concerned with explaining how systems work and how new elements are incorporated into social systems than in grand theories of underlying causes of change.

Modern cultural evolutionists display a variety of viewpoints, but they generally look for certain uniformities in social change and for some of the factors that account for these uniformities. Wittfogel explains certain phases of early civilization in terms of the geographical problems and possibilities of exotic river valleys. White sees the increasing amount of energy available to man as the basic factor that unfolds new possibilities. Parsons emphasizes the importance of greater general adaptability in evolving social systems and the ideologies that support them.

Nearly all explanations of social change have a degree of plausibility, but none is complete enough to satisfy all critics. What makes theory difficult is that social change can be analyzed by viewing any of several factors as prime causes: the drift toward gesellschaft society, new socialization patterns, the intricate division of labor, war and struggle, industrialization, population growth, and many more. All such developments are closely interrelated and are, perhaps, most easily understandable in modern technical societies if viewed from the perspective of the derivative effects of inventions. The automobile makes a good starting point for demonstrating how one invention can affect all the institutions of a society.

Although the analysis of an invention clarifies much about social change, it is not to be concluded that invention is the one and only cause of social change. To clarify this, an analysis of various factors contributing to change has been used—invention, diffusion, crises, and deliberate promotion of change through law. These factors must be weighed against resistances—habit, fears, costs, vested interests, and attitudes and beliefs. Resistance often leads to the disparities in rate of change called cultural lags.

The vast majority of social change takes place without violent revolution, but sometimes a wide gulf between aspirations of the people and their present condition can lead to such upheavals. Uniformities in great revolutions are found by such analysts as Brinton, Davies, and Parsons. Parsons also sees an adaptive transformation that prevents the revolution from being as complete as its supporters would have hoped. Nevertheless, old orders are never completely restored.

The pace of change has become rapid enough to be disturbing to many people, and sometimes a nostalgia for the past is expressed. Sociology, however, must concern itself with an understanding of social systems that cannot be made to stand still or to move backward. Sociologists seek to explain the reasons for social change and its probable direction, but they do not claim to have a special ability to evaluate.

index